100
HIKES in™

UTAH

100 HIKES in™

UTAH

Steve Mann & Rhett Olson

THE
MOUNTAINEERS
BOOKS

Published by
The Mountaineers Books
1001 SW Klickitat Way, Suite 201
Seattle, WA 98134

First edition, 2001

Published simultaneously in Great Britain by Cordee, 3a DeMontfort Street, Leicester, England, LE1 7HD

Manufactured in the United States of America

Project Editor: Julie Van Pelt
Editor: Doris Cadd
Cover and Book Design: Jennifer Shontz LaRock
Layout: Mayumi Thompson
Mapmaker: Gray Mouse Graphics
Photographers: Steve Mann and Rhett Olson

Cover photograph: *Sandstone cliffs reflected in Lake Powell near Llewellyn Gulch*
Frontispiece: *Looking across the slickrock on the Red Mountain Traverse*

Library of Congress Cataloging-in-Publication Data
Mann, Steve, 1956-
    100 hikes in Utah / Steve Mann and Rhett Olson.— 1st ed.
      Includes index.
      ISBN 0-89886-758-4
    1. Hiking—Utah—Guidebooks. 2. Utah—Guidebooks. I. Title:
One hundred hikes in Utah. II. Olson, Rhett, 1974- III. Title.
GV199.42.U8 M36 2001
917.9204'34—dc21

                                                  00-012472
                                                     CIP

TABLE OF CONTENTS

SOUTHWEST

SOUTH CENTRAL

KEY TO MAP SYMBOLS

═══════	interstate	⌂	building
▬▬▬▬	paved road	⁚	buildings in town
══════	dirt road	▲	campground
-----------	main trail	⌗	picnic area
···············	alternate or unhiked trail	▪	shelter
· ▬ · ▬ · ▬	boundary (park or wilderness area)	⌂	backcountry campsite
· ▬ · ▬	powerline	☗	lookout
•—————•	ski lift	⚐	microwave tower
(84)	interstate highway	✕	mine
(97)	U.S. highway	) (	saddle or pass
(530)	state route	] [	footbridge
[169]	Forest Service road	•—•	gate
Ⓟ	parking	⚓	boat anchorage
✚	airstrip	♀	spring
▲	high point or mountain peak		river or stream
•	point of interest		waterfall
♦	ranger station		lake, reservoir, pool

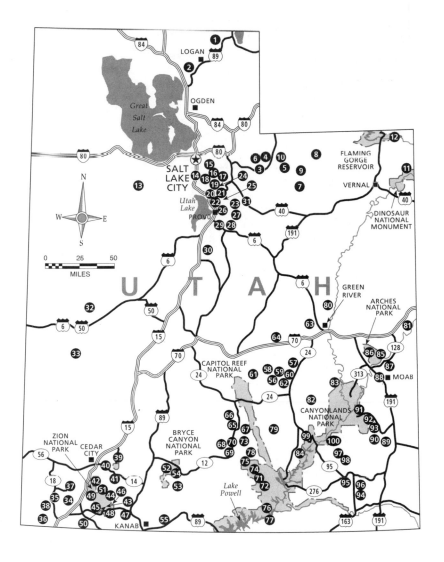

ACKNOWLEDGEMENTS

We thank our wives, Charlotte Mann and Julie Olson, for their support while we made our home in the backcountry for over 250 nights during the three years spent preparing *100 Hikes in Utah*. We love them all the more for allowing us to pursue our love of Utah's wilderness.

Also thanks to our frequent hiking companions John "Walt" Walter, Jeff Porcaro, Matt Smith, and Darren Scruggs. Special thanks to Mike McConnell and Jeff Porcaro for sharing their passion for the outdoors with us. This book would have never happened without them.

Our thanks to Project Editor Julie Van Pelt for her patience through our many questions and manuscript changes, and to our editor Doris Cadd and all Mountaineers Books editorial staff for their thorough editing and proofreading.

We also want to thank the people at MapTech, DeLorme, and National Geographic for providing Terrain Navigator maps on CD-ROM, the Utah Gazetteer road atlas, and Trails Illustrated maps, respectively. We recommend each of these products, along with U.S. Geological Survey topographic maps, for road access and backcountry trail navigation.

INTRODUCTION

Few other states can match the geological diversity of Utah, which sits at the junction of three geophysical regions: the Rocky Mountains, the Colorado Plateau, and the Great Basin.

UTAH'S ROCKY MOUNTAINS

Utah's mountains formed through two types of natural events. First, the main part of the Rockies (including the Wasatch) resulted from uplifting at the junction of tectonic plates—huge plates of the earth's crust floating over the earth's inner core. Over millennia, during much colder eons of Utah's prehistory, glaciers carved deep canyons and basins into these mountains. Areas such as Little Cottonwood Canyon, just southeast of Salt Lake City and home to several of Utah's world-renowned ski resorts such as Snowbird and Alta, teem with evidence of profound glacial shaping.

The Rocky Mountains, which run from north to south through the state, have their principal manifestation along the populous Wasatch Front, in and around Salt Lake City. Utah's main population is centered in the Wasatch Front's glacier-scoured valleys, such as the Salt Lake, Utah, Heber, and Cache Valleys. The Wasatch mountains also form the eastern boundary of the Great Basin. The Great Basin stretches south and west toward the West Coast.

Other mountains, especially in southern Utah, "sprang" into being through volcanic eruptions over millions of years. Southeastern Utah's Henry and La Sal Mountains have volcanic origins. Volcanic activity is also evident in Southwestern Utah, near St. George, Cedar Breaks National Monument, and Zion National Park.

The Uinta Mountains of northeastern Utah is one of the few North American ranges to run east–west. Uinta peaks reach higher than any in Utah, topping out at the 13,528-foot Kings Peak, located in the center of the 456,700-acre High Uintas Wilderness Area, the largest wilderness area in Utah. More than a dozen peaks over 13,000 feet, and many more over 12,000 feet, grace this true alpine wonderland.

THE COLORADO PLATEAU

The southern half of Utah lies within the Colorado Plateau, a vast region encompassing the upper third of Arizona. One very interesting isolated region here is a narrow swath of land that stretches across northern Arizona called the Arizona Strip, which ends at the plateau's magnum opus the Grand Canyon. The Colorado Plateau also encompasses parts of western Colorado and northeastern New Mexico.

Once the bottom of an ancient sea fed by melting northern mountain glaciers, the Colorado Plateau began as deposits, which formed sedimentary layers. With climatic warming, the sea dried up and wind-blown dust settled in multicolored strata, or layers. This relatively soft sedimentary sandstone is disposed to geologically rapid erosion from wind and water, which warp and shape the land into fantastic, unimaginable patterns and formations.

Erosion's seemingly random effects and the striated coloration of the sediment combined to create today's Colorado Plateau, one of the most amazing and scenic places on earth. Add to this landscape—gnarled and whirled by nature's forces—its inhospitable environment for humans, and you have one of the most awe-inspiring, remote, and wild areas left in North America.

Across the plateau water created narrow slits penetrating hundreds, even thousands, of feet vertically into sandstone. The resultant canyons, called slot canyons, can be narrow enough for you to touch both sidewalls by stretching out your arms while looking up at thousand foot cliffs towering above you. Slot canyons are some of the premier hiking destinations of the plateau, attracting hundreds of thousands of tourists. You'll find several of the best slot canyon hikes among the 100 hikes in this book.

In other areas, such as Bryce Canyon National Park, the erosive effects are much grander in scope, although not necessarily in beauty. Bryce's spires, hoodoos, and ledges resemble a vast fairyland of color, where an entire mountaintop of cool-colored alpine meadows, wildflowers, and stately pines erodes away into a grand panorama of flaming reds, oranges, and purples.

Just about everyone has heard of some of these areas—Zion National Park, Bryce Canyon National Park, Capitol Reef National Park, Canyonlands National Park, Arches National Park, the recently designated Grand Staircase-Escalante National Monument, Cedar Breaks National Monument, the Paria River Wilderness Area, and Glen Canyon National Recreation Area. They are nature's theme parks on the Colorado Plateau.

THE GREAT BASIN

The Great Basin stretches across Western Utah, through Nevada, and into Eastern California, and north into parts of Idaho, Oregon, and Washington. A hot, dry, mainly desert area, the Great Basin includes California's Mojave Desert, Death Valley, and Utah's Bonneville Salt Flats. Sand, salt, dust, sagebrush, cacti, jackrabbits, desert tortoises, lizards, and prairie dogs frequent this barren expanse. But don't be fooled; despite the Great Basin's arid character, it has its own charms, beauties, and wonders—you may just have to look a little harder or travel a little farther.

WEATHER AND CLIMATE

Utah's climate is as diverse as its landscape. In the winter, you can expect to see snow blanket the state from the mountains of the south to the valleys of the north. Because the state is fairly dry, the second driest in the nation, the snow is considered some of the best powder on earth. In the summer months, the days are warm and the nights are cool.

Utah's dryness, especially the low relative humidity, sometimes surprises hikers from more humid climes. An important effect of the dryness is the unexpected range of daytime high and overnight low temperatures. Dry air allows daytime heat to dissipate quickly, so while the daytime may be very hot, the temperature drops quickly once the sun sets. (Summer thunderstorms can also drop the temperature, sometimes 20 to 30 degrees in just a few minutes.) Take along a jacket and lightweight long pants, even in summer.

Utah's dryness also requires increased water consumption—more on this in the section on water.

As you find your way to the upper elevations, the temperature drops. As a rule of thumb, you can usually count on the temperature dropping 4 degrees Fahrenheit for every 1000 feet you gain in elevation. As you venture into the desert regions of southern Utah, you will find that the temperatures are usually much warmer than in the north. Remember that some hikes may begin in a lowland desert but ascend to a higher elevation where the temperature may be lower than you expect, especially when combined with nighttime cooling.

Weather Safety

Utah's environment is such that heat-related injuries are a real concern. When the body overheats, the blood vessels swell to help expel the excess heat. This decreases the amount of blood flow to the brain. If a person is dehydrated, there is less blood volume, which compounds the problem. One's best defense against the threat of heat exhaustion and heat stroke is proper hydration, discussed in detail later.

Symptoms of heat exhaustion are an increased heart rate (usually unnoticed by the victim), nausea, and faintness accompanied in some cases by sweaty skin. To treat heat exhaustion, the person affected should sit or lie down in a cool spot with the legs elevated. After the cooling process has begun, an effort to rehydrate the individual should begin. The individual should refrain from physical activity for the day and should not resume activity until adequately hydrated.

Heat stroke is more serious than heat exhaustion. It can have long-term effects and is sometimes fatal. People with heat stroke have very high body temperatures. They often suffer delirium, irrational behavior, and convulsions. Other things to look for are increased heart rate and breathing, hot skin, and shock. When treating heat stroke, time is of the essence. The individual should be rapidly cooled down. After shading the person from the sun, use water and circulated air to cool the person off. Alcohol rubs and ice should be avoided. However, massaging the limbs can be beneficial in getting cooled blood to the internal organs.

In the case of heat stroke, immediately begin the cooling process and then try to get professional medical help. Be aware that many of the hikes in this book are remote; the nearest medical facility is often many hours away. Make sure members of your party are familiar with basic first aid. The best advice is to practice sound preventative measures rather than deal with serious injury.

Lightning

Along with Utah's thunderstorms comes the threat of lightning. Nature's display of power and light can be breathtaking, but it can also spell disaster for those who are unaware of how to protect themselves. Lightning is the leading nature-related cause of death in Utah. While hiking, you can do several things to help lower the danger of a lightning strike. First, keep in mind that lightning usually strikes the tallest object in an area. It is also attracted to metal objects and items near or on water. Follow these basic thunderstorm rules:

• Avoid shelter under a lone tree or widely scattered trees. You are much more safe if you find shelter in a low area under smaller trees gathered close together.
• Avoid being the tallest object in an area such as on an open hilltop. If you are in an open area and lightning threatens, get on your knees and curl up into a ball; but do not lie flat on the ground. It is best to have your shoes or boots as the only contact point with the ground, otherwise a nearby lightning strike could rise up out of the ground through your body.
• Avoid being in or near water.
• Take off your pack, which may have metal in the stays or frame.
• Be especially careful in summer; the majority of lightning strikes causing human injury or death have occurred during the months of June, July, and August.

Flash Floods

While hiking in Utah, it is important to understand that there are two primary types of flooding. The first is caused by the melting snowpack. As the snow melts, streams and rivers begin to swell in depth and current. This runoff usually peaks in May, but can fluctuate from year to year. Fast- moving water can be very dangerous. Six inches of fast moving water create enough force to knock a person off his or her feet; 2 feet are enough to pick up and move a vehicle. Although floodwaters caused by snowmelt can be very dangerous, they are often easy to recognize and avoid.

The second type of flooding occurs when strong thunderstorms deluge an area with heavy precipitation in a short amount of time, resulting in flash floods. Unlike the runoff from melting snow, a flash flood is very unpredictable and can easily catch you off guard. Because water flows in the path of least resistance, low-lying areas, especially narrow canyons, are most susceptible.

Although flash flooding is difficult to predict, there are things to watch for. When setting camp, be wary of low-lying areas, especially dry creekbeds. *Never camp in a dry wash or creekbed!* Watch for telltale signs of flash floods, such as debris against rocks or along the base of trees or brush, or water stains along cliff walls. These signs help you gauge the high water mark. Always make camp well above these indicators.

Also know the local weather forecast; although weather predictions are not always accurate, they can give you a general idea of what weather is likely. It is especially important to watch the weather closely when hiking in the canyons of southern Utah. Slickrock doesn't absorb water, so a little rain goes a long way. Many of the canyons have tributaries that start miles away from where you plan to hike. Be aware of the weather around you because, although it may be sunny where you are hiking, rainfall miles away can be filling the canyon above you.

In narrow canyons where flash floods are common, plan ahead when weather threatens. Keep your eyes on canyon walls to spot exit routes or high benches where you could wait out rising waters. *Never enter a slot canyon during threatening weather.* Every year in Utah, newspaper articles relate the tragic stories of hikers who entered canyons despite warnings from local authorities. Remember, rainstorms over high mesas or mountains out of your view produce flash floods sometimes 50 to 100 miles downstream.

Should you find yourself in a flash flood–prone canyon during a rain, watch the stream for a sudden change in color or clarity. Keep an eye out for small debris, such as small twigs or pine needles, on the stream's surface. The final sign of an oncoming flash flood is the roaring of the water and rumbling of rocks gouging the canyon walls. When you see, or hear, any of these sudden changes, floodwaters are very close. *Immediately get to higher ground.* Although you may think you won't recognize the signs, you will—as long as you are watchful. If no high ground is available, wedge yourself into a crack in a cliff wall or behind a point where the cliff wall juts out. Do not attempt to outrun the flood either upstream or downstream. Of course, the best advice is to avoid this situation altogether by staying out of such areas when there is any chance of wet weather.

Hypothermia

One of the first steps in preventing hypothermia is learning to recognize it. It is often associated with winter activities, but it is equally likely to occur in the summer months, especially when water, wind, and high elevation are involved. Deep pools in dark slot canyons are often so cold as to bring on hypothermia.

The first signs of hypothermia are cold hands and feet. It is common for movement in the hands to become difficult, shivering often follows. Shivering is your body's way of heating itself back up. As the body's core temperature continues to fall, the body starts to become weak, and you may experience mild confusion. Hypothermia can be serious, but you can do several things to protect yourself.

Keeping yourself dry and warm is the name of the game in hypothermia prevention. To keep warm the body needs energy. Food and water fuel the body to produce heat. Proper clothing is also important. Dress properly for physical activities in the outdoors by wearing layers. When engaged in activity, you can peel off layers to minimize sweat that will saturate garments and reduce their insulating capacity. On the other hand, as your body begins to cool off, you can add layers to regulate your temperature.

If you do experience hypothermia, find some way to dry yourself off, warm yourself up, and stay out of the wind. If you are unable to find immediate shelter, change into dry clothes, if possible, and exercise the major muscles of the body (i.e., in your legs, back, and shoulders) to produce heat. Don't ignore persistent shivering. It is better to detect hypothermia early, before it becomes serious.

SEARCH AND RESCUE

Not too long ago there was a story of a young couple who decided to venture into the backcountry of southern Utah. Soon they realized they were lost, but they didn't worry because they had a cell phone and a global positioning system (GPS). They called the ranger station (it was pure luck that their phone had service) and gave them the coordinates listed on the GPS. The rangers explained to the couple how to get back to their vehicle at the trailhead, but the couple did not have a map to reference.

Fortunately the couple was found, but their adventure illustrates that a GPS does not eliminate the need for a map and knowing how to use it. Along with inflicted embarrassment came a fee from the county for the search and rescue services. Hikers must assume responsibility for their activities—from knowing how to help yourself to shouldering the cost of a rescue. Also, unlike these lucky hikers, you will *not* get cell phone reception on the majority of the hikes in this book.

We have provided what we feel is a sufficient description of all 100 trails that will aid in familiarizing you with the area, but these descriptions and accompanying, maps do not replace the need for a good, detailed area map. Purchase either United States Geological Survey (USGS) topographic (topo) maps or other maps listed in the trail descriptions. Printed topo maps from computer CDs, such as those from MapTech, also provide good reference.

BACKCOUNTRY DRIVING TIPS

Many of the trailheads for Utah hikes are remote and involve driving long distances on less frequently maintained backcountry roads. These roads pose their own challenges: sometimes getting from the trailhead back to pavement is more difficult than the hike! Here are a few backcountry driving tips:

- Avoid clay roads when wet. An otherwise passable dirt road can quickly turn into a slick mire. Roads in southern Utah are especially susceptible to this transformation. After a rainstorm, the dry, clay-based roads you drove so easily in the morning turn into a slippery, car-bogging clay paste. Passenger cars frequently find the wet clay impassable, and occasionally even four-wheel drive (4WD) vehicles become mired.
- Watch out for sandy patches, especially in hotter weather. If you decide to pass a sandy spot, keep your speed up. Remember, if you get stuck on a remote road, you may be there for a while.
- Don't take your passenger car on roads that require 4WD or high-clearance vehicles (HCVs).
- Carry a shovel in your car. You can dig your vehicle out of sand or mud or use it to level out high spots that might high center you.

WATER

One of the most important topics to discuss before you hike Utah's trails is water. For those familiar with Utah hiking, it is amazing how unprepared and uninformed newcomers can be to water requirements and water safety. Three aspects of Utah hiking—low humidity, scarcity of water sources, and potential water contamination—make water preparation critical; the lack of proper preparation could be fatal!

Yes, most of Utah technically qualifies as a desert, meaning hot and dry weather in the summer and cool or cold and dry weather in the winter. Very low humidity levels are not uncommon in summer months, and average levels range around 15 to 20 percent. Combine hot temperatures with that dry air, and you'll find yourself needing much more water than you would in more humid regions.

How do you know if you're hydrated? The easiest method is the basic urine test. If your urine is clear, you are well hydrated. The more yellow your urine, the less hydrated (more dehydrated) you are.

Rangers in national parks like Grand Canyon and Zion tell horror stories about tourists who start out on strenuous hikes in 100-degree-plus weather with a pint or two of water or soda. Those same tourists get to the bottom of a deep canyon, sometimes miles from the nearest water, and realize they're in big trouble. Faced with 1000-foot vertical climbs, exposed to the sun, and without water, unprepared hikers have suffered heat exhaustion, stroke, and even death.

The recommendation is to plan on a gallon of water per person per day when hiking in Utah under average conditions. With extreme heat or more strenuous trails the amount of water you need increases. That doesn't necessarily mean that for 2 days you need to carry 2 gallons—or about 16 pounds—of water. What it does mean is that you should know about *guaranteed* water sources on your chosen trail. During drought years, seemingly reliable springs and streams often dry up. Check with local authorities for water conditions before you begin your hike.

Water Recommendations

In addition to the 1-gallon-per-day recommendation, here are a few other water tips:

- Carry a lot of extra water in your car. This serves a double purpose. First, when you get back to your car from the hike, you'll have plenty of drinking water. You will be especially thankful for that water should you run out before reaching the car. Second, should your car get stuck, you will have sufficient water to last until help arrives. Since many Utah trailheads are remote, you can't count on someone finding you quickly.
- Drink all you can for several hours before embarking on your trip. The more water you take in the more hydrated your body will be.
- Use a hydration reservoir on your pack. You are more likely to take more frequent drinks if you don't have to stop and retrieve a bottle from your pack. In very hot weather, waiting to drink until you are thirsty means you've waited too long. At that point your body has already started to dehydrate. Continuing this pattern for long will reduce your energy as the day wears on or, worse, lead you toward heat exhaustion.

Water Safety

How do you assess the safety of backcountry water? Old adages state that where the water runs fast, especially over rocks, it's safe. Not true. Our advice is to assume all water is unsafe. That's perhaps an extreme position, but it is clearly the safest. Recent studies of water contamination of waterways in the United States have suggested that as much as 90 percent of the water contains either *Giardia lamblia* or *Cryptosporidia*. These waterborne parasites cause diarrhea, stomach bloating, vomiting, and other nasty symptoms. Although rarely fatal, they can have dangerous consequences when combined with other factors such as water shortage and heat.

These two parasites are found in the water supply principally because of beaver, cow, and human feces contamination. In Utah's canyons, cattle often graze along the streams during the winter and near mountain streams and springs in the summer. Many streams also have active beaver populations.

Water Treatment

Purifying water can be accomplished in three ways: filtering, treating, or boiling. But before we discuss these methods we need to clarify the objectives. In southern Utah's canyon country you not only want to make the water safe by removing or killing parasites, you also usually want to make the water palatable by removing sediment. Most southern Utah streams are filled with sand and other minerals.

Which purification method is the "best"? As you'd expect, it depends. Boiling is highly effective at making water safe, but is less convenient, requiring the use of fuel and a stove, which generally means you'd only boil while at your evening camp. Another problem with boiling is that it does not remove sediments. Iodine tablets are the most convenient, but they can introduce an iodine taste and do not help with the sediment problem. Filters work well for both parasites and sediment, but in heavily sedimented waters, the filter can clog quickly.

Our recommendation is to carry fresh water for day hikes or use iodine tablets or filters for longer day hikes. For overnight or longer trips we recommend filtering, especially in southern Utah. Mountain streams typically do not contain heavy sediments found in red rock canyon waters, so boiling is acceptable in many mountain areas. We usually try to carry enough water for half a day or more and then refill water bottles by filtering when we stop for lunch. When you have time for a longer stop, look around a little for a location with clearer water. Alternatively, you can allow water to settle so that many of the sediments fall out, reducing potential clogging of your filter.

In many canyons, the best, coldest, and cleanest water often drips from seeps along the canyon walls. Although this water may be clean enough to drink straight, we place a bowl on the ground to collect water while we eat, and then filter the accumulated water. We normally take along a collapsible bowl for this purpose.

ESSENTIAL GEAR

Whether day hiking or backpacking, you should always have the Ten Essentials with you: extra clothing, extra food, sunglasses, a knife, firestarter, first-aid kit, matches in a waterproof container, flashlight or headlamp, maps, and compass.

Take a jacket, even in summer, in case you are stranded overnight. After a hard day of hiking your body will have to work overtime to keep you warm when the temperature falls at night.

Your first-aid kit doesn't need to be large, but you should have some means of cleaning and caring for a wound until you are out of the backcountry. Even if you are only planning to hike for a few hours, it is wise to have water and food. Should you get lost or hurt, adequate water can sustain you until help arrives.

WILDERNESS ETIQUETTE

Every hiker should follow the basic etiquette of wilderness travel. Wilderness is disappearing at an alarming rate. You can be part of the problem or part of the solution. The tenets of responsible backcountry visits are well known, but far too many hikers still do not follow them. Here are the "rules" embraced by the Leave No Trace program:

- Follow the most worn trail. Do not shortcut across switchbacks. When there is no trail, hike on rock or in a stream.

- Camp at least 200 feet from any water source. That means no camping right on the shore of a lake or on the banks of a stream. Do not dig ditches; use a ground tarp or thin plastic for rain protection under your tent. Do not camp in highly vulnerable areas, such as alpine meadows. If there's an existing worn campsite, use it. Camp on rock to reduce damage to vegetation.
- Fires are unnecessary and wilderness etiquette prohibits them. Fires scar the ground, remove deadwood needed by flora and fauna, are unsightly, and cause air pollution, and the smoke damages your high-tech gear. In summer, campfires are often prohibited because of fire danger. Use a backpacking stove.
- Pack it in; pack it out. Take all of your garbage out with you. In fact, good etiquette advocates removing garbage left by others, too.
- Dig a cat-hole about 6 inches deep for feces. The best location is in organic soil where waste decomposes more quickly. Take a thick sealable plastic bag to pack out toilet paper. Always make sure you are at least 200 feet from any water source.
- Hike in small groups. Most areas have maximum group sizes, often around twelve. We recommend groups no larger than six.
- Avoid walking on cryptogamic soils—a dark crust on sandy desert soils. The crust reduces erosion and helps retain moisture.

USING THIS GUIDEBOOK

Each trail description in this book begins with a summary information block containing the most important aspects of the hike, including the distance you'll cover, estimated time to complete the hike, best hiking season, elevation, difficulty rating, recommended maps, and land management administration. Following the summary information are detailed descriptions of the route to the trailhead and of the hike itself.

Distance

All distances are approximate. We've done our best to accurately estimate distances, a task greatly simplified by use of the MapTech maps on CD-ROM. However, the frequent twists, turns, and ups and downs of most backcountry trails make map-based estimates imprecise. We have attempted to correct for the varied terrain, but use the distances provided as estimates.

Each hike is listed as oneway, loop, or round trip. One-way hikes require two vehicles or a shuttle; loop hikes begin and end at the same point, but involve little retracing of your course; a round trip means you hike to your destination, then return back to the trailhead over the same path.

Hiking Time

Time required for a trip is based on an average hiker in good physical condition. For occasional hikers, allow more time, especially on the more difficult hikes.

Season

Utah offers hikes year-round, but you need to choose the right hike at the right time. Low desert hikes can be brutally hot in midsummer. Mountain hikes, especially those over 10,000 feet, can be snowy all year except for late July through early October. Follow the recommendations for the best hiking experience.

Elevation

Two aspects of elevation—altitude and elevation gain—need to be considered in your hike plans. If you are not accustomed to a higher altitude, you'll quickly notice yourself getting short of breath after what would be an easy hike at a lower altitude. Elevation gain also influences a hike's difficulty level—the toughest hikes are those with a large elevation gain. For example, a 5-mile hike with a 5000-foot elevation gain is extremely strenuous, whereas a 10-mile hike over relatively flat terrain is easy to moderate. The elevation gain or loss measure listed for each hike takes into account all ups and downs. Elevation gain represents total feet climbed over the course of a trip unless otherwise indicated. Many hikes in this book are descents to canyon bottoms and lose rather than gain elevation. In cases where elevation loss is more significant than feet climbed, a measure is given for the former.

Difficulty

Each hike is rated as easy, moderate, or strenuous. Factors determining the rating are elevation gain, distance, and terrain. Although subjective, the ratings give a general idea of the trail's difficulty level.

Maps

A map showing directions, landmarks, and key features accompanies each hike. However, these maps cannot take the place of detailed topo maps, which are essential to your safety. USGS topo maps that cover the hike area and other recommended maps are listed. You should always take detailed maps even on short trips.

Land Management Agencies

This section lists the state or federal land management agency (or agencies) with jurisdiction over the hike. Contact information for each listed agency is in the appendix.

Hike Descriptions

A detailed description of the hike follows the summary information. This description includes directions to the trailhead, all major junctions, water sources along the trail, and distances between these landmarks. Remember that water sources vary from year to year, so be sure to check with local authorities before counting on springs or small streams.

The descriptions include some alternate routes and side trips for those who wish to explore more than the main trail. You'll also find information about any required permits, such as for hikes in the national parks.

A NOTE ABOUT SAFETY

Safety is an important concern in all outdoor activities. No guide-book can alert you to every hazard or anticipate the limitations of every reader. Therefore, the descriptions of roads, trails, routes, and natural features in this book are not representations that a particular place or excursion will be safe for your party. When you follow any of the routes described in this book, you assume responsibility for your own safety. Under normal conditions, such excursions require the usual attention to traffic, road and trail conditions, weather, ter-rain, the capabilities of your party, and other factors. Because many of the lands in this book are subject to development and/or change of ownership, conditions may have changed since this book was written that make your use of some of these routes unwise. Always check for current conditions, obey posted private property signs, and avoid confrontations with property owners or managers. Keeping informed on current conditions and exercising common sense are the keys to a safe, enjoyable outing.

The Mountaineers Books

NORTHEAST

1 | NAOMI PEAK

Distance: 7 miles round trip
Hiking time: 2.5 to 4 hours
Difficulty: moderate
Season: late June to October
Elevation gain: 1940 feet
Map: USGS Naomi Peak
Land Management Agency: Wasatch-Cache National
Forest, Logan Ranger District

From the center of town in Logan, about 1.5 hours north of Salt Lake City off I-15 on US 89, at the intersection of 400 North and Main Street, follow US 89 northeast of town toward Bear Lake for about 21.5 miles to the Tony Grove turnoff. Follow the paved road 6 miles to the Tony Grove Campground and trailhead. As you near the end of the road, ignore the sign for Backcountry Trailheads, which leads to the horse staging area. Continue another mile, passing the turn to the campground, to the paved parking lot where the road ends. Don't let the number of cars at the trailhead fool you. Most people are there for the lake—fishing, boating, and picnicking—so you'll have most of the trail to yourself.

Tony Grove Lake sits in a beautiful setting at the base of a series of rocky

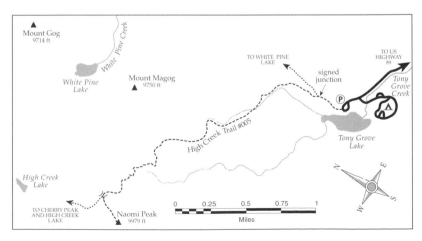

23

Rocky ledges above Tony Grove Lake

ledges, with rugged Naomi Peak to the west. The peak you see from the trailhead is Mount Magog, not Naomi Peak. As you leave the trailhead, follow any of the several trails heading west. About 0.25 mile up the trail is a sign and trail junction. Take the left-hand trail, also called the High Creek Trail #005, to Naomi Peak. The trail to the right goes to White Pine Lake.

You begin crossing a series of meadows, each a little higher than the previous. Each meadow is separated by a rocky shelf, which you ascend as you move from one meadow to the next. For the first mile or so, the shelves are small, then you ascend a larger main shelf to a bigger meadow. Crossing this meadow, you begin to ascend to a large basin at about 9000 feet. After you reach the top of a ridge, which forms the lip of the basin, you drop about 100 to 150 feet into the bottom of the basin, which is surrounded by tall, rocky cliffs. Dozens of white-tailed birds are visible in the trees and as you climb to the top of Naomi Peak. You'll see them catch and ride the wind currents near the cliffs.

After crossing the basin, you start to ascend the headwall of the cliff band toward a saddle at 9700 feet. From the basin you rise steadily, but not too steeply, zigzagging your way up a ridge and across rocky outcroppings. When you reach the saddle, you'll see the Naomi Wilderness Area sign, which was lying on the ground when we were there. The ridge is the boundary of a wilderness area that extends westward, but does not include the trail from Tony Grove up to the ridge.

The trail from the saddle continues west toward Cherry Peak and High

Creek Lake, descending 1000 feet to the lake. From the saddle you can see Mounts Gog and Magog to the north and northeast. A faint trail along the ridgeline to the northeast overlooks a basin below Mount Magog, a worthwhile short hike.

To reach Naomi Peak, turn south at the saddle for 0.25 to 0.5 mile, and 200 to 250 feet up, to the top of the peak. The west face of the Naomi summit ridge, below the peak, is very steep, rocky, and windy. During our visit, the wind chill here was a full 20 degrees cooler than at Tony Grove Lake just under 2000 feet below, so make sure to bring proper clothing.

The view at the top is spectacular—wild, rugged country in every direction. Beautiful peaks stretch into the distance northward into Idaho, eastward into Wyoming, and south toward the Wasatch Range. On very clear days you might even make out the outline of the Raft River Mountains in northeastern Utah along the Idaho border.

The descent back to the lake is quick and easy. For great multiday explorations, try High Creek Lake and beyond for high country, rugged terrain, and a lot of solitude. Or, you can catch the trail north to White Pine Lake and beyond to Doubletop Mountain and on into Idaho.

2 | WELLSVILLE CONE/ BOX ELDER PEAK

Distance: 9.5 miles round trip to Wellsville Cone; 11 miles round trip to Box Elder Peak
Hiking time: 5.5 to 8 hours
Difficulty: strenuous
Season: July to October
Elevation gain: 4220 feet to the cone; 4640 feet to Box Elder Peak
Maps: USGS Honeyville, Wellsville
Land Management Agency: Wasatch-Cache National Forest, Logan Ranger District

Between Logan and Brigham City, turn off US 89 onto SR 23, and head north through Wellsville to Mendon. At the south end of Mendon, turn south where a road crosses SR 23 diagonally at 5900 West and 1800 South Streets. About 150 feet down the road, turn right onto a dirt road, just before the first house on the right. An old small Forest Service sign indicates national forest access. At the first main fork (0.8 mile), keep right. At the following two forks, at 1.3 and 2.2 miles, go left. The first parking area is near a corral (a fence around a single tree), after a cattle guard. HCVs may proceed about 0.5 mile farther to a second smaller parking area, but

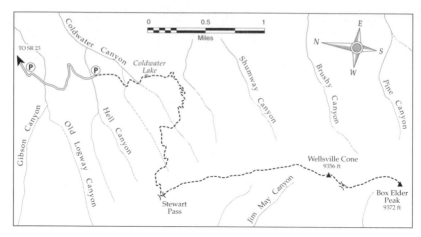

passenger car travelers may choose to stop here because the road is rough in spots. The Forest Service reports recent road improvements that may make it easier to get to the upper parking area.

From the lower parking area, follow the double track road at the west side of the clearing about 0.5 mile to another clearing. From this upper lot, the trail starts up an old dirt road now blocked by logs. It quickly turns into a single track. Proceeding upward, the trail traverses a ridge southward about 0.25 to 0.5 mile to Coldwater Lake—actually more of a cattle pond. The trail leaves the lake at the south end, then ascends a ridge. Topping the ridge, turn westward and start the long ascent to Stewart Pass.

The climb is hot and dry, with many long switchbacks, ascending the faces of several different ridges. For most of the climb you are exposed to the sun. Please do not shortcut the switchbacks! Help keep the trail in good condition by sticking to the main trail.

When you top out at Stewart Pass, a welcome cool breeze blows up the west face of the range. Even on hot days the breeze can be cool, so bring a jacket. Hawks and falcons float in these breezes on the west face. The Wellsville Range is a known migratory birding area. You may want to bring binoculars for better views of the raptors.

The clearly marked trail follows the ridgeline to the south, rising gently at first toward the cone. You may be fooled—two peaks appear to be of nearly equal height, but the back peak is the cone and is several hundred feet higher than the foreground peak. Box Elder Peak is not yet visible as you move along the ridge near Stewart Pass.

The trail doesn't go to the top of the Wellsville Cone. At the last switchbacks, as the trail finally turns around to the west face of the cone, a faint trail cuts to the left to the top. If you miss it, you can cut cross-country (off-trail) once the trail turns to the southwest toward Box Elder Peak.

Looking down from the trail near Wellsville Cone

Continuing on to Box Elder Peak from the cone, the trail drops into a saddle, then switches back up a steep slope. On the return trip, you'll realize how steep a climb you've made and how hot and dusty the trail can be. Be sure to bring plenty of water.

3 | YELLOW PINE CREEK

Distance: 4.5-mile loop
Hiking time: 3 to 4 hours
Difficulty: moderate
Season: December to early March
Elevation gain: 780 feet
Maps: USGS Hoyt Peak; Trails Illustrated Wasatch Front/
    Strawberry Valley
Land Management Agency: Wasatch-Cache National
    Forest, Kamas Ranger District
Special requirements: snowshoes

From the town of Kamas take SR 150 toward Mirror Lake. About 6 miles east of Kamas, you'll see a fee station in the center of the road up ahead. Just before the station, turn left (north) into the Yellow Pine Creek parking area and trailhead. Although you can park without going through the fee station, you do need to pay the day-use fee to use this trail.

The upper sections of the Yellow Pine Creek Trail pass through a steep-walled valley subject to avalanches. This hike combines sections of the Slate Canyon Trail and lower Yellow Pine Creek Trails with an off-trail route over the less steeply sloped ridge that separates the two canyons. Because this is an off-trail route, we recommend that you take the USGS map.

There is usually a trail of packed snow heading due north up Slate Creek, although with fresh snow you'll have to make your own trail. The trail follows an old jeep trail, now obscured by snow, passing through a fence over a buried cattle guard. A sign at the gate indicates the Slate Creek watershed area. Follow the creek upcanyon for about a

Snow at Yellow Pine Creek

mile, where the canyon forks. You can see that the drainage to the north-northwest (left) meets a steep headwall about 0.5 mile ahead. The stream runs in the fork to the right, more to the northeast.

Begin the off-trail route by traversing the stream-bank on the side of the creek. Use good judgment here, avoiding any avalanche-prone slopes. We chose to traverse the left streambank, which is steep but only about 10 to 15 feet high, and gently sloping above that. Routefind your way up the drainage until the stream starts to turn from northeast to due north. On the USGS map you'll be on the northeast shoulder of a ridge labeled with an elevation of 7687 feet at the peak.

Turn to the southeast following the ridgeline, trying to maintain your elevation. Once you cross behind Ridge 7687, the slope above you becomes less steep. Work your way up the ridge. Your goal is to get on top of the ridge between the 7600- and 7800-foot contour lines, then cross the ridge to the steep flank above the west side of Yellow Pine Creek. Try not to push too far north. The upper ridge top above 8000 feet becomes steeper, as does the drop into Yellow Pine Creek. Traverse and ascend the ridge for the better part of a mile.

The top of the ridge is serene. The deep snow here makes for a white-powder wonderland where few ever venture, especially in winter. Many pines and aspens grace both the slopes and ridge tops. Although the main road is only a mile and a half south, you'll feel as if you've come upon a completely undiscovered spot.

Avoid descending into Yellow Pine Canyon—the side slopes are too steep and avalanche prone. Stay on the ridge above the canyon, following the shoulder south-southwest. You'll have great views of Yellow Creek below and of the mountains to the south

Continue down the ridge top above the canyon. After about 0.5 mile, the canyon widens and the side slopes lessen. In another 0.25 mile, you drop back into the canyon and pick up the snow-packed trail heading down. Continue down the trail watching for a junction. At the canyon mouth, one trail heads left, more to the south, to the Yellow Pine Campground. Turn right (west) and follow the trail back to the Yellow Pine Creek trailhead.

4 | NOTCH MOUNTAIN/IBANTIK LAKE

Distance: 10 miles one way
Hiking time: 1 to 2 days
Difficulty: moderate
Season: July to early October
Elevation gain: 2430 feet
Maps: USGS Mirror Lake; Trails Illustrated High Uintas
  Wilderness
Land Management Agency: Wasatch-Cache National
  Forest, Kamas Ranger District

Take SR 150, also known as the Mirror Lake Highway, east from Kamas. This is a U.S. Forest Service fee area, with fee stations right on the highway. About 25 miles from Kamas is the turnoff to Trial Lake. Follow the road past the dam, then to a fork. Take the right fork to the Crystal Lake trailhead, which serves both the Crystal Lake Trail (to the west) and the Notch Mountain Trail (to the north).

If you choose to do this hike as a one-way trip, you'll need a second vehicle or mountain bike at the Bald Mountain Pass trailhead, another 5 miles east of Trial Lake. In summer these trails get high usage, so placing a mountain bike at the trailhead may be risky.

Heading north from the Crystal Lake trailhead through the pines, you'll pass just west of Trial Lake, then gain about 300 feet over 1.25 miles to Wall Lake. You pass just below the lake, crossing the stream that drains from it. After following the contour of the lake for about 0.25 mile the trail turns east. This section is not well marked; use the maps to help ensure you're on the right trail.

In another 0.25 mile, the trail turns north and begins the ascent to the Notch, a low pass between two peaks of Notch Mountain. Over the next mile the trail passes several smaller lakes, some of which you may not notice. In 1 mile you reach tree line in a flat area at the base of the Notch. Several lesser-visited lakes are to the west. You gain another 100 feet over the next 0.25 mile reaching the pass at the Notch, which offers unbroken views for miles in almost every direction. The wind blows strongly here, so bring a jacket.

The trail drops quickly off the north side and is usually wet with rivulets produced by melting snow lasting into late July. The trail is clear, but rocky as you drop 400 feet over the next mile to reach Ibantik Lake, a watery jewel nestled at the base of the steep cliffs of the east peak of Notch

Cliffs above Ibantik Lake

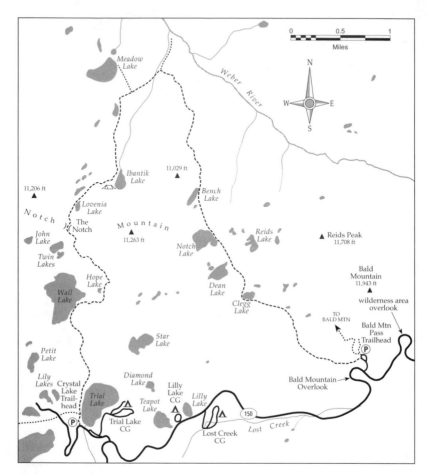

Mountain. Several good camping areas are west and south of the lake, with good streams to filter water. Of course the lake water also can be filtered. If you have a single vehicle, this is a good turnaround point. From the trailhead to Ibantik is 4 miles one way.

From Ibantik Lake, the trail continues north-northeast, descending 400 feet in the next mile to a fork. The left fork dead-ends in about 0.5 mile at Meadow Lake, another good camping spot less traveled than Ibantik Lake. The next 0.5 mile—and 200 feet elevation loss—brings you to another trail junction and the low point of the trail. Here you turn right and start to gain back the elevation lost over the last 2 miles.

This section is steep, gaining 800 feet in the next mile. The trail skirts the east side of the cliffs that frame Ibantik Lake. From the high point, the trail flattens and passes Bench (0.75 mile) and Notch Lakes (1 mile). The final stretch is 2.5 miles, passing several lakes and gently sloping 500 feet up to the Bald Mountain trailhead at 10,800 feet.

5 | NATURALIST BASIN

Distance: 13 to 15 miles round trip
Hiking time: 2 to 3 days
Difficulty: moderate
Season: late July to September
Elevation gain: 980 feet
Maps: USGS Mirror Lake, Trails Illustrated High Uintas Wilderness
Land Management Agency: Wasatch-Cache National Forest, Kamas Ranger District

The hike to Naturalist Basin begins at the Highline trailhead, just past Mirror Lake on SR 150 about 35 miles east of Kamas. The signed turnoff is about 4 miles north of Mirror Lake and less than 0.25 mile north of the Butterfly Campground. The trailhead has restrooms and ample parking, but no overnight camping.

Naturalist Basin is one of the most visited locations in the High Uintas Wilderness. If you're looking for solitude, this may not be the best choice; however, the natural beauty of its lakes, waterfalls, and meadows—combined with its easy access—make Naturalist Basin a premier hiking destination.

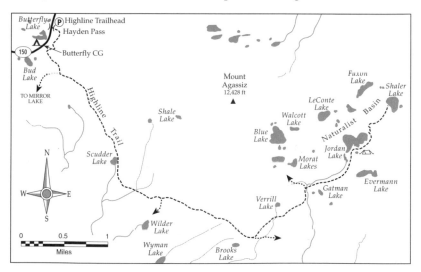

Leaving the Highline Trail toward Naturalist Basin

After descending 200 feet in the first 0.75 mile, a trail joins from Mirror Lake to the south. Continue on the Highline Trail to the southeast for 1.5 miles, passing through pine forests to arrive at Scudder Lake.

The next 0.75 mile of the trail levels as it turns east. At the 3-mile mark, you reach a fork. The south (right) trail leads to Wilder and Wyman Lakes. Continue straight ahead (left at the fork) on the Highline Trail.

Over the next 1.25 miles the trail ascends to another fork. Leave the Highline Trail (right), turning left (north) to Naturalist Basin. The trail climbs in the next mile up into the basin to a junction and a beautiful view of a large meadow at the base of a rocky ledge. The left trail heads to Morat and Blue Lakes; Blue Lake lies slightly above tree line, so camping is best at Morat.

The main trail continues to the right, crossing a stream to several possible destinations. After about 0.5 mile, just before ascending a hill, you can turn off-trail to the right to Evermann Lake, which gets a little less traffic than the lakes right on the trail. At 1 mile from the stream crossing, you reach Jordan Lake, the largest in the basin and the source of the stream you crossed earlier. The best camping is on the south and west sides of the lake.

The final on-trail option is to ascend the steep ledge behind Jordan Lake up 200 feet and 0.75 mile to Shaler Lake at 10,900 feet. Since Shaler Lake is above the tree line, it is not recommended for camping, but it makes a great short hike from your camp.

6 SMITH AND MOREHOUSE TRAIL

Distance: 12 miles round trip
Hiking time: 1 to 2 days
Difficulty: moderate
Season: July to October
Elevation gain: 2760 feet to saddle; 3150 feet to Island
  Lake; 3570 feet to Big Elk Lake
Map: USGS Erickson Basin
Land Management Agency: Wasatch-Cache National
  Forest, Kamas Ranger District

From Heber City, northeast from Provo and southeast of Salt Lake City, go north on US 40 and turn right onto SR 32. Go 10 miles to a junction in Francis—a gas station on the corner says Uinta Junction. Turn north, going through Kamas and on to Oakley. At 7.7 miles, turn right at the sign for Smith and Morehouse and Weber Canyon.

Go 11.6 miles to where the pavement ends. Straight ahead is the Thousand Peaks Ranch. Turn right and follow the signs to Smith and Morehouse Recreation Area for 1.7 miles to a fee station at the lower campground. Continue on (no fee for hiking) another 0.3 mile to the reservoir, then 1.7 miles to the upper campground, above the lake. Turn left at the fork at the entrance and follow the signs the last 0.5 mile to the trailhead parking area.

The wide trail begins with a large wooden bridge over Smith and Morehouse Creek. After the bridge, you go through a hiker's gate (be sure to close it securely). The trail climbs steeply for about 0.25 mile, then levels out to a gradual gain through thick pine forest. At 1.5 miles an open meadow affords views of the rocky peaks up ahead. In another 0.5 mile, you'll hear the sound of a stream on the left as the trail approaches it. Watch

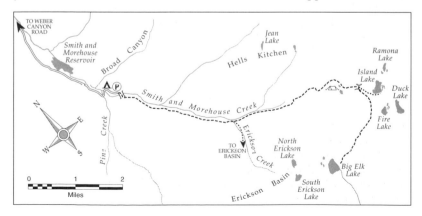

Wildflowers near Big Elk Lake

for faint trails going left over to the stream, where the water cascades down rocky ledges.

A few hundred yards past the cascades, you reach the trail junction. The left trail goes up toward Island Lake; the right goes to Erickson Basin. Stay left.

A little farther up the trail, is a stream crossing with a sign marked "Trail." Cross the stream and walk over the logs to avoid 100 feet of wet marsh and mud. After a short, moist, and flat meadow, the trail starts a 1.5-mile uphill section to a saddle between two bald and rocky peaks. You'll find great views back down onto Smith and Morehouse Canyon and of the peaks to the east and west, but you can't see much beyond the immediate basin.

Thinning forest, lush green meadows, tiny brooklets of crystal clear water (always filter), white rock outcroppings, and a few small lakes grace the saddle area. We recommend camping off-trail at one of the lakes in the saddle.

From your camp you can make side trips to Island and Big Elk Lakes. Island Lake lies about 1 mile south on the main trail. To reach Big Elk Lake watch for a trail sign just before dropping off the south side of the saddle. The sign indicates the path going west, crossing behind the peak on the west side of the saddle. The trail to Big Elk Lake is faint, but well cairned.

You'll find many more people at both Big Elk and Island Lakes, which have easy access from nearby roads to the south.

The USGS map shows a trail going west from Big Elk Lake to Erickson Basin, creating an enticing loop hike, but we do not recommend this trail. Not only is it poorly marked, but erroneously placed cairns will also guide you off the trail, potentially forcing a long cross-country trek back to the proper trail.

7 | BROWN DUCK LAKE

Distance: 14 to 20 miles round trip
Hiking time: 2 to 3 days
Difficulty: moderate
Season: late July to October
Elevation gain: 2365 feet to Brown Duck Lake
Maps: USGS Kidney Lake; Trails Illustrated High Uintas
    Wilderness
Land Management Agency: Ashley National Forest,
    Roosevelt Ranger District

The Moon Lake Campground serves as the trailhead for this hike on the south edge of the High Uintas Wilderness Area. Take SR 87 north off US 40 in Duchesne (pronounced Dew-shane) in northeast Utah. A little more than 15 miles from Duchesne, turn off 87 north to the town of Mountain Home. Head north through town, following the signs to Moon Lake. The trailhead

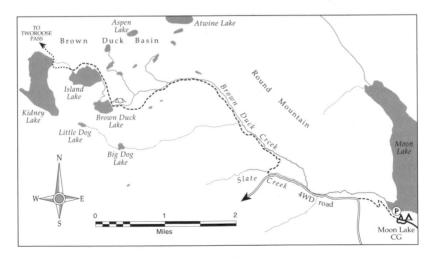

Along the Brown Duck Lake Trail

is on the left side of the road before you reach the campground about 33 miles from Duchesne.

Ignoring the trail that takes off west from the center of the parking area, go north, following a line of telephone poles through the trees. This section of the trail skirts around the campground and other developed areas around Moon Lake and adds about 0.75 mile to the hike. As the trail approaches the northwest corner of the campground, right against the lakeshore, is a four-way trail junction: to the east is the campground, to the north the Lake Fork Trail follows the lakeshore, and to the west the Brown Duck Lake Trail starts up a series of switchbacks ascending the ridge.

After 400 vertical feet and just over 1 mile, the trail joins with a dirt road and continues to the northwest, soon paralleling Slate Creek. The dirt road ends in about 1.25 miles where the trail forks. Take the right fork, which crosses the stream shortly after the junction, then turns to the northeast.

It's about 4 miles through the forest to another fork just short of Brown Duck Lake. Go left to the lake, where your options for camping and exploring abound. You can circle 0.5 mile around to the west side of the lake where fewer people camp, or follow the trail to one of the many higher lakes—0.5 mile to Island Lake or 1.5 miles to the larger Kidney Lake.

A good destination for a day hike from a base camp at one of the lakes is Tworoose Pass, about 4 miles from Brown Duck Lake. You can follow the high, rocky ridgeline to the south to a peak marked 11,567 feet on the Kidney Lake USGS map at 2.25 miles from the pass, and Duck Peak at 2.75 miles.

8   KINGS PEAK

Distance: 28 miles round trip
Hiking time: 2 to 4 days
Difficulty: strenuous
Season: late July to early October
Elevation gain: 5680 feet
Maps: USGS Gilbert Peak NE, Bridger Lake, Mount Powell,
    and Kings Peak; Trails Illustrated High Uintas Wilderness
Land Management Agency: Wasatch-Cache National
    Forest, Mountain View Ranger District

Travel east on I-80 into Wyoming. About 35 miles east of Evanston exit the freeway at Fort Bridger (exit #39). Travel south on Wyoming SR 414 to Mountain View. In town turn onto SR 410 west. Six miles down the road the paved road makes a sharp bend, and a gravel road breaks off straight ahead. Turn onto the gravel road, heading south for 12 miles until the road forks. Go left; the right fork goes to China Meadows. Follow the road signs to the Henrys Fork trailhead, about 10 miles from the fork.

From the Henrys Fork trailhead follow the trail to the southwest, staying on the right side of the Henrys Fork River. After about 6 miles the trail takes a quick jaunt to the east for a lone crossing of the river on a small footbridge. The terrain then opens up to welcome you to Henrys Fork Basin and views of Flat Top Mountain, Mount Powell, Gilbert Peak, and Kings Peak.

The numerous lakes here are great for fishing and camping, and the area

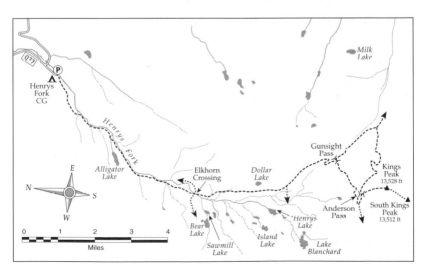

Looking up at Kings Peak from Anderson Pass

is heavily used. Please use the principles of Leave No Trace as you access this area.

Continue southward through the basin past Dollar Lake. A series of switchbacks at the head of the basin takes you to Gunsight Pass, where you can either continue on the well-marked trail that drops in toward Painter Basin and then turns to the west toward Anderson Pass, or you can head southwest from Gunsight Pass through the rock bands to your right. Cairns mark the way through the cliff bands and the meadow at the top, but this route is more strenuous and dangerous and saves little, if any, time. As you head toward Anderson Pass, Kings Peak and South Kings Peak are on your right.

At Anderson Pass you leave the trail and begin the climb to the highest point in the state at 13,528 feet. The summit of Kings Peak offers great views of Garfield Basin to the west and Painter Basin to the east. For those with energy to spare, continue southward to South Kings Peak to bag another 13,000-foot peak.

9 | HIGH UINTAS TREK

Distance: 54 miles one way
Hiking time: 6 or more days
Difficulty: strenuous
Season: mid-July to September
Elevation gain: 5500 feet
Maps: USGS Hayden Peak, Explorer Peak, Oweep Creek, and Kidney Lake; Trails Illustrated High Uintas Wilderness
Land Management Agencies: Wasatch-Cache National Forest, Kamas Ranger District; Ashley National Forest, Roosevelt Ranger District

For a serious backpacking trip into the heart of the High Uintas and awe-inspiring alpine scenery, this is the hike. Follow the directions for Hike 5, Naturalist Basin, to the Highline trailhead, near Mirror Lake. This hike requires a shuttle vehicle at the Moon Lake trailhead. See Hike 7, Brown Duck Lake, for directions to this trailhead.

Day 1. The first day of this weeklong trek takes you to Naturalist Basin, described in Hike 5. At 7 miles, day 1 is the shortest of the trip. Beautiful Naturalist Basin sets the stage for the alpine beauty and wilderness adventure that awaits you.

Day 2. Begin by hiking back to the Highline Trail, about 2 miles. When you reach the junction, head east toward Rocky Sea Pass. In 1.75 miles you reach a trail junction. The popular Granddaddy Lakes region lies to the south. Keep heading east. You begin the ascent to the pass by climbing 500 feet in 1.25 miles. You then arrive at a trail junction to Four Lakes Basin, which also lies to the south. Continue east another 1.25 miles to Rocky Sea Pass, at 11,350 feet.

The descent down from the pass is rocky and steep. Take your time here—a hiking stick or poles are helpful. After dropping 600 feet into the basin, you reach a junction at about 1.75 miles from the pass. The Highline Trail heads east. Go north on the trail to Black Lake, about 1.25 miles ahead. The junction to Black Lake is signed, but the 0.25-mile trail down to the lake is primitive and steep. If you prefer not to make the steep

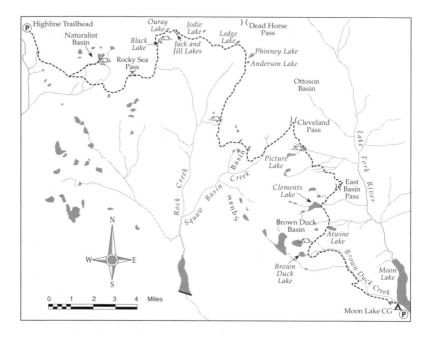

descent to Black Lake, follow the description for day 3 to a stream where you can camp at a water source. Total distance for the day is 9.5 miles.

Day 3. You need the Trails Illustrated map to make sense of the trails today—they do not show up on the Explorer Peak USGS map. Ascend the 0.25 mile from Black Lake back to the trail junction, a great warm-up activity for a cool morning. Head north, passing the Rosalie Lake Trail turnoff, then turn east (right) on Trail 123 to Ouray and Jack and Jill Lakes. Shortly after the turn, and about 1 mile from the Black Lake junction, you pass a small stream.

The trail here becomes faint in places, but is generally easy to follow. Consult the map often. The entire basin is wet and wild, and you have to cross several streams. About 3 miles from the Black Lake junction, you reach a junction with Trail 122. Turn southeast to return to the Highline Trail in about 1 mile.

At the Highline Trail, turn east toward Dead Horse Pass. Go 1.75 miles east to a trail junction just short of Ledge Lake. This beautiful area marks the last time you'll be on the Highline Trail and the beginning of a long section with far fewer hikers.

At the junction, head south to Phinney and Anderson Lakes and toward Squaw Basin. There is a sign, but it has fallen over and may be hard to spot. Over the next 4.5 miles the trail passes through mostly marshy flatlands at the base of a huge rocky, barren ridge. Although the trail becomes faint and overgrown, cairns mark the entire trail, and from each cairn you can see the next one up ahead. The day ends after about 5 miles, as you come upon a small jewel of a lake ringed by tall pines. The stream that feeds it emerges from the rocks at the base of the ridge just 100 feet from the lake. Wildflowers abound along the short stream course. Total distance for the day is 10.5 miles.

Day 4. Continue south from the lakeside camp, soon ascending the south end of the ridge you've been following for more than half a day. It's about 1.75 miles from camp to the top of the ridge, an ascent of about 500 feet. Your climb offers great viewpoints of Rocky Sea Pass to the west and the Rock Creek drainage, including the Black Lake area, to the northwest. From the ridge top you can see into Squaw Basin to the east.

Drop down into Squaw Basin to the first trail junction. Follow Trail 66 eastward toward Squaw Lake and Cleveland Pass. It's 2.5 miles of mostly downhill hiking, past Squaw Lake to the junction with Trail 63, which takes off to the northeast for Cleveland Pass.

Trail 63 skirts the northeast edge of Brown Duck Mountain as it climbs 800 feet to Cleveland Pass. From the junction in Squaw Basin to the pass is 3.5 miles. Take careful notes of the surrounding terrain as you near the top, as the next junction can be confusing. It'll appear that you're back-tracking, but you actually head down the opposite side of the northern-most extension of Brown Duck Mountain.

Arriving at Cleveland Lake, Trail 62 cuts off to the southwest across flat marshy ground with short sparse grasses and lichen-covered rocks. Watch for cairns across the flat meadows. The trail quickly drops down into the trees, where the trail is quite eroded. Go 2 miles, dropping 500 feet into East Basin, and make camp near three small lakes just northeast of Picture Lake, ending another 10-mile day.

Day 5. East Basin has only one trail through it; follow it southeast to-ward East Basin Pass. Get your legs stretched out early—the rise to the pass is the steepest climb so far. About 3.5 miles of more gentle terrain

Conquering Rocky Sea Pass

precede the climb, then—mercifully—it's only a 0.5 mile to climb the 400 vertical feet to the top. Although the grade is only 20 percent, it feels like straight up.

From the top it's 5 miles to Brown Duck Lake, passing first Clements Lake then Atwine Lake. Numerous cows graze this area, so the closer you get to Brown Duck Lake, the messier the trail gets. Just before the lake, you have to cross the stream on logs. The stream is wide and full, so use caution. Shortly after the stream, you reach a trail junction. Turn west and hike 0.25 mile or so to find a campsite. Total distance for day 5 is 9.75 miles.

Day 6. The last day brings you to the trailhead at Moon Lake. Refer to Hike 7, Brown Duck Lake, for the 7.5-mile trail down to Moon Lake.

10 | CHRISTMAS MEADOWS TO KERMSUH LAKE

Distance: 14.5 miles round trip
Hiking time: 1 to 2 days
Difficulty: moderate
Season: July to September
Elevation gain: 1990 feet
Maps: USGS Christmas Meadows, Hayden Peak; Trails Illustrated High Uintas Wilderness, Uinta Mountains, Kings Peak
Land Management Agency: Wasatch-Cache National Forest, Evanston Ranger District

Take SR 150 out of Kamas. Pay your fee at the recreation fee collection station a few miles out of Kamas. After 47 miles and just after the Stillwater Campground, you'll see a sign for Stillwater Road. Turn right and follow

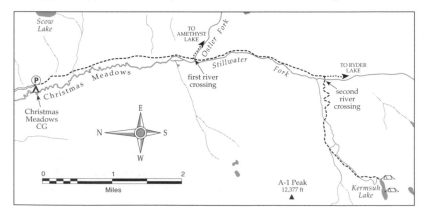

Crossing log bridge

this well-graded dirt road for 4 miles to the Christmas Meadows Campground. Depending on snowfall and spring temperatures, snow may remain until mid-July. Check with the Evanston Ranger District office for the latest conditions.

The trail starts out along the fringes of Christmas Meadows among aspens and pines. To the right is an open meadow, where lush greenery surrounds a slow-running stream. Watch for moose feeding in the meadows below.

For the first 2.5 miles, until the Amethyst Lake Trail cutoff, the trail is fairly smooth with relatively little elevation gain. In the early summer months, expect several muddy sections; traverse them by crossing logs and rocks.

Just after the Amethyst Lake Trail intersection, is the first crossing of the now substantial stream. Downstream, a log bridge with a log handrail makes crossing here easy. Over the next 2 miles the trail begins to gain elevation and becomes more rocky. Several meadows open up to great views of the mountains above. Occasionally, avalanche paths can be seen, evidenced by piles of dead wood at the base of a bald spot on the mountainside.

At 4.5 miles, the trail splits once more. The trail to the left continues to Ryder and McPheters Lakes. Follow the trail to the right toward the river for the second major stream crossing. A log offers the promise of a dry crossing—at least for those with good balance. Notice that the USGS map inaccurately shows the trail on the north side of the stream from Kermsuh Lake—the trail is on the south side.

After crossing the Stillwater Fork, the trail makes its way upward, gaining almost 1000 feet over the next 2.5 miles to Kermsuh Lake. A series of switchbacks over rocky terrain sometimes makes the trail difficult to follow, but small rock cairns show the way. The stream from Kermsuh Lake is audible here, and the river, rushing through a deep gorge, is sometimes visible.

Soon the trail levels out and makes its way through a series of meadows connected by a slow-flowing, fish-filled stream. After another slight elevation gain, the trail quickly makes its way to the east end of Kermsuh Lake, which offers several fine camping spots along its east and south sides. Look for signs of glacial movement, such as striations in the otherwise smooth rock, at the south end of the lake. The small lake, nestled at the base of a large cirque, offers plenty of solitude.

11 | JONES HOLE

Distance: 8 miles round trip, 0.5-mile side trip to falls
Hiking time: 5 to 6 hours
Difficulty: easy
Season: March to October
Elevation gain: 550 feet
Maps: USGS Jones Hole; Trails Illustrated Dinosaur National
     Monument
Land Management Agency: Dinosaur National
     Monument

In Vernal in northeast Utah, head east on 500 North Street. About 1 mile from town turn northeast on a paved road signed to Jones Hole. The road

Cliffs above the Jones Hole Fish Hatchery

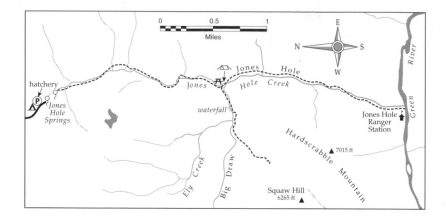

weaves its way north and east, then turns due east over Diamond Mountain at nearly 8000 feet, where snow may linger in early spring. From Vernal to the Jones Hole Fish Hatchery is about 40 miles. Overnight parking is available at the fish hatchery, or in the last mile or two before the parking area on several dirt roads heading north (left).

The trail starts at the south end of the fish hatchery. Go down the paved road between the fish tanks and toward a chain-link fence. At the east corner of the fence is a trailhead marker showing some photos and a trail map. From here the trail follows the stream down its tree-lined course. The vegetation along the stream is lush and green, contrasting with the high cliffs.

After the trail crosses a footbridge over to the west side of the stream, a footpath heads to the right up against the side wall. This side trail leads to two Indian rock art sites with explanatory signs.

At about 2 miles, the trail forks at a camping area, the only area for overnight camping with a permit from the Dinosaur National Monument Visitor Center, about 1 hour from Jones Hole. The fish hatchery has no jurisdiction over monument lands, which you entered when you started the foot trail.

The main trail continues along the stream south toward the Green River. A worthwhile side trail forks to the right and goes up Ely Canyon. About 0.25 mile up is a small pool and waterfall. You can follow the trail above the waterfall and up Big Draw to an area called the Labyrinths that consists of a series of deep canyons reminiscent of the Moab area. In 1 mile the side trail ascends 600 feet to the top of the cliffs, giving views in all directions.

Back at the camping area, continue 2 more miles downcanyon to the river. The canyon deepens and widens as you approach the river. Although the river is wide and shallow, its current is swift. In summer, Jones Hole's sandy riverbank with its campground is off limits to campers, being reserved for rafters. From late September to late April, backcountry camping is allowed at the Jones Hole river site with a free backcountry permit.

12 | LITTLE HOLE

Distance: 7 miles one way
Hiking time: 3.5 to 4.5 hours one way, or overnight
Difficulty: easy
Season: March to November and winter dry periods
Elevation gain: 440 feet
Maps: USGS Dutch John, Goslin Mountain; Trails Illustrated
  Flaming Gorge NRA and Eastern Uintas
Land Management Agency: Ashley National Forest,
  Flaming Gorge Ranger District

Take US 191 north out of Vernal. From fall through spring, watch out for storms. US 191 skirts the east edge of the Uintas Mountains, which catch the moisture from many west-to-east traveling storms, depositing snows even when the Wasatch Front and Uinta Basin are clear. As you near the dam, you'll reach Greendale Junction. Follow US 191 east toward Flaming Gorge and Dutch John. During off-season months, stop at the Flaming Gorge Lodge to pick up your day-use permit. From spring to fall, you can pay the fee at the booth near the trailhead.

Immediately after crossing over Flaming Gorge Dam (heading east), turn right, descending toward the base of the dam and the boat launch. Park at the upper end of a large, day-use parking area part way down. There is no overnight camping at the launch or upper parking

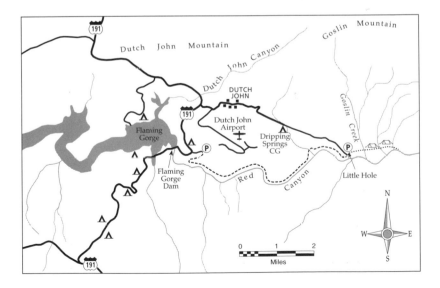

Resting along the Green River

areas. Look for the signed trailhead on the far side of the road, opposite the top end of the parking area. Begin your hike there.

If you have two cars, park the second car at Little Hole. From the dam, continue a few miles north on US 191. Turn off the highway and head for Little Hole and Dripping Springs Campground. Stay on this dirt road for a 20- to 30-minute drive to Little Hole at the road's end.

Extending along the banks of the Green River, from Flaming Gorge Dam to Little Hole, this well-worn trail is a good family hike—it's easy to follow and restrooms are available. Fishermen have used Little Hole since the days of John Wesley Powell's expedition in 1869 as a pullout and launching point for boats and rafts and as a trailhead. The entire length of the hike is blue ribbon trout fishing, but no bait is allowed.

From the parking area it's about 0.25 mile and 200 feet down a series of switchbacks to the river. At the trail junction, turn downstream. Make note of the sign at the trail junction so you won't miss it on your way back. If you do pass it, you end up at the boat launch and can walk up the road to the parking lot.

Tall ponderosa pines grace the river course. At first the canyon walls are high, but they then slope back away from the river. As you move downstream, the walls close in. From mile 3 to mile 6, the cliffs are high, steep, and narrow, causing several rapids in the river. The trail is wide and sandy, and there are boardwalks in rough sections and over the water. You cross one stream near milepost 5. For almost the entire distance, the trail parallels the river. In one short section around mile 4, it climbs up above the river along a bench, where the river canyon is at its narrowest.

For an overnight trip, you can continue past Little Hole to any of the thirteen camps farther downstream. Camp 1 is less than a mile from Little Hole, and there are four more camps along the river in the next mile. Goslin Creek is a running stream just before the first camp. You can also use Green River as a source for drinking water. All water should be filtered or treated for drinking.

13 | DESERET PEAK

Distance: 7.5 miles round trip
Hiking time: 4 to 6 hours
Difficulty: strenuous
Season: July to October
Elevation gain: 4170 feet
Maps: USGS Deseret Peak East, Deseret Peak West
Land Management Agency: Wasatch-Cache National
Forest, Salt Lake Ranger District

Take I-80 west out of Salt Lake to the Tooele/Grantsville exit (#99). Take SR
36 south about 3.5 miles, then turn west onto SR 138 toward Grantsville.
On the west edge of Grantsville watch for the brown Wasatch Forest
Service sign. Follow this road south for just over 5 miles, and turn west
(right) onto the signed road up South Willow Canyon, which passes
through two interesting rock gorges, the Lower Narrows and the Upper
Narrows. After 7 miles, you arrive at the Loop Campground. The trail starts
at the far west end where the road loops back to the east.

The trail heads due west through thick forests of pine and aspen, accented
with columbine and penstemon. The first 0.75 mile takes you up 500 vertical

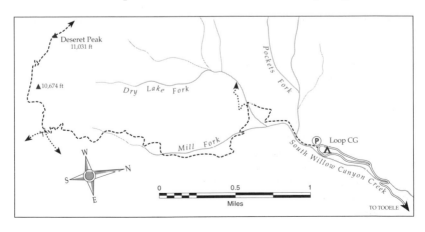

The final climb up to Deseret Peak

feet to a trail junction at a stream crossing. Straight ahead is a rocky slope, and to your right a high rocky cliff. The South Willow Lake Trail heads west up the slope and traverses the slope above the cliff. The Deseret Peak Trail cuts to the left, or east, to work its way 0.5 mile up a ridge by following the Mill Fork drainage. As you switchback up the ridge, you have good views back to the north and east, down toward the trailhead.

Topping the ridge, the forest thins out, offering a clear view up into a long cirque with sheer 1000-foot cliffs and a saddle at its farthest point, just southwest of, and below, Deseret Peak. The trail continues its constant rise, gaining 1800 feet in 1.75 miles as it approaches that saddle. In summer, wildflowers and grasses green up the moist meadows, a stark contrast to the arid valleys below.

As you near the top of the valley, the last 0.25 mile climbs a series of steep switchbacks to the saddle. The trail to the peak cuts to the right, or west. Other trails continue south and east for those who seek more distance and greater solitude. Although you've already topped 10,000 feet at the saddle, another 1000-foot climb awaits in the final 0.75 mile to the peak. Across its full length, the summit ridge affords views of the barren, white Salt Flats to the west. Nearing the top, sheer, jagged cliffs fall away to the east (right), where raptors nest in the rocky crags.

14 | GRANDEUR PEAK

Distance: 6.25 miles round trip
Hiking time: 2.5 to 4 hours
Difficulty: moderate
Season: June to October (summers are hot)
Elevation gain: 3060 feet
Maps: USGS Sugar House; Trails Illustrated Wasatch Front/
   Strawberry Valley
Land Management Agency: Wasatch-Cache National
   Forest, Salt Lake Ranger District

From I-215 heading toward the east side of the Salt Lake Valley, go to the 3300/3900 South exit, which puts you on Wasatch Boulevard. Follow Wasatch Boulevard to 3800 South, where you'll see signs for Mill Creek Canyon. About 3.5 to 4 miles upcanyon, you'll see the Church Fork picnic area on the left. The canyon is a fee-use area. The fee is usually collected as you leave the canyon.

You can either park on the road or in the small lot at the trailhead, which is reached by a narrow road that winds about 0.5 mile and gains 250 to 300 feet of elevation. The picnic/camp spots are reserved for picnickers. If you

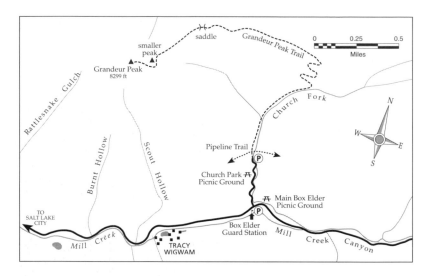

park along the road at the campground entrance, add 1 mile round trip to the trailhead from your car.

Gates to the picnic/camp area close from 10 P.M. to 7 A.M. In summer, you may want to start early to avoid the heat, so park on the road. It's also possible to hike on summer nights with a full moon and headlamps. You'll be rewarded with great views of Salt Lake City.

The trail begins following a stream upward. At 0.1 mile, the trail crosses the Pipeline Trail, running perpendicular to the Grandeur Peak Trail, which zigs to the left, then continues upcanyon, following the stream uphill. Follow the stream for close to 1 mile, then the trail turns left up a steep slope, into a set of long switchbacks up a ridge face. The trail breaks out of the trees into scrub oak some 10 to 12 feet tall, offering less shade.

The trail zigzags up the ridge, goes to the east of some rocky crags, then heads back to the west passing directly beneath the outcropping. Continuing west, the trail makes a long straight traverse up to a saddle, where you top the ridge and get your first views of Salt Lake City. The trail follows the ridgeline, ascends to a smaller peak below Grandeur Peak, then cuts around its southeast face, getting steep in several places.

Near the top are many side trails. The Forest Service is trying to restore the natural vegetation in the area, so stay on the main, most developed trail. On top, you'll enjoy great views of the entire Salt Lake Valley, from the Great Salt Lake and Antelope Island on the northwest to Point of the Mountain on the south. To the west lies Deseret Peak, due north is Ogden Peak with its silver-domed transmitting station, and to the northeast is Mountain Dell Reservoir. Far off in the distance eastward, the bare-topped High Uintas reach skyward. Mount Raymond and Gob-

Looking down on Salt Lake City from the peak

blers Knob dominate the southeast view, with rugged Mount Olympus to the southwest.

15 | GOBBLERS KNOB

Distance: 8 miles round trip
Hiking time: 6 to 8 hours
Difficulty: moderate
Season: July to October
Elevation gain: 3920 feet
Map: Trails Illustrated Wasatch Front/Strawberry Valley
Land Management Agency: Wasatch-Cache National
    Forest, Salt Lake Ranger District

From I-215 in Salt Lake City, take the 6600 South exit. Head east and drive up Big Cottonwood Canyon 8.5 miles to a small pullout on the left (north) side of the road. A sign indicates the Butler Fork trailhead.

Following the canyon up about 0.5 mile past the Mount Olympus Wilderness Boundary sign, the trail splits, one fork going right to Dog Lake, the other left to Mill A Basin. Go left. The slope increases as you ascend a set of switchbacks up the ridge.

At a trail junction on top of the ridge, the main trail goes north (right). Take

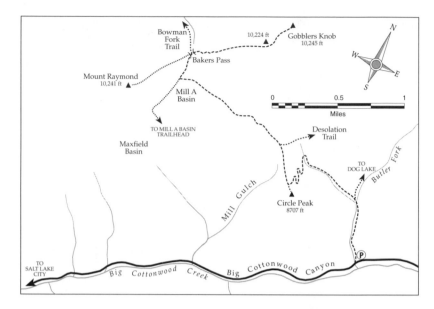

the trail to the left for a worthwhile 0.25-mile side trip to the top of Circle Peak at 8707 feet, and great views up, down, and across Big Cottonwood Canyon.

From the junction the main trail continues another 0.5 mile along the ridgeline to the north. As you approach the steep flank of Gobblers Knob, the trail meets the Desolation Trail coming from Dog Lake to the east. Turn west (left) to traverse across Mill A Basin.

The elevation gain is less across the basin, but you're still pulling uphill. You can see Mount Raymond to the west as you approach it through stands of aspen. Soon you arrive at another junction. The trail straight ahead goes west to join with the Mill B North Fork Trail. At the junction turn right (north) to ascend Bakers Pass at over 9300 feet. The climb gets steeper quickly as you work your way up to the saddle.

From the pass you can go west to Mount Raymond, or east up Gobblers Knob. Take the east trail, ascending to first peak at 10,224 feet. About 0.5 mile east, the highest peak rises to 10,245 feet. Both have excellent views of downtown Salt Lake City, Mill Creek Canyon, upper Big Cottonwood Canyon, and south to the Alpine Ridge. To the south and a little east you can see the tram at the top of the Snowbird Resort. To the east you can see the tall peaks of the High Uintas Wilderness Area.

To ascend Mount Raymond, follow the ridge west from Bakers Pass. The elevation gain and distance are about the same as to Gobblers Knob, but sections are steeper, requiring you to scramble on the narrow ridge near the summit.

Descending back to the trailhead is much easier. For those with the

Fall aspens below Bakers Pass

luxury of a shuttle vehicle, you can descend to the Bowman Fork trailhead in Mill Creek Canyon or down to Alexander Basin.

16 | LAKE BLANCHE

Distance: 6 miles round trip
Hiking time: 4 to 5 hours
Difficulty: strenuous
Season: July to early October
Elevation gain: 3160 feet
Maps: USGS Mount Aire, Dromedary Peak; Trails Illustrated Wasatch Front/Strawberry Valley
Land Management Agency: Wasatch-Cache National Forest, Salt Lake Ranger District

From I-215 in Salt Lake City, take the 6600 South exit. Follow SR 190 up Big Cottonwood Canyon for approximately 4 miles. A parking area, signed Mill B South Fork Picnic Ground, is located just before the road reaches a tight S curve. On busy weekends and holidays, you may have to park along the main road.

From the parking lot, a blacktop trail runs upriver a short distance. After about 1000 feet, a dirt path, the Mill B South Fork Trail, cuts off to

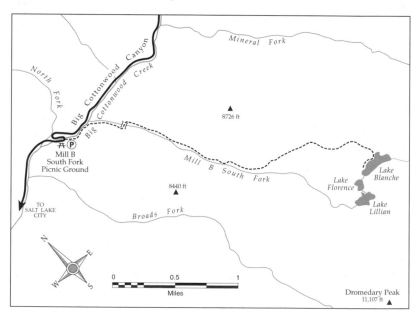

High peaks above Lake Blanche

the right. A sign here provides updates on current area restrictions.

The trail heads south on the west side of a small stream that runs down from the lakes above. After crossing a footbridge, the trail stays to the east of the water the rest of the way up the canyon. To the west, large slab walls keep guard over the canyon.

The trail maintains a steady ascent for nearly 2000 feet until it arrives just south of Lake Blanche, at the base of the cirque. Grand views of Dromedary and Superior Peaks open up above, as well as of Lakes Blanche,

Florence, and Lillian. Along with the wonderful view, the rocky slab south of Lake Blanche is interesting for striations in the rock, worn and smoothed by ancient glacial activity.

Small trails encircle the lakes, allowing for closer inspection. Between Lake Blanche and Lake Florence a small waterfall (or rapid) travels from one lake to the next. At the southwest end of each lake, old retaining walls are reminders of when these lakes were used as a watershed area. The hike's proximity to Salt Lake City affords little solitude, but its beauty is fair compensation.

17 | LAKE CATHERINE

Distance: 3.25 miles round trip
Hiking time: 2 to 4 hours
Difficulty: moderate
Season: July to early October
Elevation gain: 1675 feet
Maps: USGS Brighton; Trails Illustrated Wasatch Front/
    Strawberry Valley
Land Management Agency: Wasatch-Cache National
    Forest, Salt Lake Ranger District

In Salt Lake City, take I-215 to the 6600 South exit. Signs indicate the way to the ski resort areas. You want to head up Big Cottonwood Canyon to the Brighton Ski Resort. Follow SR 190 east up Big Cottonwood Canyon for approximately 14 miles to the town of Brighton. At the end of the road, before it loops around the town, is the Brighton Ski Resort. Park at the south end of the parking lot, near a brown lodge.

The trail begins between the Brighton Lodge and Molly Green's Pub

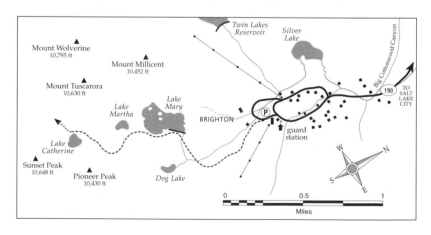

Alpine wildflowers

and follows a tree-cleared path, used in winter as a ski trail. The shade of pine trees makes the upward hike pleasant. After about 0.25 mile the trail turns and heads west toward Lake Mary. At the base of the dam at Lake Mary, the trail crosses a stream, which often covers the trail with a small amount of water. However, the water doesn't warrant any special footwear.

The trail skirts the east side of Lake Mary, the largest of the nearby lakes, and quickly comes upon Lake Martha. However, the trail does not run as close to this lake, before starting another brief ascent up to Lake Catherine.

The crystal clear waters of Lake Catherine reflect the image of nearby Sunset and Pioneer Peaks, which top out at just over 10,000 feet. The trail continues up the ridge toward the peaks, making it possible to get a bird's-eye view of the lakes. Climbing to Sunset Peak adds just less than 2 miles and 300 feet in elevation to the trip. Alternately, you may follow the path over the ridge to the west into Albion Basin and on into Alta.

18 RED PINE LAKE

Distance: 7 miles round trip to lake; 8.5 miles round trip to Peak 10,897
Hiking time: 4 to 7 hours
Difficulty: moderate to lake; strenuous to peak
Season: late spring to late October
Elevation gain: 3110 feet
Maps: USGS Dromedary Peak; Trails Illustrated Wasatch Front/Strawberry Valley
Land Management Agency: Wasatch-Cache National Forest, Salt Lake Ranger District

Take I-15 south from Salt Lake City to the 90th South exit. Head east on 90th South to the mouth of Little Cottonwood Canyon, following the signs

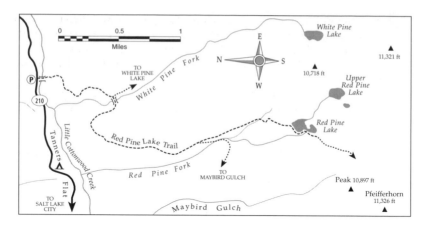

to the canyon's famous ski resorts: Alta, Solitude, Brighton, and Snowbird. Proceed upcanyon 5.5 miles to the White Pine Lake trailhead sign, a little more than a mile after the Tanners Flat parking area. Watch closely for the sign once you see Tanners Flat, as it is easy to miss. The White Pine Lake and Red Pine Lake Trails share the same trailhead, which offers nice restroom facilities and ample parking.

The two trails start together, following a paved trail from the restroom area, immediately crossing a bridge over Little Cottonwood Creek and heading south through a forest dotted with wildflowers. About 0.75 mile from the parking area, the trails split—White Pine Lake Trail is to the left; Red Pine Lake Trail veers to the right, or west, and crosses a footbridge as it passes across marshy bog land. Near the split, a sign indicates that you are entering the Lone Peak Wilderness Area, Utah's first.

The trail turns west and north, back toward the parking lot, as it ascends up the forested ridge separating the two drainages. Although not steep, the constant rise puts you well above the road by the time you reach the northern extremity of the ridge. The trail rounds the ridge, and follows it to the west, paralleling the road below. Along the ridge's north face, vegetation and wildflowers abound.

After about 0.5 mile, the trail begins to round the ridge and head back to the south, into Red Pine Canyon. Occasional glimpses of the stream below are accompanied by its constant roar. This is an excellent area to stop and enjoy the view up and down Little Cottonwood Canyon. As you work your way along the ridge, occasional views of the Salt Lake Valley are visible westward.

Heading due south, the trail continues to ascend, and you begin to see a transition from pines to aspens. The trail steepens, becoming rockier. You top out after another mile, near a jutting cliff on your left, and join Red Pine Creek on the right. Snow often remains from here to the lake into late June or early July.

A trail breaks off to the west, crossing a bridge over Red Pine Creek, to make its way to Maybird Gulch, the next drainage to the west down Cottonwood Canyon. Keep on the trail to the left, or east side, of the stream. From here to the lake the slope lessens, and works its way through a canopy of mixed pine and aspen.

After about 0.5 mile, the trail levels out as you top the ridge, which forms the north boundary of Red Pine Lake. Cresting the ridge, you find several good camping spots back away from the lake.

As the lake opens up before you, you get your first full view of the mountain bowl above the lake, which tops out near 11,000 feet. To your right, the highest peak in back is the Pfeifferhorn (Little Matterhorn on some maps), and in the foreground, an unnamed peak at 10,897 feet (elevation shown on the Trails Illustrated Uinta National Forest map). Straight ahead looms White Baldy, and to the left are the American Fork Twin Peaks.

From the ridge crest at lakeside, you see a worn trail rounding the east edge of the lake, and above that a ridge. The ridge outlines the northern edge of Upper Red Pine Lake, a smaller alpine lake on rockier ground in another glacial bowl to the southeast. Although it's difficult to see where the upper lake lies, look for a small stream entering Red Pine Lake from the southeast, which drains the upper lake. Follow the stream up; there isn't a well-defined trail, so be prepared to do some boulder hopping. Despite the lack of a trail, getting to the upper lake is not difficult.

Although there is no trail, the ascent to the lip of the glacial bowl to

June at Red Pine Lake

Peak 10,897 is well worth the effort. The steeper terrain of the bowl consists of rugged rock slides, so if you want to climb to the ridge, it's best to hike in early June and bring crampons to ascend the snowfields. Ascend either the long slope to the southwest or along the tree-lined ridge just to the left. You'll be rewarded with views of Little Cottonwood Canyon to the north , Salt Lake Valley to the west, Mount Timpanogos to the south, and Utah Valley to the southwest.

Because of the danger of avalanche, be cautious attempting the peak in early spring. You can call the Utah Avalanche Forecast Center before attempting to summit the ridge or peak (see Appendix). Later in the spring or in early summer, the consolidated snow makes an easy pathway to the top for those with crampons and ice axes. Red Lake Canyon is also a popular approach to the Pfeifferhorn.

19 | LAKE HARDY

Distance: 13 miles round trip
Hiking time: 8 to 12 hours for day hike, 2 or 3 days for backpack
Difficulty: extremely strenuous
Season: July to October
Elevation gain: 4930 feet
Maps: USGS Lehi, Draper, Dromedary Peak; Trails Illustrated Uinta National Forest
Land Management Agency: Uinta National Forest, Pleasant Grove Ranger District

Get off I-15 at the Alpine exit (#287) and head east on SR 92 for 5.4 miles to a stoplight at the intersection of SR 92 and SR 74 (also 5300 West Street). Turn left (north) onto SR 74 and follow the road 2.0 miles through Alpine. Turn right onto Pioneer Drive (600 North), then go 0.3 mile to a T intersection with Grove Drive. Turn left (north) and follow this road as it weaves east and north through town. After 1 mile the road makes a sharp 90-degree turn to the east. After 0.2 mile the road parallels a chain-link fence lined with large white boulders. After another 0.2 mile, the road forks at a large yellow road sign with double arrows.

Take the left fork onto Oak Ridge Drive into a subdivision of large homes. Go 0.15 mile to the second street on the right, which may be signed Alpine Cove Drive. Turn onto Alpine Cove Drive. Go 0.2 mile to Aspen Drive and turn right. A gate marks where the road turns to dirt. No parking is allowed before the gate where the pavement ends. If the gate is closed, this likely means the area is closed to hiking. If the gate is open, stay on the road, which crosses private property. In less than 0.25 mile you

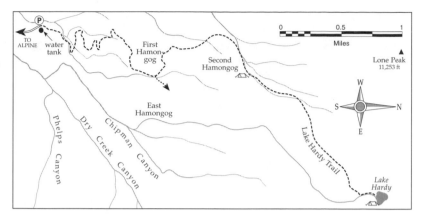

arrive at a water tank and pullout for parking. Those with an HCV can proceed another 0.4 mile to where the road makes a 90-degree turn and starts a steep ascent. Park just before the turn.

The trail follows the road to the boundary of the Lone Peak Wilderness Area. As you start out, look high up on a tall ridge to your northeast and you'll see the steep road cut into the ridge. Soon you'll be on that road headed up toward the First Hamongog (the Biblical term for meadow), where the road ends and the trail begins. The Lehi USGS map shows this section the best, but it's pretty easy to just follow the 4WD road. The Trails Illustrated map shows the trails to Lake Hardy, which are not shown on the USGS maps; we've chosen this trail for the scenic beauty of the Second Hamongog, a worthwhile destination in itself.

The next section is a couple of merciless miles of steep ascent on a hot, dry dirt road, with little shade and no water, but some good views of Utah County. When you get to a large fenced area with "No Trespassing" signs, you're getting close. The road deteriorates into a rutted mess, especially early in the season when water runs right down the road. It's easy walking, but miserable driving, even for 4WDs.

After 2.5 miles and 1500 feet up, you arrive at the Wilderness Area boundary and the First Hamongog, a beautiful meadow with a perennial stream running on its south edge. The trail starts at the parking area and heads west (left) out onto the face of the mountain, with additional overlooks of Dry Creek Canyon and northern Utah County. The next 2 miles take you to the Second Hamongog, one of the most pleasant meadows you'll find anywhere. The Hamongog is actually a terminal moraine—the endpoint of ancient glacial scouring. The leading edge of the debris pushed by the glacier formed a semicircular lip that protects the Hamongog. Two seasonal streams run near the northeast edge of the meadow. The nearer dries up by midsummer, but the second runs much longer. If you're backpacking, this area makes a great base camp for a second day ascent to Lake Hardy.

The trail leaves the Second Hamongog on the east edge and heads out

Overlooking Utah County from unnamed peak

through the aspens. Another trail heads to the north, crossing the two streams, bound for Lone Peak. The Lake Hardy Trail soon breaks out of the trees for a long steep climb. The trail stays on the west side of a ridge that drops from the high peaks above all the way to the Hamongog.

The terrain is rocky and open. For much of the summer a stream flows down to your left (west). After 1.5 miles of climbing and 1700 feet up, the trail cuts right (east) and crosses the ridge. Once over the ridge, you cross a marshy area with wildflowers. Snow covers this area into mid-July most years. Lake Hardy sits at the base of rocky cliffs about 0.5 mile up ahead, and nearly 2000 feet above the Second Hamongog, but it's hard to see until you're right on it. The stream draining from the lake is a dead giveaway of the lake's position. Work your way laterally as much as possible—try not to lose elevation or you'll be gaining it back soon.

Do not camp right at the lake. The vegetation is very fragile and is too frequently used already. Try to camp back from the lake a few hundred feet or more. To get from the trailhead to Lake Hardy in 1 day is a good day's work in anybody's book. For most it should be done as a 2-day trip. The descent is long, but obviously easier.

Several day trips are possible from the lake. You can mount an ascent on Lone Peak, although there is considerable exposure and scrambling on your way to the top. A much simpler, but rewarding trip is to the top of one of two small pyramid-shaped peaks unlabeled on the maps. From them you can see down into Bells Canyon and out toward Salt Lake City, with great views southward of all of Utah County. To get to the top, go back on the trail until you are away from the steep cliffs bounding the lake. Head up these slopes working your way along high ridges. The western of the two peaks is easiest to reach.

20 | DRY CREEK

Distance: 7.5 miles one way
Hiking time: 6 to 8 hours
Difficulty: strenuous
Season: July to October
Elevation gain: 4380 feet
Map: USGS Timpanogos Cave, Dromedary Peak; Trails
     Illustrated Uinta National Forest
Land Management Agency: Uinta National Forest,
     Pleasant Grove Ranger District

Follow the directions for Hike 19 to the yellow double-arrow road sign. At the sign take the right fork, crossing a stream, then immediately take a left on Grove Drive. This road is paved for 0.4 mile, then turns to dirt as it passes through fenced land posted no trespassing on either side. The dirt road makes its way another 0.2 mile, getting rockier and rougher, but still passable by passenger cars. Just after the road enters some scrub oak, it turns hard left into a posted national forest parking area.

Previously an old road that followed a pipeline, this trail is now closed

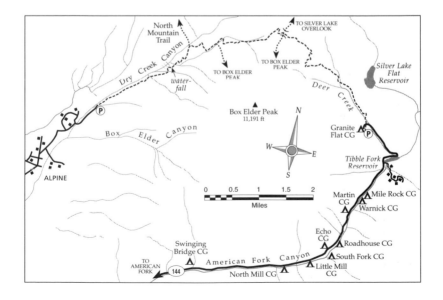

The granite peaks of the Alpine Ridge

to motorized vehicles, but still draws a good deal of equestrian traffic. Although the name suggests a dry hike, most of the ascent up the west side to the pass follows one of the larger west-draining streams in Utah County.

Leaving the trailhead, the trail parallels Dry Creek up the valley between Box Elder Peak to the south and Lone Peak and the Alpine Ridge to the north. For the first mile or so, the open trail works its way up through the scrub oak bench before entering a forest of tall pines. You can hear the stream flowing at the base of the valley even though it is several hundred yards from the trail.

The trail climbs steadily through the forest. After about 1 mile you reach a small clearing with a seasonal stream passing at the far end of the meadow. Continue upward. About 1.5 miles from the trailhead, the stream is louder, and the trail steepens as you leave the pines. In spring and summer a large stream crosses the trail. After the crossing, look to the left to see Dry Creek and a falls. Several trails to the left approach the falls. Take the trail that branches left at the point where the main trail takes a sharp turn to the right to ascend up a rocky ledge.

The narrow trail over to the falls crosses two small streams. Be careful as you near the falls, which are really more of a cascade than a waterfall. Just up from the cascade is a pool with lush vegetation.

Back on the main trail, continue upward. At about 2.5 miles, you top out at a basin. A signed junction indicates that the North Mountain Trail takes off to the north (left) heading over toward the Hamongogs and Lone Peak (Hike 19). A large rock outcrop jutting up just north of the trail makes a great viewpoint and rest stop.

The trail alternates between pines and aspens as it climbs 0.5 to 0.75 mile to another larger meadow sitting at the base of Box Elder Peak. In the early summer, the meadow teems with wildflowers. The trail becomes less distinct in the meadow. The Dry Creek Trail makes a sharp left in the middle of the meadow, while the Box Elder Trail continues across the meadow to the southeast.

Turn left and follow the trail through aspens and up a ridge, reaching the 9000-foot level. When you top the ridge, a large alpine basin opens up to you. You can see the peaks of the Alpine Ridge along the northern ridge top. As you approach tree line, the terrain opens up significantly, making for spectacular views. The trail turns into an old 4WD road, which ascends northeast, then east. After a long climb, a total of 4.5 miles from the trailhead, you finally reach the top, a saddle at 9700 feet with great views in all directions. You can see the Uinta Mountains on the eastern horizon, Mount Timpanogos and Box Elder Peak to the south, and the entire Alpine Ridge to the north, including the peaks of some of the Little Cottonwood Canyon ski resorts.

A faint trail to the northeast along the ridge heads for the sheer cliffs overlooking Silver Lake, about 1.5 miles away. To the southwest, a trail ascends Box Elder Peak, over 1200 feet above. The descent route goes southeast from the saddle, working its way down a steep rocky ledge and descending a long series of switchbacks. The trail down to Tibble Fork Reservoir is steep and hot. While you should plan on 4 to 6 hours to make it from the trailhead to the pass, it takes only 2 hours to make it the final 3 miles down to the Granite Flats Campground.

21 | THE RIDGE TRAIL

Distance: 23.5 miles oneway
Hiking time: 3 days
Difficulty: strenuous
Season: mid-July to October
Elevation gain: 8290 feet
Maps: USGS Aspen Grove, Brighton; Trails Illustrated Uinta National Forest or Wasatch Front/Strawberry Valley
Land Management Agencies: Uinta National Forest, Pleasant Grove Ranger District; Wasatch-Cache National Forest, Salt Lake Ranger District

Take the 800 North Orem exit (#275) off I-15. Follow 800 North Street (also SR 52) east through Orem to the mouth of Provo Canyon. At the mouth of the canyon, the road splits—stay left and head up the canyon on US 189.

From this junction it is 6.5 miles to the turnoff to the Sundance Ski

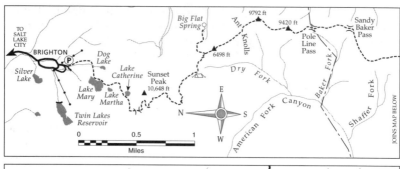

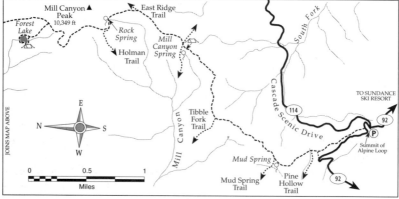

Resort, on SR 92, also known as the Alpine Loop. Go past the ski resort (3.2 miles) and Aspen Grove (4.7 miles), to the junction with the road heading to Cascade Springs (8.3 miles). Stay left on 92 another 0.4 mile to the summit and a large parking area on the left side of the road.

Water is key on this hike. The few water sources are widely dispersed and sometimes far from any place to camp. Late in the year, or in years of low rainfall, some of the springs may dry up. Check with the Forest Service for current information.

The Ridge Trail, or Forest Service Trail 157, starts on the north side of the parking area and immediately crosses the road. This well-worn, single track follows the ridge that divides Utah County from Wasatch County north to the backside of the Alpine Ridge—the mountains that form the south side of Little Cottonwood Canyon. The Ridge Trail is also part of the Great Western Trail.

After about 1 mile through meadows and pine forests, a side trail cuts left heading back a short distance to the Alpine Loop Road below the parking area. In another 0.25 mile the Pine Hollow Trail also cuts off to the left, heading west for a couple miles to rejoin the road.

After a series of mild ups and downs over about 1 mile, you arrive at a junction with the Mud Spring Trail to the west (left). The Ridge Trail turns a little more to the east and crosses over to the west side of the ridge to more open terrain, then stays on top of the ridge.

From Mud Spring to the Mill Canyon Trail is about 1.5 miles, with two 200-foot ascents. Along the way you pass the Tibble Fork Trail. Mill Canyon is the location of the first water source, a spring about 600 feet to the left of the trail down a dirt road.

You may decide to camp at Mill Canyon or continue on to the next suitable campsite about 5 miles ahead at Forest Lake. The next water source is Rock Spring, about 2 miles ahead. The spring sits in the middle of a rocky talus slope midway up Mill Canyon Peak. To continue means you will have hiked 10.5 miles and gained another 1600 feet in elevation—a very long day. If you stop at Mill Canyon, you've started with a short day, leaving 2 long days ahead. For a 3-day hike, we recommend continuing on to Forest Lake; otherwise, consider a 4-day trip.

From Mill Canyon the trail begins to rise, gaining 1100 feet to Rock Spring in about 2 miles. The spring, consisting of a trough and a pipe, can dry up, so plan accordingly. The Trails Illustrated map shows that near Rock Spring you cross the Holman Trail (to the west) and the East Ridge Trail, an alternate route to your destination. These routes are hard to spot—don't be concerned if you miss them. Just continue straight on the main Ridge Trail.

Leaving Rock Spring, the trail rises and falls, eventually rounding a ridge and small pass, and then drops quickly for a view of Forest Lake.

Utah penstemons decorate the Ridge Trail

Continue to a trail junction, about 2.25 miles from Rock Spring, where you take the Forest Lake side trail. This spur drops almost 700 feet over 0.75 mile down to the lake. There is a 4WD road to the lake, so you may find other campers there.

Day 2 is dry until just short of your camp spot, so take enough water for a full day of backpacking. In the morning, ascend to the main trail and head for Sandy Baker Pass. Over the next few miles, you climb to a peak, drop to a saddle, and then climb to another peak. At Pole Line Pass, about 2.75 miles from where you rejoined the main trail above Forest Lake, the trail joins with a road.

The trail is difficult to follow here. The road ascends up a ridge, then turns slightly to the east and begins to descend. Before the ridge top, the trail breaks off to the left, crossing out into a sheep pasture and switches back up through a grove of aspens. Watch for a Forest Service trail marker and a faint path through tall grasses.

The trail stays up on the ridgeline between Pole Line Pass and Ant Knolls. Beautiful views are present to the east and west. You climb from about 8800 feet to 9800 feet, but when you reach Ant Knolls—1.75 miles from Pole Line Pass—the short climb to its summit, just to the right of the trail, is worth the effort.

Both sides of the ridge steepen as you continue along the ridge top. About 1 mile past Ant Knolls, you see Big Flat—a large meadow below you to the east. Soon you reach a signed trail junction. The only water on day 2 awaits down in the meadow below.

Stash your pack in the trees near the junction, and take your empty water containers and filter with you down to the spring in Big Flat, about 0.75 mile. Fill up from the pipe of this reliable, perennial water source. You'll need enough water for the rest of day 2 and to lunch of day 3.

Once you get water, hike back up to the fork on the ridge, and retrieve your packs. A good campsite is located right on the ridge top just back up the trail from the junction, but it is often very windy and the vegetation is delicate. Alternatively, you can begin a steep descent down the ridge to the floor of a dry canyon, 0.5 mile from the junction. A road coming up the canyon ends right at the best camping area.

Day 3 is shorter, but involves a long climb up the Alpine Ridge, then down the other side to the Brighton ski resort. The trail steadily ascends 2 miles through a wide cleft in the rocky ridge above you to the ridge top. This area—one of the highlights of the trip—is full of alpine meadows, wildflowers, and jagged rock outcrops, but no water. You climb from 8900 feet at the campsite to 10,385 feet at the ridge top. You can choose to take a spur trail and continue the climb to Sunset Peak at 10,648 feet. The main trail drops down to a junction with the Albion Basin Trail 0.5 mile past the ridge top. Go right at the junction past Lake Catherine and Lake Mary. From the junction down to the Brighton Ski Resort is about 2 miles.

22 GROVE CREEK TO BATTLE CREEK LOOP

Distance: 8.5-mile loop
Hiking time: 4 to 6 hours
Difficulty: moderate
Season: June to October
Elevation gain: 3580 feet
Maps: USGS Timpanogos Cave, Orem; Trails Illustrated
  Uinta National Forest (best) or Wasatch Front/Strawberry
  Valley
Land Management Agency: Uinta National Forest,
  Pleasant Grove Ranger District

This loop can be hiked in either direction, but we recommend starting from the Grove Creek trailhead. Using two cars saves about 1 to 1.5 miles of dirt road hiking between the two trailheads. To reach the Grove Creek

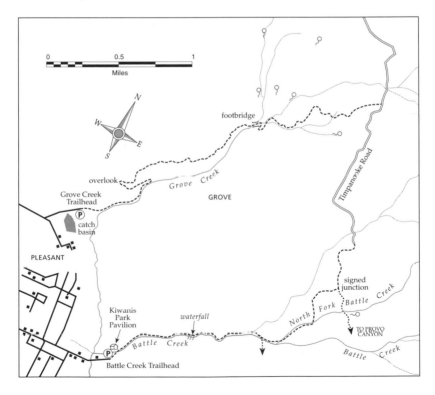

Cascade along Grove Creek

Trailhead, get off I-15 at the Orem 1600 North/Lindon exit (#276). Turn right and go about 0.5 mile to a stoplight. Turn right onto Geneva Road (SR 114) and follow the road under I-15 into the town of Pleasant Grove.

At State Street turn right. Proceed 1 block and turn left at the Purple Turtle restaurant. Go north for approximately 1 mile to 500 North Street, also named Grove Creek Drive. Turn right (east) and follow this road for a couple of miles. The street reaches a 90-degree turn with a chain-link fence straight ahead. Dalton Avenue goes to the right; Grove Creek Drive jogs to the left, following the fence line, and enters the Mahogany Ridge housing development. This area is growing rapidly and changes often, but the canyon mouth is about 0.25 mile straight ahead. Park along or at the end of Grove Creek Drive and walk to the trailhead at the canyon mouth.

The instructions for reaching the Battle Creek trailhead are nearly identical. After turning left at the Purple Turtle, look for 200 South Street, or Battle Creek Drive. This road takes you a couple of miles and ends at a parking area just past a water tank and at the pavilion in Kiwanis Park.

The Grove Creek Trail heads due east up the canyon, alongside a moderate stream. At first the trail follows a dirt road, which forks then rejoins about 150 feet ahead. Where the two roads meet at the upper end, the trail leaves the dirt road and ascends up a steep hillside to the left. If you miss the turn, the dirt road dead-ends at the stream after about 100 feet.

The trail is steep as it works its way up a rocky ledge, and although wide, the loose rock makes it difficult. After about 0.25 mile, you top out at a fence line. A sign indicates the Timpanooke Road is about 3 miles. The trail continues upcanyon another 0.25 mile, then makes a hairpin turn, heading back west, away from the stream and seemingly back the way you came. This is part of a very long switchback that takes you steadily up, eventually reaching an overlook of the entire Utah Valley; walk 50 feet up a small rise for the best view.

Now the trail heads back east for about 1.5 miles, high up on the north side of the canyon. You can hear the stream's roar, but rarely catch any glimpse of it some 200 feet below. Two sections of the trail have some exposure. The trail is 3 feet wide with a rock wall on the inside and a steep 30-foot drop off on the outside. Those with severe vertigo will likely be uncomfortable.

After about 1.5 miles, the trail reaches a bridge over the stream. This wonderful spot is a common turnaround point for those seeking a short day hike. It's also a cool spot for a break—cascading water crosses bare rock here sending a mist into the air and cooling the entire area. Just below the bridge a series of short waterfalls is visible from the trail.

From here the trail switches back through the pines and up into some grassy meadows to a large, fenced spring, a little over a mile from the bridge. Avoid crossing the fence, which was erected to prevent polluting the spring. From here the trail steepens for a final 0.25-mile climb to the Timpanooke Road. Follow the road south for about 1 mile as it crosses a large, relatively flat shelf. In summer you may encounter 4WDs along this road. Before reaching the Battle Creek Trail junction the road ends, and a single track trail continues straight ahead. Follow the track about 0.5 mile to a signed trail junction in the middle of a green, grassy meadow.

Turn down the Battle Creek Trail, which once into the canyon, stays right along the stream. At first you descend through a series of alternating shelves and meadows. At times the trail gets overgrown with grasses, but it's easy to follow.

Careful observers may notice signs of a huge avalanche that rumbled through this area from high up on the steep slopes of Mount Timpanogos in the late 1990s. After crossing several meadows and dropping into the head of Battle Creek canyon, the trail drops quickly down, descending the same elevation as the Grove Creek Trail, but doing it in a mile less distance.

Shortly after crossing a footbridge, you pass the first short waterfall roaring down a very narrow sluice and dropping 10 feet. Another 0.5 mile downstream is another section of cascades, this time right next to the trail. Be careful here, especially with children—trying to approach the water on the slick wet rock can have disastrous results.

Another 200 yards and you reach the highlight of Battle Creek—a 60-foot waterfall over a sheer rock cliff. Be careful, as more than one person has gone over the edge trying to see the falls from the top while standing in the stream. The trail bypasses the falls against the rocks on the right (north).

Another 0.5 mile down the trail and you arrive at the Kiwanis Park and parking area. If you have two cars, this is the end of your hike. Otherwise, take any one of the several dirt roads heading north along the base of the mountain. Numerous roads crisscross the area—just remember that you don't want to lose much elevation. It's about 1 mile back to the Grove Creek trailhead. As you proceed, keep looking at the mouth of Grove Creek Canyon, the next canyon to the north and try to head in that direction. Soon you'll see the catch basin and parking area.

23 | MOUNT TIMPANOGOS

Distance: 16.6 miles round trip
Hiking time: 7 hours minimum
Difficulty: strenuous
Season: mid-July to October
Elevation gain: 6210 feet
Maps: USGS Aspen Grove; Trails Illustrated Wasatch Front/
  Strawberry Valley or Uinta National Forest
Land Management Agency: Uinta National Forest,
  Pleasant Grove Ranger District

Mount Timpanogos (pronounced Timp-an-oh-gus) looms large, dominating the eastern skyline of Utah Valley. The trail to the top begins at Aspen Grove. Take the 800 North Orem exit (#275) off I-15. Follow 800 North (also SR 52) east through Orem to the mouth of Provo Canyon. Right at the mouth of the canyon the road splits. Stay left and head up the canyon on US 189.

From this junction it is 6.7 miles to the turnoff to the Sundance Ski Resort on SR 92, also known as the Alpine Loop. Turn left onto SR 92, a narrow winding road that passes the ski resort, many cabins, and large family recreation center on the 5-mile ascent to Aspen Grove. The trailhead is at

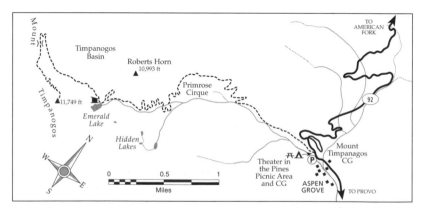

Rocky Mountain bighorn sheep near the peak

the Theater in the Pines Picnic Area and Campground, a large signed parking area on the left just past the fee station.

The obvious trail starts heading due west from the parking area. Just before entering some trees, a sign indicates you're entering the Mount Timpanogos Wilderness Area. For the first mile, the trail ascends gently to a waterfall, then starts into a long series of steep switchbacks that climb to the rim of Primrose Cirque, passing another waterfall along the way. Early in the season, when snow covers the ground, this waterfall melts out the snow from below, creating a "killer snow hole." At least one hiker has been killed, and several others injured, when the snow caved in beneath them, causing the hikers to fall 30 feet or more into near-freezing water.

As you climb toward Emerald Lake, you pass numerous waterfalls. From the trailhead, you climb 3200 feet over 5.25 miles to Emerald Lake, a jewel of a lake in a scenic location. From the lake it is about 3 miles to the summit.

The trail crosses the basin and meets a trail coming up from the basin to the north, then traverses a narrow ledge with some exposure at a place some call "the cat walk." Although it sounds ominous, the trail is several feet wide with plenty of room. After the cat walk, you cross a wide boulder field that necessitates hiking boots.

At the base of the final ridge the Timpanooke Trail joins in from the right (north), then the trail rises sharply to a saddle at the lowest point in the ridgeline. As you top the ridge at the saddle you're greeted with a fantastic view of Utah County. Watch for Rocky Mountain bighorn sheep near the saddle—this area is one of their favorites.

The trail crosses over to the face of the mountain, traversing a narrow worn path across slate-covered slopes below. The trail then beelines for a large rock outcrop ahead and climbs right up its face on a series of steps. The last 0.25 mile follows just below the ridgeline to the metal shelter at the peak. At the summit a cool wind and views in every direction await you.

24 | SNAKE HOLLOW

Distance: 5 to 8 miles round trip
Hiking time: 3 to 5 hours
Difficulty: easy to moderate
Season: December to March
Elevation gain: 1520 feet to junction; 2220 feet
    to Big Flat
Maps: USGS Brighton; Trails Illustrated Wasatch Front/
    Strawberry Valley
Land Management Agency: Wasatch Mountain State
    Park; Uinta National Forest, Pleasant Grove Ranger
    District
Special requirements: cross-country skis and/or snow-
    shoes

Snake Hollow sits just above Wasatch Mountain State Park, site of the 2002 Winter Olympics cross-country skiing events. From the south, coming up Provo Canyon on US 189, turn north onto SR 113 at the east end of Deer Creek Reservoir toward Charleston. Continue north into downtown Midway, following the signs to Wasatch Mountain State Park. After 4 miles, at the intersection with Main Street in Midway, turn left on SR 224. The road first heads due east, then makes a 90-degree turn north. After 2 miles, it skirts the southwest edge of the Wasatch Mountain Golf Course, before heading up Snake Hollow. The paved road passes a powerhouse (signed) in another mile. Proceed 2 more miles to a large parking area at the Mill Flat trailhead.

The trail follows a wide dirt road, which ascends up Snake Hollow from the parking area. On winter weekends, snowmobilers head up the

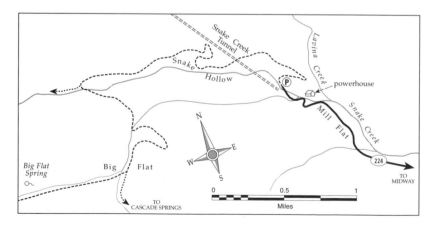

Winter quiet among the aspens

snow-covered road seeking fresh powder in the high mountain bowls to the west.

At 2.5 miles a road breaks off to the left and works its way along the mid-elevation foothills and ridges all the way back to Cascade Springs 10 to 15 miles to the south. This road is used by snowmobile tours from nearby resorts. It gains access to the Big Flat area by following the road about 1.5 miles south, then turning east. Big Flat is a large meadow and a great area for off-trail snowshoeing and winter camping.

The road to the right continues 1.25 miles up Snake Hollow to the base of steep ridges and bowls. Avalanche danger can be very high on these slopes, so exercise caution.

25 | ALPINE LOOP

Distance: 8.5 miles round trip
Hiking time: 3.5 to 5 hours
Difficulty: moderate
Season: December to March
Elevation gain: 2110 feet
Maps: USGS Aspen Grove; Trails Illustrated Wasatch Front/ Strawberry Valley
Land Management Agency: Uinta National Forest, Pleasant Grove Ranger District
Special requirements: cross-country skis and/or snow- shoes

The Alpine Loop Road goes from above the Sundance Ski Resort, over a pass, and down into American Fork Canyon, traversing the backside of Mount Timpanogos. In winter, this road is closed at the Aspen Grove trailhead, making the road from Aspen Grove to the summit a great

Snowshoeing the Alpine Loop

cross-country ski excursion. For instructions on getting to the trailhead, see Hike 23 to Mount Timpanogos. In winter, there's a large parking area where the road ends at a large snowbank. There is no day-use fee charged during winter months.

Begin by heading up the Alpine Loop Road. Snowmobiles are allowed on the road, and the traffic is usually light. Conditions are best during the week and after a recent snowfall.

The road switches back up the mountainside, but the country is

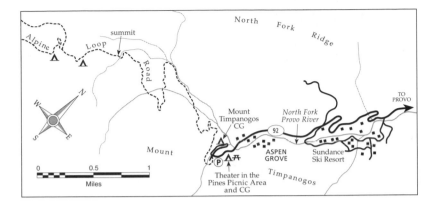

generally open with good views and little avalanche danger. At about 3.75 miles you reach a fork. The road to the right drops down to Cascade Springs. Continue on the main road (left) another 0.5 mile to the summit of the Alpine Loop Road. A fenced parking area is on the left.

From the summit you have three options. For most, this is a great place to stop, rest, eat lunch, take in the views, and then return to the Aspen Grove parking area. For advanced skiers, it is possible to ski down the American Fork (AF) Canyon side of the summit, but you'll need a second car to pick you up there. The road down the AF side is steeper, with deep drop-offs along sections of the road. The third option is to do a little backcountry skiing or snowshoeing. The Ridge Trail (Hike 21) begins on the north side of the road opposite the parking area and follows the ridgeline in relatively level terrain for several miles, ideal for snowshoeing. Be prepared for some routefinding, because the trail will be under several feet of snow.

26 | CASCADE SADDLE

Distance: 11.5 miles round trip
Hiking time: 6 to 8 hours
Difficulty: strenuous
Season: July to October
Elevation gain: 3930 feet
Maps: USGS Bridal Veil Falls; Trails Illustrated Wasatch Front/Strawberry Valley
Land Management Agency: Uinta National Forest, Pleasant Grove Ranger District

Take the 800 North Orem exit (#275) off I-15. Follow 800 North Street (also SR 52) east through Orem to the mouth of Provo Canyon. Right at the

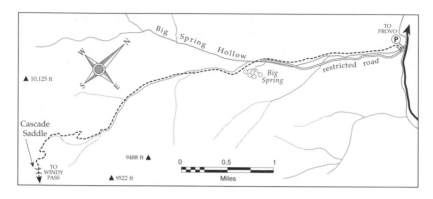

mouth of the canyon the road splits. Stay left and head north up the canyon on US 189.

From this junction it is 5.6 miles to the turnoff to the south fork of Provo Canyon and Vivian Park. Turn right (south) and proceed 3.3 miles to a turnoff signed "National Forest Access." Turn right and follow the road 0.2 mile to a large parking area.

The foot trail begins at the west side of the parking area. About 100 feet down the trail you cross a footbridge. On the far side is a sign stating it is 1.8 miles to Big Spring and 5 miles to the saddle. At Big Spring a rope and tire swing out over a pool in the stream and several concrete pads in the area are remnants from when the spring served as a scout camp. The trail continues to parallel the stream up a draw, until it crosses Big Spring Hollow to follow another side drainage to the right.

As the trail steepens, you see signs of the frequent avalanches that keep the trees from attaining any size. At about 1.5 miles from the springs, you arrive at the top of an intermediate ridge, marked 7666 on the USGS map, a gain of over 1200 feet from the springs.

Beginning the trek to Cascade Saddle

Your destination at the saddle is visible, but you've got another 1900 feet to climb in the next 1.5 miles. The climb through a series of small alpine bowls is beautiful, although the steepness may prevent you from fully appreciating it. The last 0.5 mile is straight up, but the ridge-top view is breathtaking. You'll see much of Utah Valley to the east and the Uinta Mountains to the west.

From here you can either return as you came, or you can hike down the west side on the Windy Pass Trail to the Rock Canyon Campground, as described in Hike 27.

27 | WINDY PASS

Distance: 7 miles round trip
Hiking time: 4 to 6 hours
Difficulty: strenuous
Season: July to October
Elevation gain: 3950 feet from road; 4200 feet from campground
Maps: USGS Bridal Veil Falls; Trails Illustrated Wasatch Front/Strawberry Valley
Land Management Agency: Uinta National Forest, Pleasant Grove Ranger District

Take the 800 North Orem exit (#275) off I-15. Follow 800 North Street (also SR 52) east through Orem to the mouth of Provo Canyon where the road splits. Stay left and head up the canyon on US 189 for 1.8 miles to the turnoff to the Squaw Peak Road on the right.

Follow the curvy road for 4 miles to a fork; go left. The pavement ends at the Hope Campground 0.4 mile ahead. Once on the dirt road, it's 5 miles to the Rock Canyon Campground turnoff. Either park at the campground, adding about 0.5 mile round trip and 200 feet of elevation gain to your trip, or continue another 0.5 mile past the campground on a very rough road where a foot trail crosses the road and Forest Service signs proclaim "No Motor Vehicles." Park along the road at the trail crossing, or continue 300 feet ahead to a second pullout.

If you park at the campground, look for a trail heading east, up toward the road from the far southeast end of the campground's loop road. The trail ascends 0.25 mile up to the roadside parking areas.

From the road the trail follows a dry drainage called Dry Fork, generally east. The well-developed trail gains elevation rapidly. A couple of faint, dead-end trails cross it within the first mile. Keep on the south side of the drainage.

After a mile or so the trail turns away from the drainage as it switches

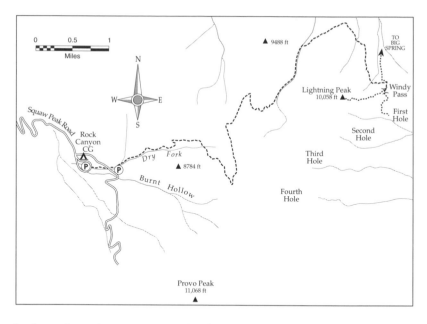

back up through aspen groves. At about 1.5 miles the trail reaches a bowl at the base of steep cliffs on three sides. A tall peak dominates the ridge directly south. Once in the bowl, the trail passes through wildflower-filled meadows with scattered aspens.

The trail crosses a first drainage, Dry Fork, and then follows a second smaller stream, filled with runoff into midsummer, up into the heart of the bowl. Stay right along the stream here, or you'll miss the trail. At the base of the cliffs and hidden behind a large rock outcrop, the trail makes a sharp, nearly 180-degree turn and starts traversing the terraced ridge to

Looking down Rock Canyon

the east. You final goal is the ridge top, another mile ahead, with spectacular views.

From Windy Pass either return as you came, or if you have the luxury of two cars, continue down the east side of the ridge. For more on this alternative, see Hike 26.

28 | SPANISH FORK PEAK

Distance: 8.5 miles round trip
Hiking time: 7 hours
Difficulty: strenuous
Season: April to September
Elevation gain: 4870 feet
Maps: USGS Spanish Fork Peak; Trails Illustrated Wasatch
     Front/Strawberry Valley
Land Management Agency: Uinta National Forest,
     Spanish Fork Ranger District

On I-15, heading south from Provo, take the Price/Manti exit (#261) and proceed south on US 89. The trailhead is approximately 4 miles from the mouth of Spanish Fork Canyon on the northeast, or left side of the road. Look for a small dirt road leading to a green gate. If you reach the large truck pullout for Pole Canyon (also known as the community of Covered Bridge Canyon), you've gone too far. Once through the gate, drive a little less than a mile on a dirt road and park your vehicle under some trees. Hike 0.25 mile farther up the road and you will see the sign for the trailhead. From the sign, follow the Sterling Hollow Trail.

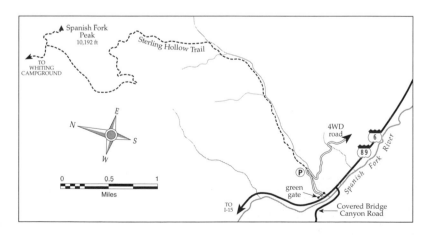

Meadows beneath Spanish Fork Peak

Spanish Fork Peak is a great day hike, but it can be an overnight hike by continuing north on the Sterling Hollow Trail past Maple Canyon Lake and down the Right Fork of Maple Canyon, ending at the Whiting Campground in Mapleton Canyon. Hiking through would necessitate shuttling.

Sterling Hollow Trail begins as a gradual climb on a trail of loose rock taking you up out of the hollow. As you begin your ascent you can look back and see US 89 and the houses in Pole Canyon. Cattle graze the area during the summer months. The trail smooths, entering into the surrounding brush, and soon running under a canopy of trees. Be wary of poison oak, common in this area and most of the mountains in Utah.

As you continue into the higher elevations, enjoy the shade of quaking aspens before crossing a large field of wild grass and flowers where the trail disappears. The USGS map shows the trail continuing up and over the ridge to the west. However, the best route is straight up through the grass. This is the hardest part of the hike; try to minimize damage to the plant life as you scramble up to the worthwhile view. Also, you may unknowingly spook a sitting pheasant or sage grouse, making your heart jump as the bird quickly flutters off.

The top of the mountain has some loose, but not dangerous, rock and a beautiful view of Utah County. Look for the mailbox embedded in a large pile of rocks; it previously held a notepad for hikers to record their accomplishment or leave messages for each other.

29 | LOAFER MOUNTAIN TRAIL

Distance: 11 miles round trip
Hiking time: 8 to 10 hours
Difficulty: moderate
Season: late June to September
Elevation gain: 3990 feet
Maps: USGS Payson Lakes, Birdseye; Trails Illustrated
Wasatch Front/Strawberry Valley
Land Management Agency: Uinta National Forest,
Spanish Fork Ranger District

In the town of Payson, drive south on 600 East Street along the Mount Nebo Scenic Loop. The road takes you just below the white "P" on the hillside and into the mouth of Payson Canyon. Drive about 12 miles to the Loafer Mountain trailhead on the left side of the road. If you pass the entrance to Payson Lakes on the right, you have gone too far.

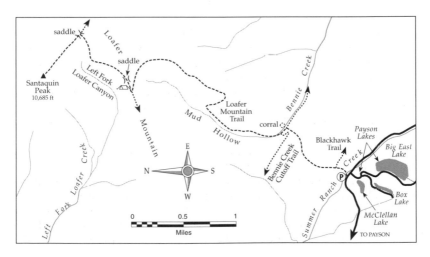

From the trailhead, the trail follows the road for a very short time and then heads north. After 0.25 mile the Blackhawk Trail enters from the right through a green gate. The trail works its way up 100 feet or so then drops after 0.75 mile to the Bennie Creek Cutoff Trail. A small corral marks the intersection. Take the left fork—as shown by the sign—to stay on the Loafer Mountain Trail, No. 098. The trail takes another short drop and reaches another signed intersection. Turn right. (Note that the USGS map is inaccurate to this point. Simply follow the trail signs.)

The trail gains just over 2000 feet in the next 3 miles. The upper reaches of the trail follow a rocky ridge void of any substantial trees, making this section hot in sunny weather. The trail soon comes to a small saddle and a great view of Utah County. This is a great spot to camp for those making this an overnight trip.

From the saddle, the trail makes its way northeast toward Santaquin Peak. After a mile, the trail reaches another small saddle. Santaquin Peak lies to the left. A great view of Utah County can be gained from Santaquin Peak by following the trail to the left for 0.5 mile. From this vantage point

The view of Payson Canyon

one can see Mount Nebo to the south, Mount Timpanogos to the north, and countless other peaks in all directions.

30 | MOUNT NEBO

Distance: 14 miles round trip
Hiking time: 8 hours
Difficulty: strenuous
Season: late June to October
Elevation gain: 3340 feet
Maps: USGS Nebo Basin, Mona; Trails Illustrated Uinta
    National Forest
Land Management Agency: Uinta National Forest,
    Spanish Fork Ranger District

Take SR 132 east out of Nephi toward Manti. Where the road forks after 5 miles, go left. Travel upcanyon another 4.5 miles just past the Ponderosa Campground. The trail begins from a parking area on the left side of the road. Although the trail to the peak is steep and very dry, expect to see deer, elk, and small game in the summer.

From the parking area, the single-track trail quickly begins its easy-to-follow ascent through scrub oak and grass. As the trail winds up Andrews Ridge, it offers a view of the looming mountain above to the northwest, and Nebo Basin to the north.

After about 3 miles, the Nephi Nebo Peak Trail enters from the left. Stay to the right and follow the trail as it begins to level out and head north. For those making this an overnight trip, there are a couple of camping spots

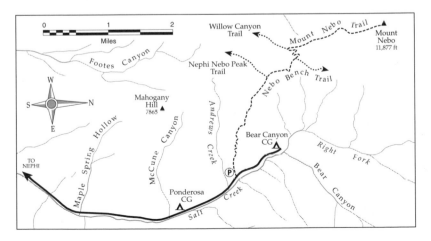

A distant Mount Nebo

over the next 0.5 mile. Seasonal water can usually be found here in early spring. The trail then enters more switchbacks up a talus slope where it connects with the Nebo Bench Trail. Turn left here and continue up another series of steep switchbacks.

The switchbacks lead to the mountain ridge where the Willow Canyon Trail enters from the left. From here the trail offers a view of Juab County below to the west and Loafer Mountain to the north. Follow the trail north, along the ridge, for 2.5 miles to the peak.

31 | DANIELS PASS

Distance: 4-mile loop
Hiking time: 2 to 4 hours
Difficulty: moderate
Season: December to March
Elevation gain: 690 feet
Maps: USGS Twin Peaks; Trails Illustrated Wasatch Front/
  Strawberry Valley
Land Management Agency: Uinta National Forest, Heber
  Ranger District
Special requirements: snowshoes

From Heber City, drive south on US 40 toward Strawberry Reservoir. About 20 miles up Daniels Canyon, you reach the summit and the Daniels Summit Lodge, a large motel and general store on the west side of the highway. Turn into the lodge complex and after passing under the log entry way, immediately turn right and follow the dirt road about 100 yards to the end. Park at the trail signs at the end of the road.

Although the trail signs indicate this trail is for cross-country skiers and snowshoers only, snowmobiles frequent the first part of the trail. Blue metal signs on trees mark the trail, which begins by dropping 100 vertical feet toward the Lodgepole Campground. The Trails Illustrated map is inaccurate; follow the blue metal signs.

About 1 mile in, you see a blue trail marker with arrows indicating a trail junction. Straight ahead the trail continues heading downcanyon to the campground, with a groomed trail looping around. For an easy trip,

An off-trail romp through Utah powder

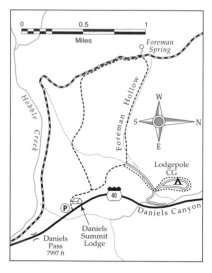

take this trail. The full loop makes for a 3.5-mile trip, with a 300-foot ascent on the way back, made easy by following the snowmobile tracks.

For a more exciting backcountry trip, turn west and begin ascending the small canyon called Foreman Hollow. Snowmobilers do not try this trail. If other snowshoers have not already made a path, simply follow the low point of the drainage west. You can't get lost—this area is bounded on all sides by roads. Just keep working your way up the drainage for just over 0.75 mile, and up about 600 feet, to a road that gets heavy snowmobile usage.

Once on the road, head south. If you follow the road 1 mile south, turn left (east) at the junction, and then go 1 mile east, you'll be back at the Daniels Summit Lodge. Most fun, however, is to go about 0.25 to 0.5 mile south on the road, then turn east and head through the powder cross-country down the gentle slope, working your way down to the east and south. Eventually you meet the trail you started on and can follow it southeast back to the lodge.

32 | NOTCH PEAK

Distance: 7.5 miles round trip
Hiking time: 3 to 5 hours
Difficulty: moderate
Season: May to early November
Elevation gain: 2910 feet
Maps: USGS Notch Peak, Miller Cove
Land Management Agency: BLM Fillmore Field Office

Drive southwest out of Delta on US 6 and US 50, passing the large, flat, often dry lakebed of Sevier Lake to the south. Just after the lakebed is a well-graded dirt road on the north side, about 41 miles from Delta. Turn north for 3.4 miles to the Miller Canyon Road and turn west. After 5 miles and just before you start to enter Miller Canyon, turn south at the junction heading up Sawtooth Canyon, through the Miller Cove area. This road is normally suitable for passenger cars (just go slow!), but conditions can

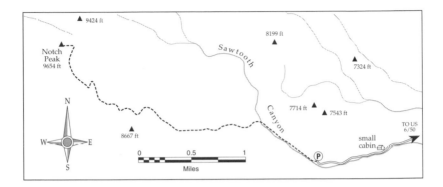

change each year. When you pass a road junction, stay right. About 2.5 miles up this canyon, you pass an old abandoned cabin, and the road worsens. Shortly after the cabin is a stand of juniper trees to shade your parked vehicle.

Follow the 4WD track up the canyon, noting the high cliff walls on both sides of the small gorge. The canyon opens up after a little less than a mile and the 4WD track splits. To the right is a more open canyon; to the left the smaller canyon follows the south cliff walls. Go left.

For the next several miles, you stay in the canyon bottom. Before long the 4WD track peters out, leaving you walking in the dry wash bottom. The walls close in and the small canyon gains a little of the character of its sandstone slot canyon cousins farther south and west.

Nearly a mile from the fork, you reach a series of rocky ledges that are generally easy to scale, but can be treacherous from November to March, when snow and ice provide tenuous footing, at best. In warmer weather this section is not too difficult. In some places you can bypass parts of the ledges by traversing up onto the hillside on the north side of the canyon; the south side consists of tall, steep cliffs. Just don't get caught on the hillside without

The view from Notch Peak

a way to reenter the canyon, which affords the easiest passage to the peak.

The canyon soon turns north and opens back up. Up ahead you'll see a saddle between two peaks. It's about 1.25 miles from the ledges to the saddle. Once at the saddle you'll be able to look over the cliff edge. Be careful—it's over 2000 feet down. Turn west and ascend a short, but steep, half mile to the top of Notch Peak. The vertical cliffs rank as the tallest in Utah, with a sheer drop of almost 1500 feet and a total drop of nearly 5000 feet to Tule Valley below.

33 | CRYSTAL PEAK

Distance: 2 to 3 miles round trip
Hiking time: 2 hours
Difficulty: easy
Season: fall to spring
Elevation gain: 700 feet
Map: USGS Crystal Peak
Land Management Agency: BLM Fillmore Field Office

From Delta, on US 6 and US 50, turn south on SR 257 about 10 minutes west of Delta, just before the town of Hinckley. You will pass through Deseret on your way to the town of Black Rock, about an hour's drive. From Black Rock, turn west (right) onto Black Rock Road, a graded dirt road suitable for passenger cars.

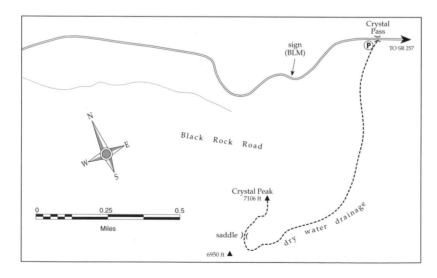

The white volcanic tuff of Crystal Peak

Although you drive 36 miles to reach Crystal Peak, you'll see it long before you arrive. Unlike the surrounding peaks, Crystal Peak is a white conelike peak that stands out like a sore thumb. From a distance the peak looks as though a lot of plant life is growing on its slopes. Closer inspection reveals that the dark spots are actually huecos, or pockets in the rock, making the hike up Crystal Peak both unusual and spectacular.

Along the northwest side of the peak are several spots to pull off the road to park. We suggest you park before reaching the BLM Crystal Peak sign.

Crystal Peak, along with all of the surrounding area, is very dry. Make sure you bring plenty of water. Avoid this area in the summer months because of the heat and high sun exposure. In addition to spring and fall, you can summit Crystal Peak during warm periods in winter when there is no snow.

From your north side parking spot, follow the base of the hill around to the east. As you round the peak's southeast shoulder, you arrive at a wash that divides the white, pocketed rock from the familiar pinyon and juniper forested ridge, with dark, "normal" soil, running west. Follow this wash upward until you reach a prominent saddle, which joins the ridge to the white rock of Crystal Peak. There is no distinct trail to the saddle, so make your way upward along the south side of the wash.

Once on the saddle, turn and head north. Stop at the saddle and pick out a route up. Look for a ravine with a gentle grade. Try to avoid any areas where climbing might be required. The white volcanic deposits are very brittle and break under the slightest weight. As you near the top, you reach a 10- to 12-foot section that requires scrambling. Be extremely cautious here. As you climb up onto the summit flat, test every hold before applying your full weight. Although the scrambling is easy, the going is slow as you exercise extreme care.

Once on top of Crystal Peak, you can see out into Nevada and the high peaks of Great Basin National Park to the west. To the northeast you see the Wasatch Range, and due east the Tushar Mountains, the second highest range in Utah. The barren desert surroundings take on a unique beauty.

Climbing down the scrambling section is much easier than the ascent, but again exercise caution. Make sure to note your path on the way up because finding your car once you get back onto flats at the base of the peak can be confusing.

SOUTHWEST

34 | QUAIL CREEK

Distance: 2 miles round trip to the pools; up to 10 miles round trip exploring upcanyon
Hiking time: 1 hour to pools; up to 5 hours for exploration upcanyon
Difficulty: easy to moderate
Season: April to October if you plan to get wet; dry hiking October to March
Elevation gain: 560 feet
Map: USGS Harrisburg Junction
Land Management Agency: BLM St. George Field Office; Red Cliffs Desert Reserve

Get off I-15 in southwestern Utah at the Harrisburg Junction, exit 16. Follow the frontage road north, paralleling the east side of the interstate, watching the signs to Red Cliffs Recreation Area. In a few miles, you'll see signs guiding you to turn left and pass through a narrow tunnel under I-15. It's a few miles to the recreation area boundary. Expect to pay a day-use fee at Red Cliffs. There's a parking area at the signed trailhead.

The first 0.5 to 0.75 mile of this hike crosses through the Red Cliffs Desert

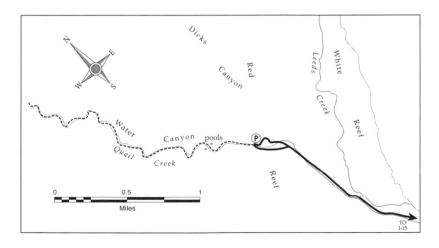

Reserve, which restricts travel to established trails. Be sure to stay on the trail or in the streambed until you reach the bypass of the narrow section described below.

The trail starts at the west side of the parking area, crossing sandy benches as it passes through open areas near the mouth of the canyon. Soon, however, the canyon walls close in. About 1 mile up the canyon, you reach an especially narrow channel through the slickrock, with two large water-filled potholes. Those in for a short hike may want to stop here to take in the sun or to take a dip in the potholes, which are large enough to swim in. To reach the upper pool, or to continue the hike, you need to by-pass the first pool by traversing a sloping section of slickrock. A short piece

Chimneying over Quail Creek

of rope and a series of carved footholds help you through this section, but don't count on the old rope to hold your full weight; rather, use it to help keep your balance. The bypass is fairly easy, but may be more than casual hikers want to attempt.

Above the pools the creek makes a sharp turn into the narrowest section of the canyon. It would appear that you can go up this section, but we recommend going around it.

To bypass the narrows, go back to just before the sharp turn and work your way up into the rocks on the north side of the creek. The trail passes between a couple of finlike vertical sandstone protrusions. Partway through this section is a large juniper tree growing in the crack between the fins. Right at that tree is another crack dropping back down toward the creek. Although it may not look promising, walk down the crack across the sloping sandstone. This route takes you back to the creekside, above the narrows.

To follow the stream, you have to chimney between the canyon walls, which are about 4 to 5 feet apart, for about 15 feet over the stream. To chimney, lean out over the water and place your hands on the sandstone on the far bank. Raise your feet up on the opposite wall so your body is nearly horizontal. Shuffle your hands and feet to move forward until you pass the obstacle. The water in the canyon is only about 4 feet deep, so in warmer weather you can wade or swim through this section.

A couple more turns in the canyon and you reach a point at which proceeding means you'll have to walk in the shallow stream for about 0.5 mile, through a section with high walls and the stream reaching from wall to wall. It is possible to ascend a side canyon, then routefind and scramble to bypass this high-walled narrows, avoiding the water during cooler weather. Above the narrow section, the stream gets smaller and the canyon shallower. The stream course supports thick vegetation, which slows your progress. Continue upcanyon until you've explored enough, or time runs out.

35 | THREE PONDS

Distance: 4 miles round trip
Hiking time: 2.5 to 3 hours
Difficulty: easy
Season: late September to early May
Elevation gain: 210 feet
Maps: USGS Santa Clara, St. George 1:100,000
Land Management Agency: Snow Canyon State Park;
   Red Cliffs Desert Reserve

From St. George in southwestern Utah, head north on SR 18 (called Bluff Street in town). It's 19 miles from the intersection of Bluff and St. George

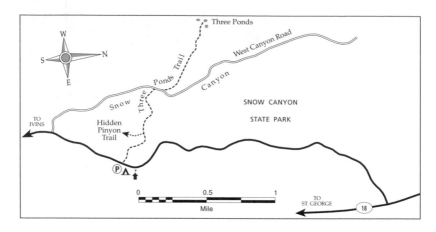

Boulevard streets in St. George to the main entrance of Snow Canyon State Park. Turn into the park and head down the canyon for 2.3 miles. The ranger station is located next to the large park campground on the left (southeast). Pull into the campground road to pay your park day-use fee. Exit the campground back onto the main road and continue 0.1 mile southwest to a large parking area on the right side. Park here.

Start out over the slickrock on a well-marked, rock-lined trail. Do not take the turn-offs to the Hidden Pinyon Trail, a shorter loop hike that traverses the slickrock near the trailhead. The Three Ponds Trail works its way up and down a few small rocky ridges. The hiking is easy and the trail wide.

After about 1.25 miles, you reach the West Canyon Road. Cross the road and follow the dry sandy wash west-northwest toward the orange cliffs. The trail stays in the wash the entire way; avoid shortcutting across the benches. In dry periods, hiking the wash bottom gets more difficult in the deep, loose sand.

Near the upper end, the wash narrows somewhat, and slickrock walls move closer to frame the canyon. The trail ends at a large pool at the base of a notch through a 50-foot wide sandstone fin. Above the large pool, sunken in the bottom of the slickrock slot, lie two deep potholes; hence, the name Three Ponds. In warm, sunny weather you can cool off by wading into the bottom pool.

Someone has carved shallow "moki steps" in the sandstone above the bottom pool, but unless you want to swim, we don't recommend using them. Instead, go left up through the rocks on an easy, worn path that crosses over the fin and drops gently down the opposite side. From the back, it's simple to look down the top of the notch onto the two potholes below. These pools may be deep and the side walls slick, so don't attempt to pass down this slot unless you have ropes and at least two people.

Looking down on the Three Ponds

From the top of the slot, turn around and head up the washbed. A couple hundred yards upcanyon a beautiful waterfall slides down a 40-foot high fall. Although it may not be perennial, in the spring there's water and a very cold pool beneath it.

On the way back to the trailhead, watch for the trail immediately after crossing West Canyon Road. The trail drops off the road, into a wash, then turns east (left) up a sloping slickrock section right beside a tree. If you continue down the wash more than 50 feet beyond the road, you're off the trail.

36 | BULLDOG KNOLLS

Distance: 2.5 miles round trip to Peak 6152; 6 miles to radio towers
Hiking time: 3 to 8 hours
Difficulty: moderate
Season: November to February
Elevation gain: 920 feet
Map: USGS Jarvis Peak
Land Management Agency: BLM St. George Field Office

Head north on Bluff Street (SR 18) in St. George to the intersection with SR 8. Turn west toward the towns of Santa Clara and Ivins. Continue past Ivins to Shivwits. West of Shivwits, you reach a junction. Turn to the south toward I-15 and Littlefield and into the Beaver Dam Mountains.

Follow the road south past a mining operation. The road begins to climb, eventually reaching a pass called Utah Hill Summit on the Jarvis Peak USGS map. There is a wide pullout on the south side of the road and a dirt road heading up into the hills. Taking the dirt road, you'll pass two microwave stations and towers. At 0.8 mile, a lesser road takes off to the right; stay left.

At 1 mile is a good turnout and parking area with a fire pit. This is a good spot to park for those without an HCV. Continuing up, there's a cut-off road on the right at 1.2 miles. You could also park here, but the pullout is smaller. At 1.3 miles, the cutoff rejoins on the right, and the road worsens. The last opportunity to pull out and park is at 1.8 miles. It's 1 additional mile to the top, a saddle on a ridge crest with a wide spot in the road big enough for two or three cars. The last mile is rocky and narrow. Once

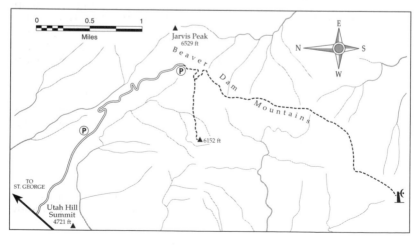

Overlooking the dry desert terrain

you start up, you're committed. A full-sized pickup or SUV can make it, but expect the sides of the vehicle to get scratched by brush on either side of the road. At the top, large rocks block further progress on the road.

The hike to the top of the highest peak in the Bulldog Knolls area is a cross-country routefind to the top of a peak overlooking the low Great Basin desert. There is no trail, so allow more time to cover the distance than you would for established trails.

Your goal is the peak topped with a microwave tower to the southwest. From the ridge top parking, set out on foot, following the old jeep trail up the north side of the ridge heading west. In about 0.25 mile, turn north up a steep grade to another ridge saddle. From this saddle turn west, off the road, and ascend cross-country about 0.75 mile to a peak marked 6152 feet on the USGS map. If you have a GPS, the coordinates are 12249795 E 4107189 N.

From this intermediate peak, you have excellent views of Red Mountain to the north and Gunlock Reservoir, just to its west, and the southwest flank of Pine Valley Mountains, behind Red Mountain. To the northeast, partially obscured by Jarvis Peak, are the salmon cliffs of Zion. Also peeking out behind Jarvis is the south end of St. George.

To the south, you see the west cliff face of the area's highest peak, which tapers to the lowland desert to the west. In the distance you can see the peaks bordering the Arizona Strip and new Parashant–Grand Canyon National Monument and the north edge of the Grand Canyon. The high mountain to the west-southwest is Mount Trumbull.

If you want a longer cross-country trip, return to the jeep trail, which descends the ridgeline to start up to the high peak. Eye the terrain ahead. The ridge to the south-southeast flows over several small hilltops, then turns slightly eastward to a higher ridge top. Look along the ridgeline southeast toward a peak. The high peak between you and highest point may appear to be your destination, but the true peak has a tower on top.

Start hiking on the jeep trail straight ahead, descending steeply about 0.25 mile to what looks like a turnaround point on the road. You are on a narrow ridge that bisects the mountains to the north and south. The road makes a sharp turn to the west and heads down a wash. Leave the road and start off-trail straight ahead (south) up the ridge. Be careful not to end up traversing the ridge instead of ascending it. Follow its backbone up to the next peak. The rise steepens and the brush thickens near the top, but requires no climbing and little bushwhacking.

The top of this ridge bears evidence of a wildfire in the late 1990s; the lack of vegetation makes it easy to routefind. Get a good look at your goal, the tower-topped peak to the southwest. Descend into the wide heavily vegetated basin between you and your goal, then back up the ridge to a front, lower peak. This section is deceptive—the distances are farther than they look. The route from here is all cross-country. Stick to the ridges when possible to avoid bushwhacks. Follow a ridge up to the foreground peak, then up a slight uphill to the peak and tower. From the top the views to west and south include the Virgin River Gorge and to the north and east the Pine Valley Mountains.

37 | PINE VALLEY MOUNTAINS

Distance: 17-mile loop
Hiking time: 2 to 3 days
Difficulty: strenuous
Season: July to October
Elevation gain: 5560 feet
Maps: USGS Signal Peak and Grass Valley; Dixie National
    Forest—Pine Valley and Cedar City
Land Management Agency: Dixie National Forest, Pine
    Valley Ranger District

Head north out of St. George on Bluff Street (SR 18), drive past Snow Canyon State Park and the town of Veyo to Central, where you'll see a junction indicating the road to Pine Valley. From Central to Pine Valley is about 8 miles. Proceed to a four-way junction with a historic white church on the right side. Turn east (left) for 1.5 miles to the Pine Valley Recreation Area fee station. At the time this book was published, there was no fee for hik-

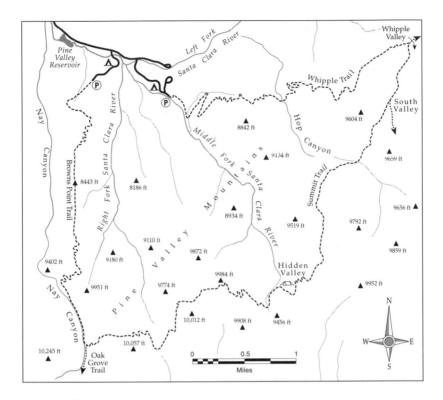

ing or backcountry camping, as long as you park at the trailhead. Stop at the fee station and let them know you are planning to hike only. If you use the established campgrounds, make sure to pay the entrance fee.

Continue on another 1.25 miles to a sign stating Blue Springs, Recreation Residence Area, and Whipple trailhead. Turn right. It's 0.75 mile to the trailhead. At a fork, keep to the left toward the "recreation residences." Do not enter the Blue Springs Campground. The Whipple trailhead has a wide parking area at the end of the road with a large entrance sign designating the Pine Valley Wilderness Area. Another road makes a hard left and continues to the residences.

The Forest Service map best shows the developed trails. Be sure to get one at either the Pine Valley Ranger Station or the Interagency Building in St. George. Also note that water can be scarce on this hike. Several streams contain water in early summer, but dry out by late July. Be careful not to hike too early, or you'll have to contend with deep snowdrifts, which often last into mid-July. Check with the Pine Valley Ranger Station for current water and snow conditions.

The trail starts wide. After just 300 feet, you'll see a sign for the Whipple Trail and an arrow pointing left (northeast). The wide trail continuing

Stream crossing in the Pine Valley Mountains

southeast is the wrong trail—take the left turn, ascending over 1000 feet to Hop Canyon. The canyon opens to a beautiful aspen- and spruce-filled bowl surrounded by rugged rock outcroppings and cliffs.

Leaving Hop Canyon, you begin another tough pull up another 1000 feet. At the top of the second climb is the junction with the Summit Trail; at the sign, continue straight ahead into Whipple Valley. The trail is very indistinct here, but heads generally southwest. Just follow the stream course up the valley, and soon you'll spot the trail. After leaving Whipple Valley, you quickly enter the spectacular South Valley. Bounded on three sides by spruce-covered ridges, this flat green meadow is a haven for wildlife, which quiet hikers may sight in the evening and early morning hours.

The trail leaves the meadow to the southwest and ascends the ridge. Topping out, you begin a descent into upper Hop Canyon, the same stream you crossed earlier, but at a much higher elevation. Campsites are few here. One final climb takes you to Hidden Valley, where a small meadow sits among tall Englemann spruce and aspens. The entire bowl sits among tall sheer cliffs and large rock outcrops. The meadow is a marshy, muddy bog in the early spring, but a few good campsites are among the trees on the meadow's east side. A small stream flows through the meadow, but the water has a bitter taste even after filtering. In the spring, a stream fed by melting snow may be found about 100 yards past Hidden Valley along the trail.

Getting to Hidden Valley on the first day makes for a long day. If you choose to make a more relaxed 3-day trip, spend the first night at Whipple or South Valley.

Leaving Hidden Valley, you climb to the highest point along the trail. It's a tough 3.5 miles to the trail junction with the Browns Point Trail. Nearing this junction, you reach the trail's highest point, arriving at the wide, flat top of a ridge. A short 100-yard walk off the trail here yields great views of Zion National Park to the east, Quail Creek Reservoir to the southeast, and Washington and St. George to the southwest.

Now begins the descent, as the trail drops into Nay Canyon. Look for blazes in the trees and occasional rock cairns. Near the stream in Nay Canyon, the Summit Trail you've been following meets up with the Oak Grove and Browns Point Trails. The Summit Trail continues to the west, up over the top of the next ridge and past the highest peaks in the Pine Valley Range. The Oak Grove Trail turns left (south) climbs up a ridge, then descends to the Oak Grove Campground on the south side of the mountains, near Leeds.

You should turn right along the Browns Point Trail. Before long, the trail veers right and up the ridge, switching back and forth for your final climb before the knee-straining 3000-foot descent.

You top out near 10,000 feet again, then finally cross the ridge to its east side and start the rapid and rocky drop to the trailhead. You can track your elevation change as you pass through various ecological zones, from subalpine fir and spruce and aspen at 10,000 feet to manzanita and ponderosa pine at the trailhead.

The Browns Point Trail spits you out at the Lion's Lodge parking area, near the Pines Campground. Just before arriving at the parking area, you cross a trail heading to the east, which shortcuts back to the Whipple trailhead, cutting almost a mile off the return to your car. If you miss the cutoff trail, simply follow the paved road out of the campground to the main road, then back up to your vehicle.

38 | RED MOUNTAIN TRAVERSE

Distance: 8 miles round trip
Hiking time: 4 to 6 hours
Difficulty: moderate
Season: February to early May, September to November
Elevation gain: 480 feet
Map: USGS Veyo, Santa Clara
Land Management Agency: BLM St. George Field Office

From St. George, take SR 18 north toward Veyo. Turn west 0.3 mile after mile marker 15 onto a good dirt road that travels under a set of powerlines and continues for just under 0.5 mile. There is plenty of room for parking at the end.

From the parking area, head southeast on a faint jeep trail. There are

Gazing into Snow Canyon from the trail

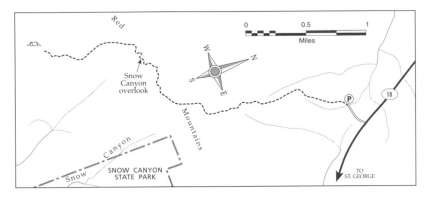

several trails around the area, but they all eventually narrow down to one road. The trail gradually begins to gain elevation. At times the juniper and pinyon trees thin and you can see back to the Pine Valley Mountains to the northeast. Along with the trees, the area is laden with manzanita, sagebrush, yucca, and barrel cactus.

After 2.5 miles the trail tops out at approximately 5150 feet. Here you can take a small detour from the trail out to the rim of Snow Canyon. The overlook offers a wonderful view of the white canyons contrasting with the red-orange surroundings. Often, sparrows and other small birds take occasion to play in the wind drafts created by the canyon.

The trail continues southwest around the west side of Snow Canyon for almost another 2 miles before disappearing into a sea of sandstone swells. For day hikers, this is a good spot to turn around, making a round trip of 8 miles.

For those looking for an overnight trip, there is ample space for camping amid the redrock. Water is sparse, so plan on carrying enough water for both days.

39 | ASHDOWN GORGE

Distance: 6 miles one way
Hiking time: 6 to 8 hours
Difficulty: strenuous
Season: June to October
Elevation loss: 1780 feet
Maps: USGS Flanigan Arch and Webster Flat
Land Management Agency: Dixie National Forest, Cedar City Ranger District

Get off I-15 in Cedar City. From the corner of Center and Main streets, turn east and head up Cedar Canyon on SR 14, toward Navajo Lake. You need

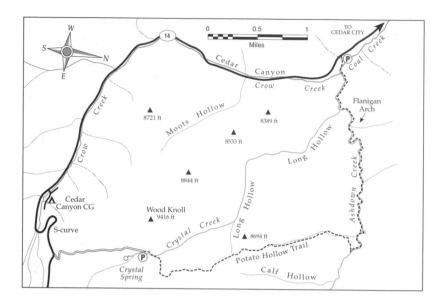

two cars for this hike. Park the first car about 7.5 miles up the canyon where a dirt road pulls off to the north (left, heading upcanyon) just before a series of concrete barriers lining a sharp curve where the road turns from east to south and heads up Crow Canyon, a narrow side canyon. The dirt road heads down the bank of the highway then upcanyon to a parking area.

To get to the trailhead, continue upcanyon. You pass the Cedar Canyon Campground and then go through a sharp S curve. Just after the S curve, there's a dirt road on the left. Take the turnoff and head about 1 mile to Crystal Spring. The road is suitable for two-wheel-drive vehicles—just go slowly.

Once in the meadows, you pass the small Forest Service sign marked "Trail," indicating the Blowhard Trail, a popular mountain biking trail. Drive past the sign about another 0.25 mile to a larger sign that marks the wilderness boundary and maps the Potato Hollow Trail and Ashdown Gorge. Park at the sign.

The trail drops slightly, following a ridgeline that heads a forested canyon. After about 0.5 mile, the trail turns left (west) along the canyon's north shoulder. The trees thin out and the trail reaches a junction. Turn right, or north, and drop off the ridge. This section of the trail is steep—rather than switchback down the ridge, the trail heads straight down. At the bottom, it crosses grassy meadows that in summer provide grazing areas for herds of sheep.

The trail meets a dirt road. Go right on the dirt road for about 0.25 mile, where you'll come upon Ashdown Creek. The rocky flood plain is a great place to take a break or stop for lunch. It's also wise to take a few minutes to scout weather conditions. If there are any rain clouds, don't continue into Ashdown Gorge. Rains high up in Cedar Breaks can produce potentially fatal flash floods in the gorge.

The narrow gorge extends for several miles, exiting the narrow section just upcanyon from your car at the lower parking area. You'll spend much of the time over the next few hours walking in the stream over rounded cobble rock. Shoes or boots with good ankle support are necessary. Although the straight-line distance is short, the many meanders of the stream make for a longer hike. Be sure to watch for Flanigan Arch

Rock pinnacle in Ashdown Gorge

high up on the north wall, about 1 mile below the confluence of Ashdown and Rattlesnake Creeks.

The gorge section deepens to over 1000 feet. A variety of plant and animal life make their home in the gorge, including delicate bluebells, wild marionberries, ponderosa pine, and many avian species.

Once you leave the narrow gorge, continue to follow the stream downcanyon. There is no trail and some boulder hopping is required. About 0.5 mile downcanyon, you'll see your car.

40 | RATTLESNAKE CREEK

Distance: 18 to 20 miles one way
Hiking time: 3 days
Difficulty: moderate
Season: July to October
Elevation gain: 2340 feet
Maps: USGS Flanigan Arch, Brian Head, Navajo Lake
Land Management Agencies: Dixie National Forest, Cedar City Ranger District; Cedar Breaks National Monument

Get off I-15 at the south Parowan exit (#75), about 20 miles north of Cedar City. Follow SR 143 into town, then follow the signs to the Brian Head Ski Resort. Continue past the ski resort to the base of Brian Head Peak. A 1-mile dirt road cuts off the pavement to the top of the peak—a worthwhile side trip if you have an extra 30 minutes. Just past the turnoff to the peak is a parking area on the opposite side of the road, next to a Cedar Breaks National Monument sign. Park here.

The trail follows the fence line—the national monument boundary—across a flat meadow, then through pine forests. It emerges on the north shoulder of the fan-shaped Cedar Breaks. At various points just after the end of the fence, you can walk about 100 feet south for great views of the breaks and of the gnarled bristlecone pines.

The trail stays along open ridges and drops more steeply, turning away from the rim and down through Stud Flat, about 2.5 miles from the trailhead. The trail crosses open grassland gently sloping downward. Watch for the faint trail and cairns marking the path. Continue across the ridge top to the edge of Rattlesnake Canyon.

The trail drops 500 feet over the next mile into the scenic canyon. Rattlesnake Creek is a perennial stream amid tall ponderosa pines, with good camping along the stream. The canyon is much warmer than the higher ridge tops.

Follow Rattlesnake Creek south to Ashdown Creek about 3 miles. Just

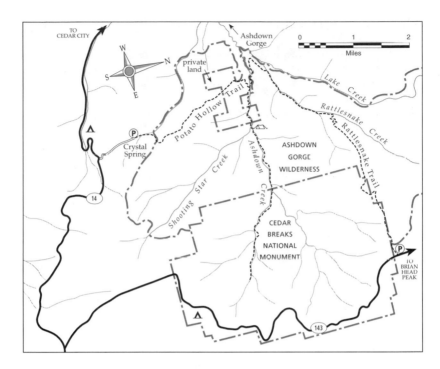

upcanyon from the confluence is some private land—be careful not to camp in this area. There is also no camping in the monument, which starts east of the confluence.

Day 2 is a full-day hike up into the seldom-visited bottom of Cedar Breaks National Monument. Just follow Ashdown Creek upstream. There are many side canyons entering, mostly from the south. At each fork, follow the main water source. There are no wrong turns—every canyon merits exploration. However, a special treat awaits where the main watercourse drops from the high cliffs above. If you do explore a side canyon, make sure you can find your way back—there are no trails and no cairns marking the right path.

Continue up the stream to where you see the canyon's end at the base of steep cliffs ahead. Waterfalls from high up spread mist over the rocks below. Notice that the stream in the canyon has more flow than the waterfalls seem to supply. The main source of the stream's flow emerges directly from under the base of the cliff— an unusual geologic feature worth viewing.

Head for the rocks at the base of the waterfall. Just to the left, and behind the fall, is a dark crack in the cliff's base. Approach the crack, but DO NOT ENTER IT! You'll hear the stream flow down in the crack, deep enough to be

Bristlecone pines—the oldest trees in North America

out of sight. The mist from the fall is cool and the rocks offer welcome shade. At the base of the cliff you are only about 0.25 mile from the road up on the rim of the breaks, but it's over 1000 feet lower in elevation.

This full-day trip can be hot and long. The stream is full of minerals; get water from one of the clear side streams. Rocks and canyon walls show millions of years of geology, and wildlife is abundant in this remote section.

On the third day, leave your camp back at the confluence of Rattlesnake and Ashdown Creeks. Go up the dirt road directly across the creek (south) from the confluence. About 0.25 mile up the road, a faint, unmarked path breaks off to the left through tall grasses. This is the Potato Hollow Trail, which ascends steeply to Crystal Spring, the end point of the hike. Your routefinding, map reading, and compass (or GPS) skills will be put to the test getting back to the trailhead. There are roads and trails not shown on any map.

The correct trail climbs a very steep pine-covered ridge to a T trail junction. Although it is tempting to head right (west), the correct trail is to the left (east). After about 3 miles and a 1250-foot elevation gain, you arrive at the trailhead at Crystal Spring, where you'll need a shuttle vehicle.

41 | CASCADE FALLS

Distance: 1 mile round trip
Hiking time: 1 hour
Difficulty: easy
Season: June to September
Elevation gain: 190 feet
Map: USGS Navajo Lake, Straight Canyon
Land Management Agency: Dixie National Forest, Cedar
City Ranger District

Take SR 14 out of Cedar City. Turn right at the Navajo Lake turnoff, 8 miles after the SR 143 junction. After 0.25 mile turn left on another less-maintained dirt road. The road winds down for a mile to reach another junction. Go left here. The trailhead is 2 miles down this dirt road. The dirt roads do not require 4WD vehicles.

This short, easy hike offers spectacular views. The trail is well used and covers very little elevation, making it ideal for novice hikers, but even experienced hikers will enjoy the breathtaking scenery.

From the trailhead, the trail heads northwest through the pines. Red cliffs line the ridge to the right. After a few hundred feet, a wood platform overlook can be found on the left side of the trail. From the overlook, loom

Wooden steps on the trail to Cascade Falls

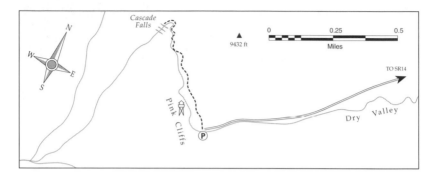

the high white and red cliff tops of Zion National Park. The West Rim of the park is especially visible. It is also possible to see the upper reaches of Orderville Canyon, to the east of the park.

Along the trail are several spots where water seeps onto the trail, creating slick spots. The slick clay and the exposure may be unnerving for some.

Soon the falls come into view as the trail begins its brief ascent to the water's head. The trail ends at a wood platform that provides an excellent view of the small falls' origins. The water forming the falls gushes out of a hole in the side of the wall. This water comes from Navajo Lake above. After seeping through sink holes, it resurfaces as Cascade Falls.

42 | SPRING CREEK CANYON

Distance: 6 to 7 miles round trip
Difficulty: easy
Season: May to October
Hiking time: 3 to 4 hours
Elevation gain: 560 feet
Map: USGS Kanarraville
Land Management Agency: BLM Cedar City Field Office

Get off I-15 at the Kanarraville exit (#51), south of Cedar City. Follow the road through town and turn left on the dirt road just after the last house on the right. The turnoff is less than 5 miles from the freeway exit. Follow the dirt road about 0.75 mile to a grassy parking area. Passenger cars may wish to park here. HCVs can follow the road up a short hill on the left. Proceed about 0.5 mile to park next to the stream. No signs mark the trailhead.

Spring Creek Canyon is an easy version of the Southwest's famous slot canyons. Although not as dramatic as Spooky Gulch and Bull Valley Gorge, Spring Creek Canyon is easily accessible, requires less of a time commitment, and is less traveled.

The narrows of Spring Creek Canyon

Start walking upcanyon. The road/all-terrain vehicle (ATV) trail goes up onto a bench on the right (south) side of the stream, crossing it a few times as it continues upcanyon. The wide trail ends a mile or more upcanyon at a thin slit between two high cliffs—the start of the slot. Enter the narrow canyon and follow the footpath. It weaves among trees and brush growing along the small stream and between the high walls, which keep the desert sun from drying out the area.

Once in the slot, continue upstream. You pass a fork at a wide spot in the canyon. The main canyon goes left. The right fork merits exploration for

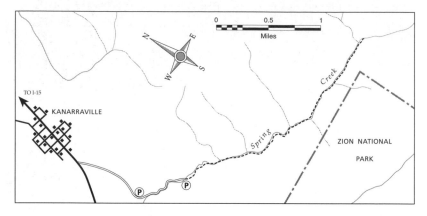

those with an adventurous inclination. After about 3 miles from the upper parking spot, you need to walk up some logs to continue upcanyon. Above the logs, the canyon begins to widen and the stream course gets overgrown with thick brush. You can continue for another mile or so to a larger fork in the canyon, but both forks eventually require technical gear to ascend.

43 | ANGELS LANDING

Distance: 4.5 miles round trip
Hiking time: 5 hours
Difficulty: strenuous
Season: March to October
Elevation gain: 1380 feet
Maps: USGS Temple of Sinawava; Trails Illustrated Zion National Park
Land Management Agency: Zion National Park

Park at the Zion National Park Visitor Center and take the shuttle bus to the Grotto trailhead. The trail heads northeast, crossing the road and then a footbridge across the Virgin River. Shortly after crossing the river, the trail intersects the trail to Emerald Pools. Turn right, heading north toward the large sandstone walls.

A series of switchbacks carved into the walls leads you up out of the lush canyon bottom and into Refrigerator Canyon. The canyon narrows and provides early afternoon shade. After a 0.5 mile is another set of over twenty switchbacks, referred to as "Walter's Wiggles." The trip up this steep twisted ramp is sure to get the blood flowing. Once on top of the "Wiggles," the trail gradually ascends, topping out at Scout Lookout about 2 miles from the trailhead, where a rewarding view of the canyon awaits.

Looking down on Angels Landing from Cable Mountain

The trail from here is not for the squeamish or faint of heart as it crosses the top of a thin sandstone fin with high exposure on both sides. Many are content with the view from Scout Lookout and turn around here. For the adventurous, a guide rail with chains aids you across this narrow section for the final 0.25 mile. Wet or icy conditions make this section of the trail very dangerous. Proceed with care.

Once upon Angels Landing, the canyon's grandeur unfolds in every direction. The view stretches north to the Virgin River Narrows and south, downcanyon, as far as the eye can see.

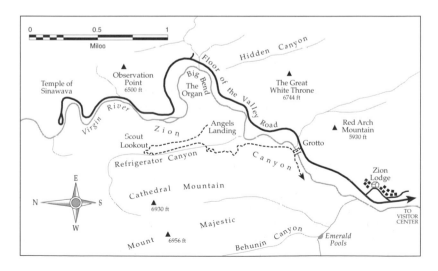

44 | THE SUBWAY

Distance: 8 miles oneway
Hiking time: 8 to 10 hours
Difficulty: moderate
Season: late May to early September
Elevation gain: 250 feet
Maps: USGS The Guardian Angels, Trails Illustrated Zion
    National Park
Land Management Agency: Zion National Park

On SR 9, drive east toward Zion National Park. Just after the small town of Virgin, turn left (north) onto the Kolob Reservoir Road. The upper trailhead is approximately 16 miles from town. Because this is not a loop hike, a shuttle or bike should be left at the lower trailhead where you will exit the canyon, about 8 miles from Virgin.

This hike is highly regulated by the National Park Service, which limits the number of hikers permitted down the canyon each day. Go to the Zion National Park Visitor Center to purchase a permit before beginning the hike.

Like most narrow canyons, this canyon has some challenges. Be aware of weather conditions before starting the hike because of extreme flash flood danger. Also, a 50+-foot rope is needed to negotiate obstacles.

From the trailhead, follow the trail for almost a mile until you reach the Wildcat Connector Trail. The USGS map calls it the Lava Point Trail. Turn left, go for a short distance and turn right at the trail heading south to the Northgate Peaks. Shortly after turning, take the faint trail that splits off to the left.

The trail drops into Russell Gulch, then crosses to the east. Follow the

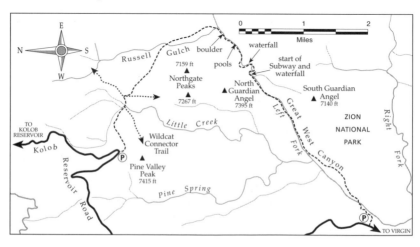

Ferns

gulch southward, staying on the east side. As the trail nears the confluence with the Left Fork, you are high above the canyon floor. The trail then takes a sudden, steep drop; make your way carefully. At the bottom, turn right and head down the Left Fork.

Scramble over the large rockfall before encountering a series of three swimming holes. Usually water begins a constant flow downcanyon from here. After the third hole, a waterfall appears. It is bypassed with the use of a rope attached to the two bolts.

The canyon walls peer from high above as the trail passes by several small springs and enters into the Subway by means of a second waterfall. A rope may be needed, for some, to bypass this waterfall.

It is easy to see why this canyon has been called the Subway. The walls are carved in a virtual tunnel with a small opening at the top, leading to the sky. Circular pools lie in the running water and make the terrain truly unique.

After about 7 miles, the trail begins to lead to the right, up off the canyon bottom. A steep ascent then leads you out of the canyon, back to the lower trailhead on the Kolob Reservoir Road.

45 | COALPITS WASH

Distance: 13.5 to 14 miles round trip
Hiking time: 7 to 9 hours
Difficulty: moderate
Season: October through March
Elevation gain: 1115 feet
Maps: USGS Springdale West; Trails Illustrated Zion
    National Park
Land Management Agency: Zion National Park

Coalpits lies west of Zion National Park on SR 9, between the towns of Virgin and Rockville. Immediately to the east of the signed bridge over

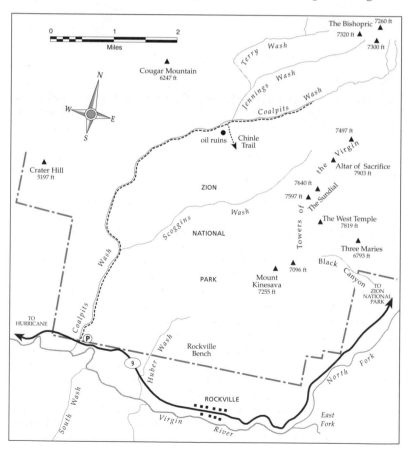

Ice-covered pool marks the upper end of Coalpits Wash

Coalpits Wash is a pullout and parking area on the north side of the road.

Situated in the lowland desert area in the southwest corner of Zion National Park, Coalpits Wash makes a great winter hike. It is teeming with wildlife, including eagles in the lowland cliffs, falcons in the canyons, and coyote and cougar.

Although cold in December through February, it is not uncommon for daytime temperatures to reach the 50°F mark in these winter months, making hiking pleasant.

The trail starts at the National Park Service fence, which forms the northern boundary of the parking area. There is a hiker's gate through the fence. The trail parallels the wash through lowland sagebrush flats with scattered cottonwood trees lining the wash for about a mile, then turns east (right) along the base of the mesa for 0.75 mile. To the east you have good views of the cliffs and spires of the West Temple and Towers of the Virgin.

A deep wide canyon, formed by Coalpits Creek, appears on the left (northwest). This is the confluence of Coalpits and Scoggins Washes. Turn north into the canyon following Coalpits Creek for about 1.75 miles. This section is rocky, so pick your path among boulders, trees, and brush. The creekbed slowly climbs until reaching the top of a mesa—a thick section of hard stone near a spring. This upper section of narrow 15-foot walls ends at a 4-foot fall over the shelf just before an alcove with maidenhair ferns. Near the top of the canyon, views open to the Bishopric, the sheer cliffs to the north.

The trail turns slightly to the east in a relatively flat basin, along the base of Cougar Mountain amid cottonwood, pinyon, and juniper. Plenty of good campsites exist on the sandy benches. If you camp here, stay well back from the stream because of flash flooding and to prevent pollution.

Back in the canyon, the stream forms several pools and small 1- to 2-foot waterfalls. Mixed with the sandstone are interesting conglomerate rocks. In about 2 miles—5.5 miles from the trailhead—you encounter the remains of an old oil rig.

Just past the oil ruins on the right (east) bench lies the signed Chinle Trail junction, which is easy to miss. Above the oil ruins, the canyon begins to narrow, necessitating frequent stream crossings. The flora changes to ponderosa pine and manzanita. Penstemon wildflowers are abundant, especially in the spring.

For most, the trail ends at a large 8-foot waterfall through two narrow sandstone buttresses or ledges, about 1.75 miles from the oil ruins. A path up onto the south ledge is difficult going. In warmer weather you can go right up the fall, but you'll get wet and the rocks are slick. In winter, the fall is iced up and water in the pool below the fall is very cold. Above the fall, the trail ends about 0.25 mile upcanyon at the base of a pouroff and high cliffs.

46 | ORDERVILLE CANYON

Distance: 12.5 miles one way
Hiking time: 6 to 8 hours
Difficulty: strenuous/technical canyoneering
Season: June to October
Elevation loss: 2600 feet
Maps: USGS Temple of Sinawava, Clear Creek Mountain;
 Trails Illustrated Zion National Park
Land Management Agency: Zion National Park

Start at the Zion National Park Visitor Center, where you pick up your hiker's permit. Call for updated information (see Appendix). The NPS stops issuing permits for Orderville Canyon around mid-October.

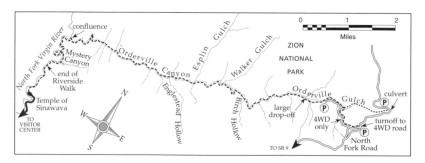

The final pool in Orderville Canyon

You either need two cars or to arrange for a shuttle with a local service. Park your shuttle car at the main parking lot. At the end of the hike, catch the bus back to your car. Area commercial shuttles charge about $15 per person and require advance reservations. For shuttle service, call Zion Canyon Transportation (see Appendix).

If shuttling yourself, drive the second car east on SR 9; continue past the park's east entrance to a sign indicating the North Fork Road, at the top of a small hill. Turn left (north) and continue 12.4 miles. The first 5 miles are paved to the Zion Ponderosa Ranch. You reach your destination at the

Orderville culvert, a large pipe under the road in the bottom of Orderville Canyon, little more than a gulch at this point.

You can park here and hike downcanyon, or backtrack about 0.75 mile to a dirt road turning west at the top of a hill. Most cars should not attempt this road, but 4WDs can make it about 1.5 miles to a parking area. Walking the road is somewhat easier than hiking along the streambed at the culvert.

Orderville Canyon is a canyoneering experience, not a simple hike. Expect to swim deep pools and rappel. Bring a 100-foot rope to avoid two very narrow and potentially deep pools. The water is cold—rarely over 50 degrees in midsummer and colder in spring and fall. Consider taking a wet suit for warmth in spring and fall. Wear boots you don't mind getting wet, because you are in the water for about two-thirds of the hike. Hightop boots or shoes protect your ankles while hiking in the river.

From your parking spot begin hiking downcanyon. There is a large drop-off in the canyon shortly after the lower parking area (about 1 mile from the culvert). Bypass this to the left on steep hiker trails. The creekbed is dry for the first few miles.

The canyon bottom narrows, but is still fairly wide with few obstacles. After about 4.5 miles you reach the confluence with Bulloch Gulch. Just above the junction, pungent sulfur-laden water trickles into the creekbed and sits in stinky stagnant pools. Water flows continuously after Bulloch Gulch.

Soon you encounter a 15-foot dryfall. Use a rope to rappel off a bolt in the left wall, or downclimb by chimneying in a crack on the left. Lower your packs first.

You'll be in the water intermittently for the rest of the day. The stream is usually ankle deep, and rarely more than knee deep, but you'll encounter several pools that require swimming. Your packs will get wet, so line them with heavy plastic, or use dry bags.

Several side canyons break off, but you should avoid exploring them during the shorter days of spring and fall because you need the time to finish the hike before dark. In summer, exploration is possible time-wise, but don't wear yourself out because the more difficult parts of the canyon lie ahead.

The second obstacle is a large chokestone jammed overhead with another stone in the creekbed, creating a 15-foot overhanging drop. Check the bolt in the left wall before trusting it. Do not trust webbing left by previous hikers; bring your own. Set a rappel line and have the first person drop into the pool at the bottom, which is usually only waist deep. Lower the packs with a rope and have the first person ferry them to the opposite bank.

After a few more obstacles, which can be chimneyed, you reach an unavoidable pool at a narrow section in the canyon. Here the steep walls are just a few feet apart with no way to skirt the deep pool behind a small,

4-foot fall. A good foothold—a hollow circle in the sandstone—juts from the watercourse. Using the hold first for your feet and then as a handhold, lower yourself without a pack into the pool and swim to the far side. As before, the first person in can ferry packs.

Before long you encounter a second unavoidable pool, larger than the others. The pool's depth makes ferrying packs more difficult, so we threw the packs from the top out into the pool where the first person down could retrieve them.

The next challenging obstacle occurs in a wider part of the canyon, which narrows to a sinuous slot with deep narrow pools. Seeps prevent you from climbing around the pools. Backtrack and look for a way to climb up on a bench 30 feet above the streambed on the left (south). A trail on the bench leads downcanyon about 300 feet to a sturdy tree with web straps around the trunk. Rappelling here avoids the two largest pools, but requires a 100-foot rope.

After this final rappel, the canyon narrows with sheer vertical walls—arguably the most beautiful section of Orderville Canyon. The walls are several hundred feet high and the canyon about 20 feet wide. It's about 30 minutes from the last rappel to the confluence with the Virgin River. There's one more pool to swim about 5 minutes from the confluence. If you have time, go up the Virgin to get views of some of its narrowest sections. Remember you have a mile of slow going in the river, and 2 miles along the paved Riverside Walk, before reaching the parking lot.

After the confluence, you are in the knee-deep water of the Virgin continuously for almost 2 miles. The rocks in the riverbed are slippery and the river current stronger than in Orderville Canyon. Trekking poles or a hiking staff will help you in this section.

47 | MINERAL GULCH

Distance: 17 miles round trip
Hiking time: 2 days
Difficulty: moderate
Season: April to July, September to October
Elevation gain: 40 feet
Map: USGS Mount Carmel
Land Management Agency: BLM Kanab Field Office

From Panguitch, follow US 89 south toward Kanab. After 54 miles you will reach Mount Carmel Junction, where SR 9 runs west to Zion National Park's east entrance. About 0.5 mile south of the junction, a dirt road breaks off to the west (right), following the east fork of the Virgin River. (Heading south,

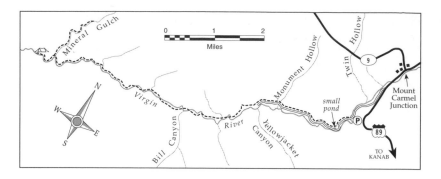

if you start up the hill, you've gone too far.) Much of the land on either side of the road is privately owned, so stay on the road when both driving and hiking. Several pullouts are on the south side of the road for camping. At a fork in the road, park and begin hiking. The BLM has started to build a signed parking area about 0.5 mile before the fork near a corral. When completed, starting at this parking area will add 1 mile to your round trip.

For the first 2 miles follow the dirt road. From the fork, follow the road to the right. The road moves along the north side of a wide valley with orange-red sandstone cliffs. Much of this land is private property, so stay on the road. After 1 mile, the road reaches a fence with a No Trespassing sign. Turn and follow the fence line down the river. From here on, you cross the river often, following an old jeep track. After another 0.5 mile the road turns south and ascends the bank up out of the canyon onto Elephant Flat. Continue down the stream.

The canyon soon narrows and although the canyon is wide and open above the streambed, you spend much of your time wading in the knee-deep water. The east fork of the Virgin River is a large creek, and the water flow is strong.

About 8 miles from the fork and trailhead, you reach a slot canyon and stream entering from the north; this is Mineral Gulch. Good campsites are on the benches near this confluence. Drop your packs here, then start up Mineral Gulch. The best sections lie within the first 0.25 to 0.5 mile from the Virgin River. In places the walls narrow to just a few feet apart and 100 feet high. Grazing is allowed here, so you may find signs of cattle through the narrows. There are a couple of small seasonal springs where fresh water seeps from cracks in the rocks in the last 0.25 mile along the river before the confluence with Mineral Gulch. The springs make much better water sources than the silty river, but you should filter the water from these springs. Most will want to camp overnight at the confluence then hike out the next day.

Mineral Gulch also makes a good base camp for explorations down into the Barracks area, farther downstream. The East Fork narrows significantly below Mineral Gulch, but you cannot follow the river past the boundary of Zion National Park, as the section known as Parunaweap Canyon is closed. The only ways out of the Barracks area are to backtrack the several miles or to go do technical climbing out of the canyon and routefind cross-country north to SR 9. This route is for experienced canyoneers only.

Log jam in a small side canyon

48 | EAST RIM TRAIL

**Distance: 10.5 miles one way to Weeping Rock;
18.5 miles round trip to Cable Mountain**
Hiking time: 2 to 5 days
Difficulty: moderate
Season: March to June, September to November
Elevation gain: 2810 feet to Weeping Rock; 3120 feet
round trip to Cable Mountain
Maps: USGS Springdale East, The Barracks, Temple of
Sinawava; Trails Illustrated Zion National Park
Land Management Agency: Zion National Park

Hiking the East Rim Trail requires a permit, obtainable at the park's main visitor center. Access the trailhead from the east entrance to Zion National Park. From US 89, east of the park, turn west on SR 9 at Mount Carmel Junction. It's about 14 miles to the park.

From the west, take SR 9 east toward the park. Instead of turning into the main park and visitor center, continue east on SR 9 through the Zion–Mount Carmel Tunnel about 11 miles to the east entrance.

A dirt road breaks off to the north immediately across from the ranger's booth at the east entrance. The road goes a couple of hundred yards before ending at a large parking area.

A trail register marks the beginning of the trail. For the first few miles, the trail—a former firebreak road—is wide and obvious. It starts across flats some distance from the cliffs to the north, heading in a generally northerly direction. After about 0.5 mile the trail turns the northeast. Sections of

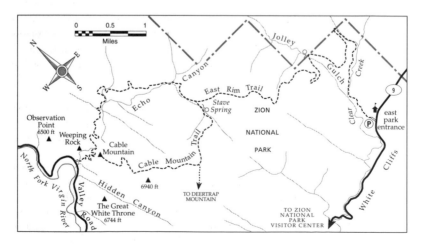

Old timbers atop Cable Mountain

the trailbed are dry sand, which make the hiking harder, but still easy.

Continuing northeast the trail starts up a canyon following a usually dry wash for most of a mile, then veers north again up a smaller side wash. A quarter mile or so up the side canyon the trail cuts left, away from the wash, ascends, and eventually heads south parallel to the trail below. Over the next couple of miles the trail works its way along the south edge of the mesa that forms the cliff bands visible from the trailhead.

The trail follows the east edge of deep Jolley Gulch about 0.5 mile, then crosses its head, where a small stream crosses the trail and drops off a 60+-foot cliff into a tiny slot canyon. Exercising extreme care, it is possible to look down into the gulch and see the floor of the interesting slot. The trail rims the west edge of the gulch south, back to the rim.

After 0.5 mile the trail turns away from the rim and the distant views of Checkerboard Mesa and lands south of the park, to work its way across several pine-covered ridges on its way to the top of Cable Mountain. In the early spring, these ridges can be covered in deep snow, even when the lower sections of the trail are clear and hot. Going up to Cable Mountain during warm spells in February can be rewarding and remote, but bring your snowshoes and check with the rangers for current trail conditions.

After 1.5 to 2 miles you top out. From here it's level walking across the mesa top through scattered ponderosa pine. Once on top, go about 1 mile to reach Stave Spring—the first reliable water source—about 6 miles from the trailhead. The spring consists of a small water pipe and trickle of water. Just north of the spring, the trail to Cable Mountain cuts off to the east. A small seasonal stream parallels this trail and offers a better water source than Stave Spring—when it is running.

The best camp spots are in the flats about 0.5 mile north of the trail junction, where a spur trail cuts off to the west to the park boundary. A few spots for small groups are along the trail toward Cable Mountain.

You have several options from Stave Spring. The first is a day hike out to Cable Mountain, which has an historic cable works used in the early

1900s to lower logs from the mesa top to the valley floor some 2000 feet below. The Cable Mountain Trail takes off to the east just north of Stave Spring. The trail is fairly easy, gaining, then losing, about 400 feet over 3.25 miles. The view from the rim is incredible—nearly 2000 feet straight down to the parking area at Weeping Rock. You can either base camp near Stave Spring and day hike out to Cable Mountain, or find a camp spot back off the rim near the old cable works. However, there is no water source on Cable Mountain.

Another option is to descend to Weeping Rock. The trail drops the 2000 feet to a parking area. From there you can use the park shuttle back to the visitor center parking area, but you'd have to arrange transportation from there to the park's east entrance. From Stave Spring the trail drops quickly over a narrow, rocky path down into Echo Canyon. In the winter this trail can be icy and slick. Following Echo Canyon to the west takes you through a great slot canyon then out onto the slickrock for a final descent down a series of switchbacks to the Weeping Rock parking lot. From the Stave Spring junction to the parking area is about 4.5 miles.

The final option is to back track out the East Rim Trail to your car at the park's east entrance ranger station.

49 | HOP VALLEY/KOLOB CANYON

Distance: 14.5 miles one way
Hiking time: 2 to 4 days
Difficulty: moderate
Season: April to June, September to October
Elevation gain: 1570 feet
Maps: USGS The Guardian Angels, Kolob Arch, Kolob
Reservoir; Trails Illustrated Zion National Park
Land Management Agency: Zion National Park

To reach the Kolob Canyon Visitor Center, travel south on I-15 to exit 40, 17 miles south of Cedar City. This section of the park features a 7-mile paved road with overlooks onto the Fingers of the Kolob, a series of cathedral buttes that jut out from the Kolob Plateau. The Lee Pass overlook is the principal trailhead for north-to-south hiking.

Make sure you get a permit for overnight backpacking. Permits for all Kolob Canyon's trails must be picked up in person at the Kolob Canyon Visitor Center within 24 hours of your departure. No reservations are accepted. You must select your campsite for each night when you pick up your permit. The visitor center has a map of the campsites, selected on a first come, first served basis.

We recommended beginning at the Hop Valley trailhead. The route

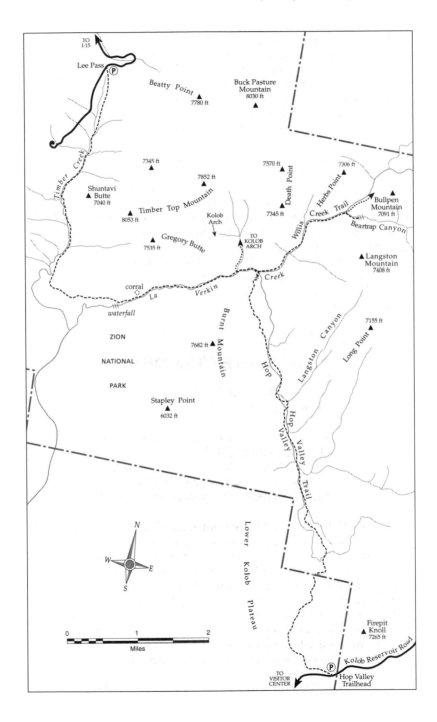

TO
I-15

Lee Pass P

Beatty Point
7780 ft ▲

Buck Pasture
Mountain
8030 ft ▲

Timber Creek

7345 ft ▲

7852 ft ▲

7570 ft ▲

Death Point

7306 ft ▲

Bullpen
Mountain
7091 ft

Shuntavi
▲ Butte
7040 ft

Timber Top Mountain

8053 ft ▲

Kolob
Arch

7345 ft ▲

Willis Creek Trail

Beartrap Canyon

Gregory Butte
7535 ▲

TO
KOLOB
ARCH ▲

Creek

▲ Langston
Mountain
7408 ft

corral

La Verkin

7155 ft ▲

waterfall

ZION

Burnt Mountain

7682 ft ▲

Hop

Langston Canyon

Long Point

NATIONAL

PARK

Stapley Point
6032 ft ▲

Hop Valley Trail

N
W E
S

Lower
Kolob
Plateau

Firepit
▲ Knoll
7265 ft

0   1   2
Miles

Kolob Reservoir Road

TO
VISITOR
CENTER

P

Hop Valley
Trailhead

requires either two cars or an arranged shuttle. The park does not offer shuttle service from this trailhead.

The Hop Valley trailhead is reached from the Kolob Reservoir Road, about an hour's drive from the Kolob Visitor Center. Get back on the freeway and continue south on I-15 to the Toquerville/SR 17 exit (#27), then follow SR 17 to the junction with SR 9 in Springdale. Next, head toward Zion National Park's main entrance on SR 9. Just after entering the small town of Virgin, a brown National Park Service sign points the way to Kolob Reservoir. The Hop Valley trailhead is about 10 miles from the turnoff in Virgin.

The first mile and a half of Hop Valley is moderately difficult hiking because the trailbed is dry sand. You cross some private land where the trail becomes a double track and soon drops into Hop Valley, where the stream begins to flow and green grasses grow on the valley floor.

The first campsites are among the pines. Shortly after campsite 1, the trail leaves the creek to start up a short incline. The view back down Hop Valley with its gleaming ribbonlike creek nestled amid the ponderosa pines and sandstone cliffs is spectacular.

After leaving Hop Valley, you descend some 500 feet into La Verkin Creek in about 0.5 mile. The junction is an ideal place to refill your water containers, take a short rest, and sit awestruck.

At the creek, you can turn west and follow La Verkin Creek back toward Lee Pass, or swing to the east and start up La Verkin Creek on the dead-end Willis Creek Trail. If you have the time, this section offers the most memorable scenery and the best chance for solitude of the entire trip. The main highlight of the 4-mile spur is Beartrap Canyon, a narrow, undeveloped side

Sunset over Gregory Butte

canyon that ends at a beautiful waterfall about 0.25 mile from the canyon mouth. For those with more time, there are campsites in both upper La Verkin Creek (above the Y junction) and near the mouth of Beartrap Canyon.

The Kolob Arch Trail, a short 0.5 mile from La Verkin Creek, breaks off to the right about 0.5 mile from the junction toward Lee Pass. This narrow canyon contains large boulders that have tumbled down from the towering cliffs, making delightful pools and a few small falls. The trail ends at a viewpoint about 0.25 mile from Kolob Arch.

About 1 mile from the Kolob Arch Trail, you pass a corral on the right (north), and the trail turns slightly northward and begins to ascend a ridge. The creek turns south, away from the trail. Timber Creek, which the trail later follows toward Lee Pass, is often dry, so this point on the La Verkin may be the last water source until you reach the trailhead at Lee Pass.

Rounding the point of Gregory Butte, the trail starts up the dry Timber Creek wash. The vegetation changes to juniper, scrub oak, and sagebrush, with a few cottonwoods and willows along the wash banks. The terrain is more open and the sun's heat more of a factor in your climb toward Lee Pass. Some sections of Timber Creek may have a small water flow, especially during the spring.

From here, you have about 1.5 miles of mostly level walking. When you rise out of Timber Creek, look ahead to a full view of the Fingers of the Kolob. The trail steepens and the washes become more rugged. Summiting one particularly rugged ridge, the trail clings to the ridge's spine. Looking back, you overlook the green Timber Creek valley below and beyond that to the mesas and low valleys of the La Verkin city and Hurricane areas. To the southeast tower the massive Gregory and Shuntavi Buttes. The final pull to Lee Pass is tough, a long steady uphill climb.

50 | UP THE NARROWS TO ORDERVILLE CANYON

Distance: 9 to 10 miles round trip
Hiking time: 4 to 6 hours
Difficulty: easy to moderate
Season: June to October; avoid during high water
Elevation gain: negligible
Maps: USGS Temple of Sinawava; Trails Illustrated Zion
National Park
Land Management Agency: Zion National Park

Go to Zion National Park, and park at the visitor center. Catch the shuttle to the Temple of Sinawava. The park collects a $20 entrance fee. No permit is required for this hike.

The Narrows of the Virgin River

This hike—suitable for children over 8 years old and for most active hikers—is the easiest and shortest way to experience the beauty of the Zion Narrows and to see the most spectacular section of Orderville Canyon. For almost 2 miles the Riverside Walk path is paved. It ends at a viewpoint where the Virgin River exits the Narrows. From here you have to enter the river and simply hike upstream. Smooth, mossy rocks cause your feet to slide and your ankles to get banged against rocks as you search for the best footing; hiking poles are strongly recommended. Anyone with knee or ankle problems, or problems maintaining balance, should stop at the end of the Riverside Walk.

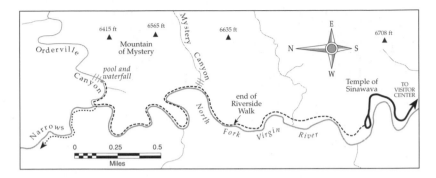

From the end of the paved trail, it's just less than 2 miles to the conflu-ence with Orderville Canyon. After 0.75 mile in the river, you pass a 100-foot waterfall on the right, the outlet of Mystery Canyon that starts on the east rim of the park. The water flow is small, but spectacular.

Orderville Canyon joins the Virgin River at a very narrow section. Both canyons are beautiful at the confluence. You can walk about 5 minutes up Orderville Canyon before encountering a deep pool and waterfall. It's im-practical to proceed beyond this point. If you are smitten by lower Orderville Canyon and have the technical experience, you can hike the en-tire canyon from the top (see Hike 46).

The confluence area is a great place to stop and enjoy lunch or a snack as you take in the sights and sounds of this almost mythical place. Once you've had your fill of the narrow canyon, return to your car by reversing your path down the stream, back to the paved Riverside Walk.

51 | WEST RIM TRAIL

Distance: 14.5 miles one way
Hiking time: 2 days
Difficulty: moderate
Season: April to early June, late September to October
Elevation gain: 1400 feet
Maps: USGS Temple of Sinawava, The Guardian Angels,
    Kolob Reservoir; Trails Illustrated Zion National Park
Land Management Agency: Zion National Park

On SR 9, drive east toward Zion National Park. Just after the small town of Virgin turn left (north) onto the Kolob Reservoir Road. About 21 miles up the road, turn right onto the Lava Point Road, which passes the south end of Blue Springs Reservoir. Drive 2.5 miles to the base of Goose Creek Knoll and the Lava Point trailhead. The trail starts here. Because this is not a loop

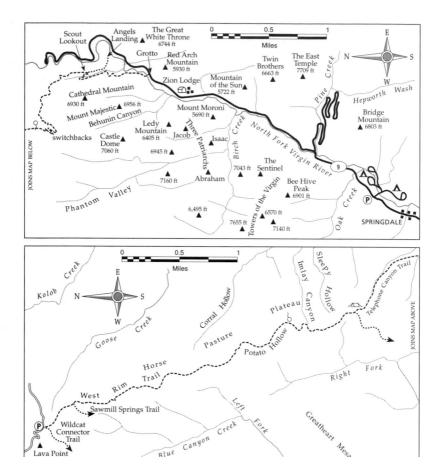

hike, it is necessary to leave a vehicle at the visitor center parking lot.

Start heading south on the trail. About 600 feet from the trailhead, the Wildcat Connector Trail (or Lava Point Trail on the USGS map) cuts off to the right; stay left. The trail loses about 200 feet in elevation in the first 0.5 mile then levels off to a more gradual descent. Lava Point looms above as you look back to the northwest.

The short Sawmill Springs spur trail veers right at the 1-mile point; again stay left. For the next 3.5 miles you cross the mostly flat Horse Pasture Plateau, then start dropping into Potato Hollow. At just over 5 miles there is a small spring at the base of Potato Hollow, a short distance from the edge of the mesa. From the spring, continue 2 miles to the junction with the Telephone Canyon Trail. This section of the trail gains about 300 feet, loses 200 feet, and then gains it back, making the last part of the 7-mile

Indian paintbrush along the trail

day the most demanding. The trail to the right makes a 3.5-mile loop around the west edge of the mesa, overlooking Phantom Valley, then rejoins the Telephone Canyon Trail. The area around the junction has several good spots to make a dry camp. This description assumes that you'll take the left trail down Telephone Canyon.

Over the next couple of miles, the trail drops about 600 feet through Telephone Canyon. At the base of Telephone Canyon is another small spring. From the spring one can see the cliffs ahead that you all-to-soon descend. Just after the spring the West Rim Trail joins in from the right.

Over the next 3 miles, the trail loses 1800 feet. Right after the trail junction, the trail drops down a large cliff through a series of switchbacks carved in the sandstone, passes beneath the cliffs of Mount Majestic and Cathedral Mountain to the south. Veering south, you walk across the top of a very narrow ridge to Scout Lookout. From here you can look down to the Zion Canyon floor, across the canyon to Observation Point, or to Angels Landing to the west. At Scout Lookout, the trail joins with the Angels Landing Trail. At the junction turn right and head down Walters Wiggles and, once at the bottom, to the Grotto. See the Angels Landing (Hike 43) description for details. From the Grotto, catch the shuttle bus to your vehicle at the parking area.

SOUTH CENTRAL

52 | UNDER THE RIM TRAIL

**Distance: 13 miles for 2-day trip; 23 miles
for 3-day trip**
Hiking time: 2 to 3 days
Difficulty: moderate
Season: June to September
Elevation gain: 4320 feet
Maps: USGS Bryce Point, Rainbow Point; Trails Illustrated
Bryce Canyon National Park
Land Management Agency: Bryce Canyon National Park

To enter Bryce Canyon National Park, turn off SR 12 onto SR 63 and into the park near Ruby's Inn, a large gas station, restaurant, and motel complex just off the highway. Be sure to go to the visitor center to get your backpacking permit. You must specify where you intend to camp each night when you pick up your permit. Also, be sure to talk with the rangers about current water conditions.

There is no overnight camping south of SR 12, even outside the park boundaries. If you arrive late at night, you'll need to camp a few miles away from the park to the east, west, or north. Bryce Canyon sits at 9000 feet and can be cool even in summer.

The park offers a shuttle from May 1 to September 30. Park at the staging area at the park entrance and catch the shuttle to the trailhead. The Under the Rim Trail offers moderate solitude and a reasonable wilderness experience considering that Bryce Canyon is a highly visited national park. For those who bristle at the sounds of motorized vehicles, including helicopters, hikes in Bryce Canyon may not be the best choice.

Under the Rim offers less of the hoodoos and spires characteristic of the park's northern hikes and the subject of most photographs of Bryce. Instead, this trail meanders through ponderosa forests at the base of the rugged 1000-foot main cliffs of Bryce. The trail crosses several ridges with spectacular views both up into the cliffs and downward into the low valleys east of Bryce.

For a 3-day trip, begin your hike at the Rainbow Point trailhead. For the overnighter, begin at the Whiteman Connecting Trail.

Plan your water storage and usage carefully; water sources are few. Iron Springs, on the south end near Rainbow Point, has reliable water, but its

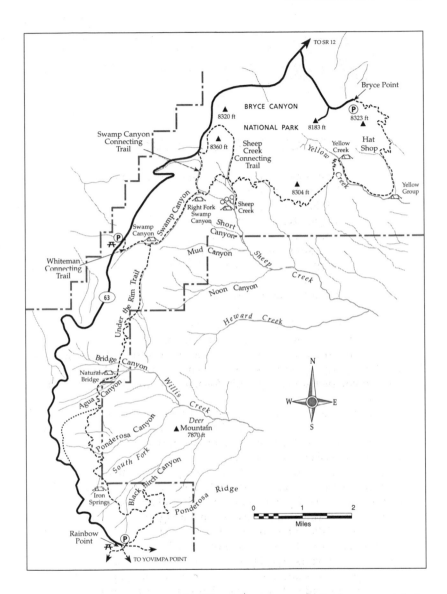

color discourages most people. Filters do not remove the heavy metals in the water. Sheep Creek and Yellow Creek campsites have the only other reliable water sources, and both are at the end of the second day (or the overnight camp).

Day 1. From the Rainbow Point parking area you descend down the ridge that forms the edge of Bryce Canyon, also called the "rim." Be sure to choose the right trail. Follow the one signed Under the Rim–Bryce Point. A

The cliffs of Bryce Canyon from Yellow Creek

short distance after leaving the trailhead, you arrive at the junction of the three sections of the Under the Rim Trail, one heading north to Bryce Point, the other two are the ends of the Yovimpa Point loop hike. The correct trail is the branch northeast toward Bryce Point. Follow the rim's edge, dropping slightly, from just over 9000 feet at Ponderosa Point to about 8700 feet at the rim's edge. As you round Ponderosa Ridge, the descent becomes steeper, ending at about 7900 feet in another mile or so. After 3 miles, you reach Iron Springs campsite. Continue along the rim for 3.5 more miles to the Agua Canyon Connecting Trail.

At the junction, head north toward the Natural Bridge campsite, which lies anther mile ahead and is your destination for the first night. There is no water here, so plan to carry enough water to last for the first 2 days. From the camp, look up in the cliffs to the west-northwest to spot the natural bridge.

Day 2. Leaving camp, the first 0.5 mile is relatively level, then you start up a large ridge. Over the next 0.75 mile you gain about 400 feet of elevation. Topping the ridge, you drop back down onto the shelf at about 8000 feet, then follow relatively level terrain for the next 2.5 to 3 miles to the Swamp Canyon Camp.

The camp sits at the base of the Whiteman Connecting Trail. For an overnight trip, you start at the top of this trail and hike about 1 mile down to the junction with Under the Rim Trail. A great viewpoint lies just to the east of the campsite, right at the junction of Whiteman and Under the Rim Trails.

From the top of the Swamp Canyon drainage, you descend into a valley at about 7700 feet. It's about 2.5 miles to the junction with the Swamp Canyon Connecting Trail and the Right Fork of Swamp Canyon campsite. At the junction, take the right-hand trail toward Sheep Creek and Yellow Creek. The trail tops a small ridge for excellent views to the east, then descends back to the Sheep Creek drainage. Here the Under the Rim Trail crosses the Sheep Creek Connecting Trail. Stay on the trail heading to the Sheep Creek campsite, which lies about 0.5 mile ahead, and is your first water source. Camp here.

Day 3. The final day is long and difficult. For a 4-day trip, you could split the final section into two easier days, spending the final night at Yellow Creek camp. Follow the trail back to the Sheep Creek Connecting Trail junction, then turn north (right) toward Yellow Creek. The 4- to 4.5-mile section from Sheep Creek to Yellow Creek has more ups and downs, but the scenery and shade improves, and its proximity to the Pink Cliffs gives a more intimate feel. The trail is also slightly overgrown in places between Swamp Canyon and Yellow Creek.

The Yellow Creek camp is an excellent site, with a lot of shade, plenty of room for three or four tents, a small year-round stream with good water, and good views of cliffs and hoodoos to west and north. The Bryce Canyon brochure warns that the water contains heavy metals that are not filtered out with pumps. For most people they pose no danger in small quantities.

From Yellow Creek the most difficult mileage lies ahead. The trail follows Yellow Creek southeast out to a point at the base of a projecting ridge, then turns to skirt the ridge's nose. At about 2.5 to 3 miles, you pass the Yellow Creek group campsite, then turn northwest and join the Right Fork of Yellow Creek. Another 1.5 miles up Yellow Creek, the trail nears the base of the rim at the Right Fork Yellow Creek campsite. The remaining 3 miles are all uphill.

The trail winds its way up the first ridge, and once on top, passes the most interesting geological feature of the trip—the Hat Shop. Here large, light-gray rocks sit on top of narrow sandstone spires, some only a few feet tall, others dozens of feet tall. The sandstone has eroded away around and underneath the harder "hat" stones. The hard top rocks have partially protected the columns underneath them, leaving these curious formations. Extending along the side of the ridge for a couple hundred feet, the Hat Shop is the highlight of the hike.

Once past the Hat Shop, you continue toward the cliff base another 0.25 mile, then start the final long ascent toward Bryce Point. To reach the top of the rim, you gain about 600 to 700 feet over the next 1 to 1.5 miles. Once on top, you have another 0.25 to 0.5 mile before arriving at Bryce Point, the end of this hike.

Make sure you contact the park before starting your trip. Trail conditions vary and parts of the trail are closed occasionally.

53 | ROUND VALLEY DRAW

Distance: 6.5-mile loop
Hiking time: 4 to 5 hours
Difficulty: moderate
Season: April to June, September to October
Elevation gain: 280 feet
Map: USGS Slickrock Bench
Land Management Agency: BLM Grand Staircase–
Escalante National Monument

Take SR 12 east out of Panguitch, passing the entrance to Bryce Canyon National Park. Continue east to the town of Cannonville, turning south in town toward Kodachrome Basin State Park. Follow the signs toward the park, but do not turn off into the park. Instead continue on the dirt road for another 6.5 miles. This road can become impassable when wet. At about 6 miles the road ascends a steep ridge, up onto the Slickrock Bench. About 200 yards after reaching the top of the hill there's an intersection with the road to Round Valley. Continue straight ahead for 1 mile to the Rush Bed Road on the right (southwest). Follow the road southwest for about 2.75 miles as it crosses the washbed and starts up the bank on the south side near a metal stock pond. Park at the pullout.

The trail begins following an old 4WD road down a dry creekbed for a little over a mile. Near the end of this section, the canyon walls rise on either side and begin to close in before a deep chasm suddenly opens up in the wash floor. The beginning of the crack is only a foot wide, but it quickly drops to about 20 feet deep. You can enter the canyon at various points, but descending right down the crack is the easiest. Just alternate between wedging your feet and your torso between the narrow walls, as you work down to the canyon floor.

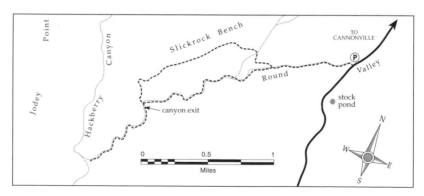

Once on the sandy bottom, you find yourself in one of the narrowest and coolest (temperature and quality-wise) slots anywhere. The walls quickly deepen to more than 100 feet. The hiking is easy—simply follow the dry slot downcanyon. From the drop-in point down to the confluence with Hackberry Canyon is about 2 miles.

The canyon remains very narrow, and in one spot the walls overhead are a mere foot or two wide, making the canyon bottom very dark. Chockstones block the way in a couple of spots; one set you climb over and

Extremely narrow section of Round Valley Draw

the other you climb under. As you approach Hackberry Canyon the draw widens considerably. The confluence is a great place for a rest break in the shade of the rocky cliffs.

To exit the canyon, head back up Round Valley Draw about 0.75 mile to a wide crack in the north wall. (You could exit here on the way downcanyon, but the extra 1.5 miles to Hackberry is worth the extra time.) Scramble up the wall, about 200 vertical feet, onto the Slickrock Bench. Look for a 4WD jeep road and follow it northeast across the bench. As the road gets farther from the draw, take off cross-country following the rim of the bench. Keep watching to the south (right) for a way back down to the head of Round Valley Draw. Drop down into the valley and back to your vehicle. From the top of the exit point back to the car is about 2 miles.

54 | BULL VALLEY GORGE

Distance: 7.5-mile loop; optional 20-mile loop
Hiking time: 6 hours; all day for the longer option
Difficulty: moderate
Season: March to May, September to October
Elevation gain: 480 feet
Map: USGS Bull Valley Gorge
Land Management Agency: BLM Grand Staircase–
  Escalante National Monument

Take SR 12 east from Panguitch. Pass the entrance to Bryce Canyon National Park and continue east to Cannonville. Turn south in town toward Kodachrome Basin State Park.

Follow the road south and east for about 3 miles. The first signed road to the right takes you to Sheep and Yellow Creeks. Continue south about

0.5 mile to a second dirt road heading right and signed "Bull Valley Gorge, 9 miles." The dirt road goes up steep inclines and across several streambeds, also crossing a concrete spillway just below a reservoir with a steep short drop off on the left. The road's clay bed becomes treacherous when wet, so avoid this road in wet weather.

After crossing Willis Creek, the road ascends steeply up a ridge and then a short distance to Bull Valley Gorge. The Gorge creeps up on you. The earthen bridge across the chasm is the giveaway. Just before the bridge is a hiker's gate in the fence. Park either at the gate or at the pullout on the far side of the bridge.

There are several entry points into the gorge, all located about 0.5 mile upcanyon from the hiker's gate. As you hike along the rim, peer into the canyon to check out the canyon floor, looking for any sign of water. If you see pools on the downstream sides of the boulders, you'll find the hiking much more difficult.

Continue to follow the trail along the rim until you reach a 12-foot drop into the canyon, right in the streambed. This is the easiest entry point. Chimney down—there may be a log at the bottom, which you can lower yourself onto. There are also two cracks a short distance downcanyon from this drop-off. One is about 20 feet, the other about 60 feet. The first (shorter) crack is only possible if there is a log at the bottom. These two entry points require climbing skills or ropes and may change with each flash flood.

After entering the canyon, you'll encounter several obstacles, all simple to downclimb—unless there are pools. Water makes footing treacherous. Take advantage of rocks and logs jammed below boulders to lower yourself, usually only 6 to 10 feet. If there are pools, you can't assess the depth or see the logs and rocks for footing. If the water is too cold or you're uncomfortable proceeding, abandon the hike here—more difficult obstacles lie ahead. If there are no pools, your passage will be much simpler. Although there could still be water ahead, it'll be less deep and less frequent.

The winding canyon deepens to over 200 feet as you approach the bridge, 30 to 45 minutes from the top. Looking up, you'll spot the remains of an old pickup, a remnant from an accident in the 1940s that now serves as the base of the bridge. The gorge narrows significantly to only a few feet across. There may be more pools, which are deeper and longer when water is present.

After the bridge, the gorge widens and deepens, reaching depths of over 400 feet. You'll encounter more obstacles, most similar in height and difficulty to those experienced early on. One large chokestone requires chimneying about 18 feet down on a steep sandstone slope to a log placed at the bottom. Less experienced hikers will want a rope here. If the log gets washed away, a rope will be required, or you'll have to search for an alternate route.

You have two exit options. First, 4 miles below the bridge you'll reach a wide spot in the canyon with large cracks ascending to both rims. A slide on the right side supports a stand of pine. To reach this point plan on 3 to 5 hours, depending on your experience level and whether there are pools to slow you down. You can exit here by climbing to either canyon rim, then rim-walk about 40 minutes back to the car.

Alternatively, you can continue downcanyon about 4 miles, to the confluence with Sheep Creek, where the canyon is 800 feet deep. Walk up Sheep Creek through a broad valley to Willis Creek, the first stream you encounter. From the confluence of Bull Valley and Sheep Creek to Willis Creek is about 4.5 to 5 miles.

Boulder hopping in Bull Valley Gorge

Turn left, following Willis Creek upstream. After 3 miles, you meet the road at a grassy parking area and then have to road walk 2 to 2.5 miles back to your car at the hiker's gate, making a loop of about 20 miles. The road portion of the hike would be very difficult in hot weather.

If you exit at the crack and return to you car, you can drive back to Willis Creek and hike a couple of miles downstream to see the best narrows of Willis, then turn back. This way you can complete both Bull Valley Gorge and Willis Creek hikes in 1 day.

55 | BUCKSKIN GULCH

Distance: 23 miles one way
Hiking time: 3 days
Difficulty: strenuous
Season: April to early June
Elevation gain: 160 feet
Maps: USGS Pine Hollow Canyon, West Clark Bench,
  Bridger Point
Land Management Agency: BLM Kanab Field Office

On US 89 east of Kanab, toward Page, Arizona, between mileposts 20 and 21, turn south to the Paria River Ranger Station. Be sure to get the latest information on route conditions before starting out. The dirt road to White House trailhead also starts here. A car or bike should be left at the trailhead for shuttling. Get back on US 89 and go east to a dirt road turnoff between mileposts 25 and 26, driving 9 miles south to the Wire Pass trailhead.

Buckskin Gulch is arguably the premier set of narrows in the United States. The gulch is long and deep, leaving few opportunities to get out. Ensure a dry weather forecast before entering and contact the Kanab BLM office for up-to-date trail conditions. Floods often change the obstacles on the canyon floor, and finding drinking water can also be a challenge—plan to carry at least 2 or 3 days' worth. There is often water in the Paria River, and water from springs can be found down Paria Canyon toward Lee's Ferry.

The first 1.5 miles through Wire Pass takes you through an extraordinarily narrow slot. Although this section is relatively free of obstacles, storms could change conditions at any time, so bring a 50-foot rope just in case. It will also be needed on day 2. Soon the canyon empties into Buckskin Gulch where you'll find some petroglyphs of mountain bighorn sheep.

Continue to the right, down Buckskin Gulch, for 6.5 miles to the Midpoint Exit. Getting there usually requires wading through deep, cold, muddy pools. At the exit, the walls are farther apart, only about 100 feet high, and the canyon is more open. It is possible to pass the exit if you're

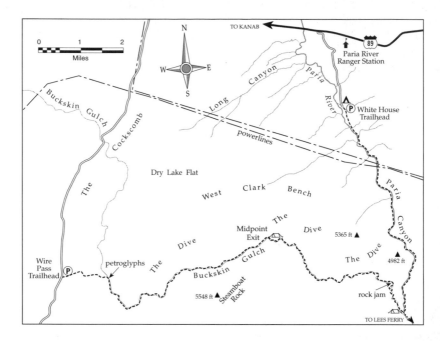

not watching for it. At the Midpoint Exit, pull up out of the canyon and onto the bench on either side for the night. Do not spend the night on the canyon floor! Getting out of the canyon will require rock scrambling and basic climbing skills. Although the walls are 100 feet high, there is only one short steep section. A rope may come in handy here, especially for descending back down in the morning.

Before entering the canyon on day 2, reassess weather conditions. The second night will be spent in the canyon.

The terrain covered on the second day is much like that of the first, with towering canyon walls and cold pools. The canyon's major obstacle is located 4.5 miles downcanyon from the Midpoint Exit. The large rock jam and dry fall is 10 to 15 feet high. Steps have been cut in the rock to the left side, but using a rope makes getting down much safer and easier. From here it is another 2.5 miles to the confluence of Buckskin Gulch and the Paria River. The second night can be spent on a large sandbar near the confluence where small amounts of flowing water can be found.

On day 3, turn north at the confluence and hike up the river. The canyon walls become shorter and farther apart than before as the trail works its way north. At 5.5 miles, a large set of powerlines passes over the canyon. From the powerlines, the White House trailhead is 2.5 miles away.

Arch along the Paria River

56 | LOWER MUDDY CREEK GORGE

Distance: 8 miles round trip
Hiking time: 2 to 5 hours, depending on where you turn around and your hiking speed
Difficulty: easy
Season: March to October
Elevation gain: 200 feet
Map: USGS Hunt Draw
Land Management Agency: BLM Price Field Office

This hike starts from the airstrip at the Hidden Splendor Mine. Follow the instructions given in Hike 58 from I-70's exit 129 to the Hidden Splendor Mine. Park at the airstrip.

This hike consists of a stroll down a high-walled gorge, some 800 to 1000 feet deep, formed by Muddy Creek. The creek meanders across the 0.25 mile wide gorge the entire 4-mile length, so you'll get your feet wet in the ankle-deep water. Other than the 100-foot drop from the airstrip down to creek level, the hike is remarkably flat, making it easy and a good introduction to the San Rafael Swell for hikers of any age or skill level.

From the airstrip, you can see the obvious gorge closing in to the south. Start by following the road off the edge and south along the creek. Once at

Sunlit cliffs over Lower Muddy Creek

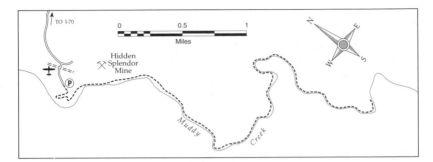

creek level, there's only one way to go. In the first 0.5 mile, mostly on the east side of the gorge, you'll find much evidence of the mining activity that gave the area its name. An abandoned building still stands. Do not enter any of the old mine shafts; traces of radioactive materials are still present.

The beautiful, high canyon walls seem to glow in the early morning or evening sunlight. The gorge ends about 4 miles from the airstrip, although you can turn around any time to adjust the hike's length.

57 | IRON WASH

Distance: 9 miles round trip
Hiking time: 5 to 6 hours
Difficulty: easy
Season: October to April
Elevation gain: 210 feet
Maps: USGS Old Woman Wash, San Rafael Desert
    1:100,000
Land Management Agency: BLM Price Field Office

From I-70, take the SR 24 exit and drive south toward Hanksville. The exit is approximately 10 miles west of Green River. While driving south on SR 24, watch for a turnoff on the west side of the road between mile markers 142 and 143. You will pass through a gate onto a dirt/gravel road. The road is passable for most vehicles, but you should keep a shovel in your vehicle to fill in any minor washouts.

Follow this road to Lost Spring, identifiable by its old wooden aqueduct. Just after the spring, the road forks. The right fork takes you into the mouth of Ernie Canyon. Follow the left fork a little more than a mile, until you come to another fork; go right. Here you will find a stock pond and a great spot to park. From here you can either hike back down the road and take the left fork, which takes you to the bottom of the wash, or hike due south cross-country for a shorter route to the wash.

At Iron Wash in the San Rafael Swell

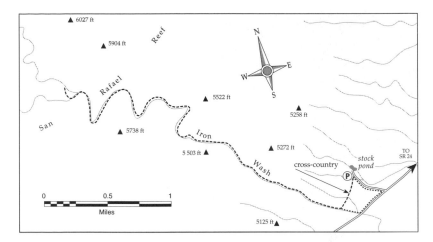

Once you have reached the wash you are on the trail. Follow the wash upcanyon. The lower sections of Iron Wash are less impressive, but as you proceed and approach the point where the canyon cuts through the San Rafael Reef, the canyon walls begin to tower up on either side. The canyon continues into the swell for about 4.5 miles and then begins to open up a little. As the canyon opens and the rock walls become black you have reached the end.

If you choose to follow the right fork at the hike's beginning, it is possible to hike out through Ernie Canyon. However, in addition to adding several miles to the hike, we found it very difficult to find our way to the top of Ernie Canyon. We suggest you day hike in from the east side, using the road from Lost Spring. Both canyons are very dry, and are best hiked in cool weather, such as during dry periods in the winter.

58 | CHUTE OF MUDDY CREEK

Distance: 18 miles one way or 20 miles round trip
Hiking time: minimum 9 hours, average 11 hours, more in
    deeper water
Difficulty: moderate
Season: April to June, September to October
Elevation gain: 560 feet
Land Management Agency: BLM Price Field Office

This hike starts at a remote and beautiful section in the middle of the San Rafael Swell. Travel west on I-70 from Green River, or east from Salina, to exit 129.

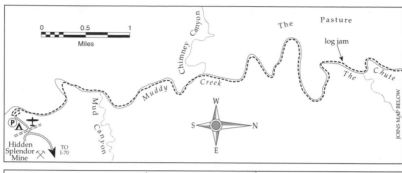

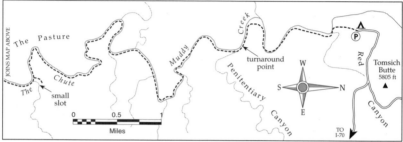

After exiting the freeway, note the odometer mileage, or reset your trip odometer. A web of unimproved dirt roads crisscrosses the swell, making it easy to take the wrong turn. Follow the detailed directions below (odometer readings may vary slightly):

Mileage	Directions
0.0	Exit 129 off I-70
3.3	Cross road and cattle guard
4.0	Road forks, head left
5.1	Junction, go toward Head of Sinbad
6.8	Cattle guard; roads cross, continue straight
10.0	Junction, head toward Tan Seep
13.0	Road to Swasey's, go straight
13.7	Junction, go right toward McKay Flat
14.6	Junction, go left toward McKay Flat
23.0	Red Canyon Loop/Hidden Splendor Junction; go to Hidden Splendor
33.2	Arrive at Hidden Splendor Mine/Airstrip

To get to Tomsich Butte, at the last junction (mile 23) take the Red Canyon Loop for 6 miles. Allow 1.5 hours driving time from I-70 to Hidden Splendor Mine. Plan on camping at your chosen starting point, either Hidden Splendor or Tomsich, so you can get an early start on this long hike.

The Chute of Muddy Creek has the feel of a technical hike: it has narrows with wall-to-wall water but no obstacles or rope work. Avoid hiking during high runoff periods, or after rains, when high water makes the hike more dangerous. In spring and fall the water is cold, so bring a wet suit. Remember that desert evenings cool off quickly, so get out before dark.

You have three options for your assault on the Chute. The easiest requires two cars; park one at the Hidden Splendor Mine, then hike from Tomsich Butte walking downstream. Without a shuttle car, you'll have to do an out-and-back hike from either Tomsich Butte or the mine.

For an out-and-back hike, you're looking at 6 miles before entering the best part of the narrows, which last about 4 miles, making the round trip 20 miles from either end. The directions are pretty simple: find Muddy Creek and start walking in it. From Hidden Splendor, you hike upstream, from Tomsich Butte, downstream. Our directions assume you are starting at the Hidden Splendor Mine. From the airstrip follow a road to the cliff edge and down a set of switchbacks. Do not drive down this road; the area below the cliffs should be reserved for foot traffic to reduce impact.

Once in the creek, you pass two canyons on the right. The second and larger of these, Mud Canyon, also has a good set of narrows, but exploration will have to wait. You also pass a sign below a large cottonwood tree indicating that upstream of this point you are in the Muddy Creek Wilderness Study Area. Take advantage of the open terrain to make good time; the hiking slows ahead. At about 4 miles, you pass Chimney Canyon entering on the left.

Pocked canyon walls in the Chute of Muddy Creek

Finally the canyon walls close in. From here you walk in the creek most of the next 4 miles, although most of the time the water is knee deep or less. The catch, of course, is the occasional pool; some can be bypassed to one edge of the stream, but a few are unavoidable. Use your poles or hiking staff to probe the murky water.

A mile and a half into the narrows, you reach the narrowest section, indicated by a log jam high overhead. Here the Chute is only 10 feet across and the stream deepens. For most hikers the water is waist to chest deep, but after storms or in wet years, you may find yourself swimming.

The canyon undulates, widening and narrowing for the next 2 miles. The deepest pools are about 0.5 mile beyond the log jam and may require swimming. The high vertical walls make this section darker and more foreboding.

About 3 miles into the narrows, a small slot opens on the right side of the canyon, found on the Hunt Draw map near the "C" in Chute and across the canyon from a knoll marked with an "X" and an elevation of "5439T." There is a 20-foot climb up a dryfall to enter this slot. Time prevented us from exploring, but others suggest it is one of the better slot canyons in the area. It is technical, so only experienced climbers should attempt the route.

Continuing up Muddy Creek, the canyon begins to open up and the sandy benches appear along the sides of the creek—indications that you are approaching the end of the narrows and the long exit hike to Tomsich Butte 6 miles farther upstream. Turn around here for a long and tiring hike back to Hidden Splendor.

59 | QUANDARY CANYON

Distance: 12-mile loop
Hiking time: 9 to 11 hours, more in deeper water
Difficulty: strenuous and dangerous
Season: late March to May, September to October
Elevation gain: 1340 feet
Maps: USGS Hunt Draw
Land Management Agency: BLM Price Field Office

The Quandary Canyon hike starts near the Hidden Splendor Mine. Follow the instructions from I-70's exit 129 to the Hidden Splendor Mine in Hike 58, the Chute of Muddy Creek. The trailhead is found 2.3 miles back up the road from the airstrip at Hidden Splendor. Park at the pullout on the south side of the road.

Although a short day hike to the top of Quandary Canyon is possible, the

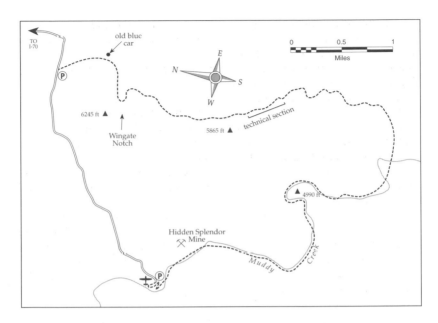

full hike is highly technical. Attempt Quandary Canyon only if you're prepared for a physically and mentally challenging day and have the following skills: rock climbing, rappelling, routefinding, and the ability to swim deep potholes. Bring your rappelling and climbing gear, including a harness, belay device, 30 feet or more of webbing, 150 feet of rope, and 25 feet of accessory cord. Climbing shoes and a bolt kit are highly recommended.

Follow the double track from the pullout southeast to an old blue car. Look up to the southwest toward a notch high above in the upper Wingate layer of the sandstone cliffs. Head west up the small drainage toward the notch. Soon you'll spot an old graded roadbed crossing under the notch and heading south. Follow the road until it tops out and passes through a narrow opening in the sandstone.

The top of Quandary Canyon is a hidden cove with pinyon and juniper trees, rocky ledges, and boulders. It is a secluded spot for a picnic or family hike—children will enjoy hiding amid the boulders or playing in the sand. Follow the small wash about 0.25 mile until you reach a 12-foot pouroff. This marks the end of the short hike and the beginning of the technical hike. The drainage begins a series of steps down into a narrow, sinuous slot.

In this first, less difficult section, obstacles include two 12-foot rappels and a downclimb of the same distance. One of the pouroffs has a large square timber wedged between the walls. Rig your webbing to the timber, and rappel down. The downclimb is through an obvious crack on the left side. If you need a rope here you should reconsider the trip. You also

Rappelling into Quandary Canyon

pass under an undocumented natural bridge, about 6 feet high.

The drainage narrows, and the obstacles get more difficult. At one point the canyon narrows to a tiny slit, too narrow for your feet to fit into the bottom. You can chimney through this section, although there is one pool you have to swim through at the bottom of this narrow section. An alternative is to backtrack a short distance to where you can walk up the slickrock on the right (west). Once on top of the canyon's side wall, walk along above the narrow slit until it makes a turn to the west. On the far right side, you'll find a small arch or pocket in the west wall. Make sure you bring at least a 150-foot rope or you will be unable to use this rappel station.

The canyon presents one difficult obstacle after another for the next 1.5 to 2 miles; most can be bypassed on the right (west) side of the canyon. As you work your way down the canyon, keep in mind the canyoneer's first rule: ALWAYS make sure you have a route out of, or around, an obstacle before you commit yourself. Conditions change so often it would be a disservice for us to imply a specific set of circumstances. You need to use your own wits and experience to make it through Quandary Canyon.

In one later section there are three increasingly deep round potholes. The third pothole is impassable. At the top of the first hole, backtrack until you find a spot to ascend to the left (east) side and bypass all three potholes, returning to the canyon bottom through some boulders.

Other obstacles include a very deep, recessed pool plunked right where the canyon narrows and makes a sharp turn to the right. The walls are sheer along the sides of the pool. You'll need to traverse a bowl on the right just above the pool, using a small ledge to hang on to. Climbing shoes help here. If this section looks too difficult, backtrack and look for an opportunity to bypass.

Later, there are two U-shaped slots in the canyon. One overlooks a 10-foot steeply angled slope, followed by an overhung dropoff about 10 to 12 feet into a pool. Use a hand rope to lower the first hiker down and determine the depth of the pool. Usually the pool is deep enough for the second hiker to slide down the slope and jump into the pool.

The other U-slot sits atop a long, sloping semicircular bowl about 40 feet high. The sandstone slopes away about 15 feet down, then drops another 25 feet to a very large pool. There are anchors on the right, or you can carefully drop your legs over the 2-foot ledge at the top of the bowl using your body for friction, then traverse west. Once you get good footholds over the ledge, there are handholds in the sidewalls to the west.

The final obstacle is a 30-foot crack. Some hikers report downclimbing the crack. Most choose to rappel the low-angle slope using anchors on the far west, or right side. The rappel is very easy.

After the technical section, it's a long hike back to your car. Exit the bottom of Quandary Canyon, then head west across some very dry and hot "badlands." Make sure to bring a lot of water. Muddy Creek water will quickly clog a filter. Continue west until you reach Muddy Creek, then follow the creek upstream. Soon you reach the mouth of lower Muddy Creek Canyon, with towering walls.

Follow the meanders of Muddy Creek upstream about 4 miles, back toward Hidden Splendor Mine. You can read the details of this section in Hike 56. Once the canyon begins to open back up, you see an old mining shack on the right (east) and a jeep trail heading up onto a bench. The airstrip is on top of that bench. From the airstrip it is 2.3 miles back to your car.

60 | BELL AND LITTLE WILD HORSE CANYONS LOOP

Distance: 8.5-mile loop
Hiking time: 3.5 to 5 hours
Difficulty: easy
Season: March to early June, September to November
Elevation gain: 860 feet
Maps: USGS Little Wild Horse Mesa
Land Management Agency: BLM Price Field Office

These canyons are located near Goblin Valley State Park in the San Rafael Swell, a large section of desert uplands formed when the earth's crust swelled and broke open like a bubble bursting. The upward thrust resulted in a reef, or set of upward sloping cliffs surrounding the formerly swollen area. This hike follows two narrow canyons within the Crack Canyon Wilderness Study Area that pass through the reef of the San Rafael Swell.

Take I-70 west from Green River to the junction with SR 24. Turn south, and drive for about 25 miles, then take the turnoff to Goblin Valley. After 11.5 miles, and just before reaching the state park, you'll see a signed dirt road heading west to Little Wild Horse Canyon. From the junction it's 6 miles to the trailhead and parking area. Do not park in the wash.

From the trailhead, follow the dry wash northward. A chockstone near the trailhead is easily climbed by most hikers, but you can bypass the chockstone by backtracking about 30 feet and walking up a short sandstone ramp on the left (west) side of the canyon.

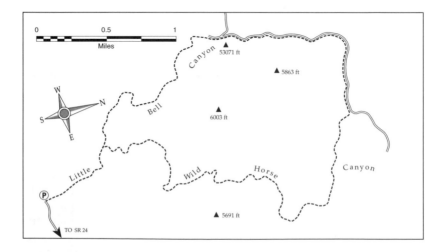

After about a 0.5 mile, the trail forks. To the left is Bell Canyon; to the right Little Wild Horse continues. You can take the loop in either direction. For those looking for a shorter hike, go right into Little Wild Horse—the more scenic of the two canyons—for a 6-mile round-trip hike. Little Wild Horse Canyon is perhaps the best easy slot-canyon hike in the Southwest, with its great narrows and no technical obstacles. After recent rains, some water may be in the canyon bottom.

Scenic narrows in Little Wild Horse Canyon

If you go left into Bell Canyon, follow the canyon about 2 miles, where it opens up as you reach the north side of the reef. Watch carefully for a right turn onto a dirt road. Follow this road as it ascends about 300 feet to the east along the backside of the reef. Although other roads are in the area, continue generally east for about 2 miles to the head of a large wash draining south.

Turn south and head down into Little Wild Horse Canyon. At first the canyon is wide and open, but soon narrows down. The narrows, averaging 4 to 6 feet wide, run for most of a mile. The canyon walls and floor are fluted and pocked, showing the erosive power of the floods that frequent the canyon. From the top of the canyon back to the trailhead is about 4 miles.

61 | UPPER CHIMNEY CANYON

Distance: 7 miles round trip
Hiking time: 4 to 5 hours, more for side canyon
    exploration
Difficulty: easy
Season: September to May
Elevation gain: 420 feet
Maps: USGS The Frying Pan, San Rafael Desert 1:100,000
Land Management Agency: BLM Price Field Office

Get off I-70 at exit 97. Write down your mileage, or reset you trip odometer. Head south. Drive 8.2 miles to a junction and go right. At 8.3 miles, keep left. There's a cattle guard and junction at 10.5 miles; go left. At 15.9 miles, go right at the fork. The next junction at 18.1 miles is signed; turn right onto Segers Road. At 19.5 miles turn left off Segers Road. Drive 0.2 mile

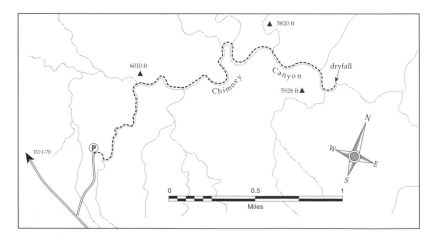

Rock formations in Upper Chimney Canyon

(19.7 total) to a dead end. Park at the round area at the end of the road.

Upper Chimney Canyon offers a different view of the western swell area. The entire plateau area is called the Musentuchit Badlands. Canyoneering author Steve Allen attributes this to early cowboys who said of the area that one "must'ent touch it."

From the round parking area, head cross-country, generally northeast, in the direction of a square-topped knoll in the distance. You are looking for a deeper wash heading mostly north. If you take the wrong one, you'll end up at a steep drop-off. Head back up and go east to the next deeper wash.

As the wash deepens and you approach Chimney Canyon, you'll need to downclimb a 10-foot ledge with seeps below. A knobby branch against the ledge helps you down. By summer, the seep amounts to little more than a few damp spots under the ledge. Follow the canyon down to its confluence with Chimney Canyon. We placed a cairn at the junction of the entry wash and Chimney Canyon to mark the spot, as this will be your exit as well. Take a minute to commit the spot to memory—several similar-looking side canyons enter along this stretch.

Follow Chimney down for the next 2+ miles, then return along the same route. The canyon usually has no water. Several side canyons merit exploration, and you may sight some wildlife in the area. Along the way you encounter a couple of short narrows. The canyon varies from 100 to 200 feet deep, but in the deeper sections the plateau walls, set back from the canyon, tower hundreds of feet above the canyon bottom. Interesting pinnacle formations spice up the trip.

As you near the end of the hike, you pass through the narrowest section of the canyon. Your hike ends at a 30-foot dryfall into a deep pool. Retrace your steps to your marked exit.

62 | GOBLIN VALLEY

Distance: 2.5-mile loop
Hiking time: 2 hours
Difficulty: easy
Season: February to May, September to November,
     December to January in warm dry periods
Elevation gain: 140 feet
Map: USGS Goblin Valley
Land Management Agency: BLM Goblin Valley State Park

Take SR 24 north from Hanksville to the turnoff to Goblin Valley State Park, just after milepost 137. Follow the paved road about 12 miles to the park entrance, where you need to pay a day-use or camping fee. After the entrance station, the road ends at a T junction. The campground, which has hot showers, is to the right and the Valley of Goblins with a pavilion-covered picnic area is to the left. The trailhead lies straight ahead, directly across the road from the T.

Goblin Valley has two trails, which you can combine into a single loop. All trails in the park are marked with yellow or blue painted rocks. From the parking area at the T junction, a rock-lined trail starts up the sandy hill

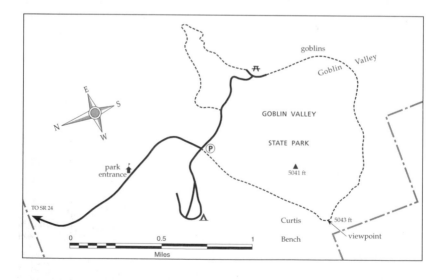

to the west, winding west then south for 0.5 mile along the Curtis Bench above the park. On the bench the trail becomes more of an old 4WD road. Soon you are approaching the south end of the bench. A trail junction marks a short spur trail to the right that goes a couple hundred yards to the south edge of the bench to a viewpoint of the Henry Mountains looming over the southern horizon.

The left trail heads over to the Goblin Valley and the rest of the loop hike. The trail drops into a tiny arroyo that deepens as it works its way off the bench and down into Goblin Valley. After a short distance the arroyo reaches a T junction. The left trail is a shorter path to the pavilion; the trail to the right winds through more of the arroyo, eventually spitting you out on the wide flat floor of Goblin Valley. There is no more trail here, but in the open valley it's easy to see the pavilion to the north. Take time to wander through the "goblins," the highlight of this trip.

Once at the picnic pavilion, look at the paved parking area immediately to the northeast of the pavilion. From the end of the pavement, follow a faint footpath to the east out along a ridge. As you start down the ridge's edge, you'll see the painted rocks marking the trail.

This section has a couple of short, steep descents on loose, rocky soils, but they aren't difficult. Working its way east, the trail drops down into a wash at the head of the Goblin Valley area. After about 0.25 mile another wash joins coming in from the west. Turn left (west) and head up the new wash, which becomes a few feet deep with sheer edges, and the trail alternates between the dry wash bottom and the benches on either side.

As you start to gain a little elevation, the little wash narrows and deepens, transforming into Goblin Valley's version of a delightful, miniature slot canyon. At its narrowest the little slot is around 20 feet deep with sloping walls about 2 feet apart at foot level. Soon you reach the head of the wash, and the paved road lies in view just ahead. Turn right on the road and walk about 0.5 mile back to your vehicle.

Goblins!

63 | MEXICAN MOUNTAIN TO SPRING CANYON

Distance: 8 to 9 miles round trip; 7 miles round trip to petroglyphs
Hiking time: 4 to 6 hours
Difficulty: easy
Season: February to early April, October to November, winter if no snow
Elevation gain: 730 feet
Map: USGS Mexican Mountain
Land Management Agency: BLM Price Field Office

Take exit 129 off I-70 west of Green River, heading north for 20 miles to arrive at the bridge over the San Rafael River and a campground. Right after the bridge on the north side of the river, the first road to the right is Mexican Mountain Road. The campground is a fee area and has restrooms, but no water.

Take Mexican Mountain Road 14 miles to its end at a parking area with a barrier blocking the road. Along the way, there is a gate you need to open to pass. Be sure to close it. There are several spots along the way to pull off and camp. Be careful not to pull off except on existing roads, as most of this region is part of the Mexican Mountain Wilderness Study Area.

At the parking area, the trail begins behind the barrier and follows the old road, now closed to motorized vehicles. You drop down toward the

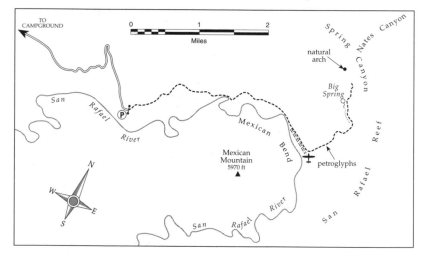

Petroglyphs at the mouth of Spring Canyon

San Rafael River, and after about a mile your path parallels the riverbank for a short distance. On the south side of the river, Mexican Mountain rises high above you. At about 1.5 miles, after you've turned away from the riverbank, you reach a dry wash. Cattle trails continue straight ahead, but they dead-end up ahead against the river. Go up the dry wash, and about 150 feet in you'll see the old road steeply ascending a cliff face.

Once on top, follow the trail/road another mile to a big stand of cotton-wood trees, which line the sides of an old airstrip. At the east end of the strip, you'll see the windsock. Near the windsock, turn left toward the large boulders, where you'll pick up the trail. Several black boulders with petroglyphs are right along the trail. Avoid touching the rocks with the petroglyphs.

From here the trail turns northward and begins to follow the Spring Canyon wash. There is a distinct trail to follow along the wash bottom. After about 0.25 mile the canyon bottom has light seasonal water. The trail occasionally crosses the small stream, but it's easy to stay dry. The wash winds its way upcanyon with 1000+-foot cliffs rising high above. As you look upcanyon, you'll soon see an arch high up in the top of the cliffs to the left (northwest.)

From here it's another 0.5 mile to the confluence of Nates Canyon and Spring Canyon. Day hikers should turn around here and retrace their steps back to the trailhead. For a shorter hike you can turn around at the petroglyphs.

Overnight trips include an opportunity to explore further up these canyons. Several dryfalls are up Nates Canyon, and another arch is up Spring Canyon. Do not count on there being water in these canyons. Take all the water you'll need. In warm weather, the road hiking section can be very hot and dry.

64 | EAGLE CANYON

Distance: 12-mile loop
Hiking time: 8 to 10 hours
Difficulty: moderate
Season: February to May, September to November, winter dry spells
Elevation gain: 1040 feet
Map: USGS Copper Globe, Sid and Charley
Land Management Agency: BLM Price Field Office

Get off I-70 at exit 114, about 45 miles west of Green River. Go south on the frontage road, following it east 1 mile to park at Justensen Flats.

Start hiking along the 4WD track running north through a concrete tunnel under I-70. The jeep trail parallels I-70, then turns north, dropping into Eagle Canyon, a distance of about 1.5 miles. Allow about 30 minutes to

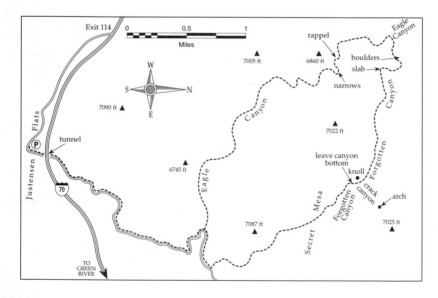

A small arch marks the exit from Forgotten Canyon

reach the canyon bottom. Once in the canyon, turn left and follow the sandy canyon downstream. About 1.5 miles downcanyon you reach a wide grassy flat, where desert bighorn sheep often graze. Approach quietly for a chance to view them.

After about 1 mile of twists and turns in the narrowing canyon, you reach a deep thin slot developing in the canyon floor. Skirt the slot on the right until you reach the 100-foot drop-off. You can rappel into the canyon at the drop-off, if there is no pool at the bottom. The route is an overhanging free rappel; a juniper tree back around the right side makes a good anchor point. If there is a pool on the canyon floor, go back to the slot and continue down the left side, past the large pine tree in the canyon bottom. There you can anchor off a tree and rappel into the canyon. Either rappel requires two 50-meter ropes or equivalent.

As you proceed down Eagle Canyon, you pass through some cool nontechnical narrows. One half mile from the rappel, coming in from the right, is Forgotten Canyon, unlabeled on maps. Forgotten Canyon is narrower than Eagle and has a couple of obstacles to surmount: (1) a series of short, class 5 boulder climbs up some rock jams and (2) a class 5.4 friction climb up a slab bypassing a dryfall. Beginners may require a rope.

As you continue upcanyon, one canyon enters from the left, then another from the right. Next, watch for a knoll that splits the drainage in two. Stay to the left of the knoll. Immediately after the knoll is a crack canyon on the left side, with a natural arch high up on the cliff wall. To see the arch you need to continue upcanyon about 50 feet past the crack. If you go too far, you won't see the arch and may miss the turnoff to the mesa top. The small crack merits exploration if time allows.

Directly across the canyon from the crack, you begin your ascent up to the top of Secret Mesa. There is no trail, so you'll need to routefind. Stay to the right of the high knolls, or domes, up above you. You cross some slickrock slabs on your way up.

Once on top of Secret Mesa, you're in a valley at the base of the ridge to your right. Follow the base of the slickrock cross-country for about a mile, staying close to the ridge. The valley floor is heavily covered with cryptogamic soils, so try to stay in wash bottoms. After about 1 mile, you reach a canyon, which you bypass by skirting its head to the south-southeast.

Rounding the canyon head, you'll see a saddle ahead to the southwest. From the saddle, you can see a jeep trail to the southeast. Drop to the left or southeast, and head for the jeep trail. As you descend, you encounter a 25-foot cliff band that has numerous easy ways down with no climbing.

Once on the road, follow the trail west (right) to the canyon bottom of Eagle Canyon. Cross the canyon, and head back up the road you entered from. This takes you back up to the tunnel and Justensen Flats.

65 | WILDCAT CONNECTOR TRAIL

Distance: 12 miles one way
Hiking time: 2 days
Difficulty: moderate
Season: late June to early October
Elevation gain: 2910 feet
Maps: USGS Lower Bowns Reservoir, Grover, Blind Lake;
   Trails Illustrated Fish Lake, North and Central Capitol
   Reef
Land Management Agency: Dixie National Forest,
   Teasdale Ranger District

Turn south on SR 12 from Torrey, near the west entrance to Capitol Reef National Park in south central Utah. Go south for about 16 miles to the Wildcat Ranger Station, where there is a large pullout and public restroom. The ranger station opens in June and closes in late September. From the dirt loop at the restrooms, follow the dirt road heading west for 0.3 mile to an old corral and cabin and an area for parking.

For the one-way hike as shown here, you need a second car at the Fish Creek trailhead, which is described in Hike 66, Blind Lake. Another option is to go partway, perhaps to one of the streams to camp, then return to the Wildcat Ranger Station trailhead.

The USGS map best shows this trail; the Wildcat Connector Trail, where you start this hike, is not shown on the Trails Illustrated map, and the junction with Trail 140 is shown incorrectly. The trail starts climbing almost

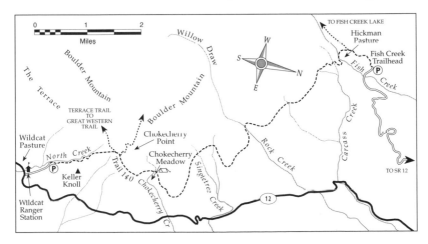

An old cabin near the trailhead

immediately, paralleling North Creek upward. At one point the trail seems to cut northeast (right) up a steep ridge side near Keller Knoll. The correct trail stays close to the stream to the left.

It's about 1.5 miles and 1150 feet up to a small flat on the top of the ridge. The Terrace Trail (#140) goes southwest. Follow an old road through the aspens west and up toward Chokecherry Point. Watch carefully for a trail sign in some brush on the right side of the road, less than 0.5 mile from the previous junction. The sign is a tall, thin fiberglass trail marker with the trail number 140 and an arrow. If you miss the turnoff, you keep climbing up to Chokecherry Point, which you know you've reached when you see the sign. If you reach Chokecherry Point, turn around and head back down to the junction with Trail 140.

From the junction at 9900 feet, the trail traverses under the "rim," the rocky ledge that forms the rim of Boulder Mountain. From the junction to Chokecherry Creek is about 1.25 miles through aspen forest and grassy meadows. As you approach the creek, the trail drops a couple hundred feet. Cows are near the stream in summer, but there are good camping spots and reliable, filterable water. All along this connector trail, you have great views of Capitol Reef to the east and relative solitude.

Over the next 2 miles to Singletree Creek, the trail drops 700 feet and gains 600 of it back. The creek usually has water. Campsites do exist near the stream, but the area lacks the open meadows of the Chokecherry Creek area.

You cross another creek, a fork of Singletree Creek, in about 0.5 mile, then quickly drop 500 feet to a flat point on a ridge. The trail cuts northwest on its way 1.5 miles to Rock Creek, the next water source. Rock Creek *should* have water, but it can go dry in lean water years. Check with the Forest Service office before you begin your hike for the current status of all the streams. The best camping lies on the far side of the creek.

From Rock Creek it is 3.75 miles to Hickman Pasture, where you meet the Fish Creek (Blind Lake) Trail. First you climb 200 feet, then descend 350 feet, then climb another 250 feet, before the big drop of 700 feet. The last 0.5 mile flattens out as you walk through the grassy meadows of the pasture. You cross Fish Creek—a perennial water source—just before arriving at the junction.

The pasture area offers great camping, but you're only 1 mile from the Fish Creek trailhead. Just follow the Fish Creek Trail (a full 4WD road at this point) down to the large parking area.

66 | BLIND LAKE

Distance: 9-mile loop
Hiking time: 6 to 8 hours or 2 days
Difficulty: easy to moderate
Season: July to September
Elevation gain: 1940 feet
Maps: USGS Blind Lake; Trails Illustrated Fish Lake, North and Central Capitol Reef National Park
Land Management Agency: Dixie National Forest, Teasdale Ranger District

Turning onto SR 12 on the east side of Torrey from SR 24, proceed 4.7 miles south, just past a road joining SR 12 from Teasdale. Near milepost 119, a dirt road signed "Great Western Trail Access" turns off to the west. Turning onto this dirt road, you should see a sign indicating that the Fish Creek trailhead is up ahead. Continue the more than 6 miles to the trailhead, a signed, large parking area at a fork in the road.

This is a loop hike on the lower rim of Boulder Mountain, a flat-topped mesa with a rocky cliff band several hundred feet high around its east side. The 11,000-foot top of Boulder Mountain is several miles wide and relatively flat. The mountain's height creates a true alpine environment in the middle of southern Utah's slickrock desert. It also creates is own weather. Hail, snow, and thunderstorms are possible throughout the summer months. Blind Lake lies at the base of the cliffs under the rim.

From the parking area, the trail follows the road to the right for a couple of miles above the Fish Creek trailhead. Those with a shuttle car can save about 2 miles of hiking by parking the shuttle vehicle at the trailhead and the other higher up the road at the Blind Lake parking area. However,

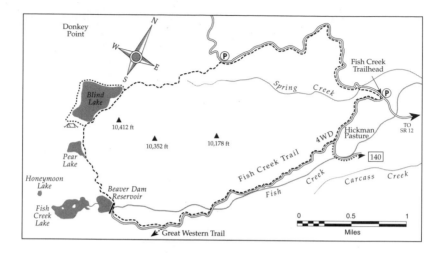

about 1 mile past the lower parking area, the road turns rocky and rough, requiring at least an HCV, if not a 4WD.

On foot, follow the road until you arrive at the Blind Lake parking area. The road rises 1150 feet between the two parking areas. Leave the road and start up the single-track trail ascending to the lake. At first the trail is gently sloped, but soon steepens for the climb up to scenic Blind Lake at 10,233 feet. This large, sky blue lake is nestled at the base of dark, rocky cliffs about 800 feet high. The area is heavily forested with pines. A trail circles the lake, and it is possible to find good camping areas back off the lake.

Follow the trail around the lake's east edge, turning south to follow the base of the cliffs for about 0.25 mile to Pear Lake, a smaller but scenic lake at the same altitude. Passing Pear Lake, the trail curves to the southeast and starts a 300-foot descent to Fish Creek Lake and Beaver Dam Reservoir.

Follow the trail across the dam at the east edge of the reservoir. On the south side of the dam, the trail joins a wide, old 4WD dirt road following Fish Creek back down to the trailhead. As you descend, after about 0.5 mile you reach a signed trail junction indicating that the Great Western Trail (GWT) ascends up onto the top of Boulder Mountain. Continue down the 4WD road.

Several meadows along the road make good campsites. Two to 2.5 miles down the dirt road, another road enters from the right in a wide grassy meadow. This road is signed as FR 140. Continue straight ahead about 0.75 mile back to the Fish Creek trailhead.

This loop can be completed as a day hike, or it can serve as a leisure overnight backpack. If you camp near the lakes, be prepared for cooler temperatures, even in summer.

A delightful mountain stream dropping off Boulder Mountain

67 | SLICKROCK TRAIL

Distance: 1 to 15 miles
Hiking time: 2 hours to 2 days
Difficulty: easy to moderate
Season: March to May, September to early November
Elevation gain: 2020 feet
Maps: Trails Illustrated Fish Lake, North and Central Capitol Reef
Land Management Agency: Dixie National Forest, Teasdale Ranger District

The Slickrock Trail follows the east flank of Boulder Mountain, paralleling SR 12 between Boulder and Torrey. Access points to trailheads are all along SR 12. However, access roads that pass through the campgrounds are closed until late May.

Head south from Torrey, or north out of Boulder. The Trails Illustrated map best shows the trail and the various access points. Where the trail crosses an access road, the trail should be signed, but some have been removed by malcontents or pranksters.

The lower end of the trail is accessed off a dirt road heading east 0.5 mile south of the small town of Grover. Turning off SR 12, you'll see a sign mentioning several destinations, including the Slickrock Trail. Just over 2 miles down this road is a junction. Take the road to the right and park in the wide grassy area. The road ahead gets steeper and rocky. Shortly after you cross the Sulphur Creek drainage the Slickrock Trail breaks off the road and heads south.

If you choose to continue south on SR 12, the next access point is on the Happy Valley Road, near milepost 113. Again, the trail should be signed. At the Singletree Campground a trail descends to meet with the Slickrock Trail between 0.25 and 0.5 mile below. At the Wildcat Ranger Station, a faint—but marked—trail heads down from the parking area and restrooms, to connect with the Slickrock Trail a little over a mile below. The road to Lower Bowns Reservoir, which leaves SR 12 immediately south of the Pleasant Creek Campground, offers access to the trail 1.7 miles down a graded dirt road. There is good camping on the south side of this road in various ponderosa pine–lined meadows.

Two roads cross the south end of the trail. The dirt road leaving from the Oak Creek Campground forks about 2 to 3 miles from the highway. Both forks cross the trail. The final road is FR 180 about 5 miles south of the Oak Creek Campground. The trail also meets SR 12 about 0.25 mile south of this turn, but FR 180 also crosses the trail about 2 miles down the road, eliminating about 3 to 4 miles of hiking.

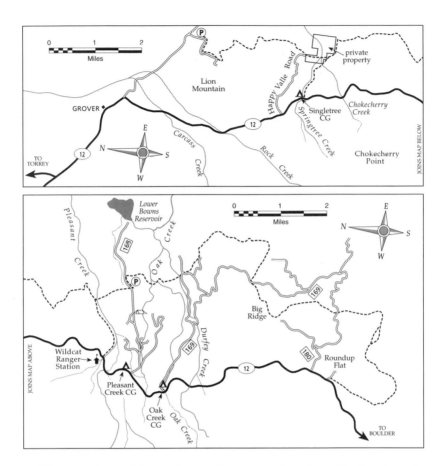

The elevations of the various trail access points along the forest roads indicate a gentle drop of only about 600 feet from the highest point, near Oak Creek, to the lowest just south of Grover. However, these elevations are somewhat misleading, as the Slickrock Trail winds its way up ridges and down into drainages and valleys all along the trail and back and forth between two ecozones: the higher characterized by tall ponderosa pine and manzanita, the other by mid-elevation pinyon-juniper forest, cliffrose, and sagebrush. The terrain varies in composition and color, from yellow-white sands and slickrock to wide green meadows, to orange-red views of the protruding slickrock below at the base of Boulder Mountain flowing into Capitol Reef National Park.

There are many options for short to long hikes along the Slickrock Trail. Short, scenic day hikes are possible between any two of the access points, either with a shuttle car or as an out-and-back hike. To hike the entire distance is best done as a 2-day backpack trip with a shuttle vehicle. Do not rely on water in the various streams that cross the trail on the map—only Singletree, Pleasant, and Oak Creeks are perennial. You could check the availability of water in various streams from your car along the access roads before beginning the hike.

For shorter hikes, we recommend Singletree and the section between Oak Creek or Pleasant Creek. These areas are fairly remote, although you can occasionally hear traffic from SR 12.

White sandstone cliffs along the Slickrock Trail

68 | DEATH HOLLOW

Distance: 21 miles round trip
Hiking time: 3 days
Difficulty: moderate
Season: March to early June, September to October
Elevation gain: 350 feet
Maps: USGS Escalante, Calf Creek; Trails Illustrated
Canyons of the Escalante
Land Management Agency: BLM Grand Staircase–
Escalante National Monument

Take SR 12 east out of Escalante toward Boulder. After about 15 miles, the road crosses the Escalante River. Just north of the river is the parking area and trailhead. For overnight trips in the monument, get a permit at the Escalante Interagency Visitor Center or at the trailhead.

The sandy trail begins by following the Escalante upriver. The canyon bottom has a fair amount of growth, but the growth offers very little shade. Expect to cross the river numerous times before reaching the Death Hollow confluence. At times, the river may be difficult to cross, depending on the season's water flow. Do not cross the river during or after storms, as flows change rapidly and are often dangerous.

At about 2 miles, the trail passes the Escalante Natural Bridge on the south wall. After another 0.5 mile the trail passes a natural arch, again on the south wall. Half a mile past the natural arch, Sand Creek Canyon enters from the north. From here, it is about 4 more miles to the confluence of Death Hollow and the Escalante.

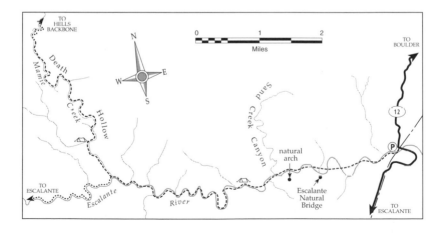

Ruins on the Escalante River approaching Death Hollow

As the trail progresses upstream, the high canyon walls begin to narrow down, foreshadowing the terrain yet to come. Several good spots to camp are found along this section of the canyon.

On day 2, plan to day hike up Death Hollow. The high narrow canyons and inviting, mossy pools make the lower sections of Death Hollow the highlight of the entire canyon. Several unavoidable pools that require swimming lay in wait—expect to get wet. This section of the canyon can be easily seen in a good day's hike. On day 3, plan to hike back out the way you came in.

This hike has the potential for several alternate routes. For those with shuttle cars, it is possible to begin the hike on the Escalante River, immediately east of the town of Escalante. A signed turnoff to the trailhead exits SR 12 near the high school on the east edge of town. The trail into the Death Hollow confluence is approximately 7 miles, about the same distance as entering from the east trailhead at the Escalante River bridge.

For those wanting to add 2 or 3 more days to their trip, hike up Death Hollow and stay near Sulphur Springs. For those with honed navigational skills, it's possible to hike down from Hells Backbone Road into Death Hollow, exiting at the trailhead on SR 12. Plan for 4 to 5 days for that trip.

69 | LOWER CALF CREEK FALLS

Distance: 6 miles round trip
Hiking time: 2 to 4 hours
Difficulty: easy
Season: September to May
Elevation gain: 370 feet
Maps: USGS Calf Creek; Trails Illustrated Canyons of the
   Escalante
Land Management Agency: BLM Grand Staircase–
   Escalante National Monument

Lower Calf Creek Falls sits just off SR 12 east of Escalante or southwest of
the town of Boulder. From Escalante, you'll see the sign to the falls and
campground a couple of miles after crossing the Escalante River bridge. Be
prepared to pay the day-use fee for hiking.

This well-developed trail is suitable for the whole family, although the
distance may be too long for children, so be prepared to carry them. Calf
Creek is a wonderful perennial desert stream, supporting a diverse wildlife population. Keep your eyes open for the beaver ponds along the
way. In the mornings and evenings you may spot wild turkeys in the canyon. Other wildlife include cougar and many species of birds.

At the trailhead an interpretive trail guide is available, which points out
locations of Anasazi ruins, petroglyphs, and a variety of desert plants. Pick
up one of the guides to help decipher the numbered signposts along the way.

This wide and well-signed trail begins near the north end of the paved
road through the campground. It follows Calf Creek up the relatively flat
canyon bottom, with sandy spots occasionally adding a little difficulty to
the hike. The canyon is wide open the entire distance, but the cliff walls
rise higher as you move upcanyon. The trail follows the stream for almost

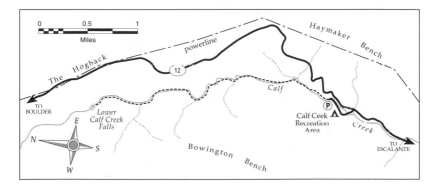

2 miles, then reaches a fork in the canyon and turns slightly east, heading up a box canyon. The upper end of this box is the falls, which is 126 feet high.

From late June to mid-September, the hike is hot, but the falls gives off a cool mist and breeze year round. In spring and fall, it's a good idea to have a jacket along, but on a hot day the cool mist will be welcome and the large plunge pool at the base of the falls makes a great place for a picnic or a cool swim.

Lower Calf Creek Falls

70 | UPPER CALF CREEK FALLS

Distance: 2 miles round trip to Upper Falls
Hiking time: 2 to 3 hours round trip to Upper Falls
Difficulty: moderate
Season: September to May
Elevation gain: 540 feet
Maps: USGS Calf Creek; Trails Illustrated Canyons of the
    Escalante
Land Management Agency: BLM Grand Staircase–
    Escalante National Monument

Follow SR 12 east out of Escalante, or south out of Boulder. The trailhead is along SR 12 between mile markers 81 and 82, 0.4 mile north of marker 81. There is no sign on the road, but there is a large rock, about 3 feet in diameter, with a blotch of white paint. A dirt road heads a short distance west to the edge of a mesa top and a trail register. There is no camping at the trailhead. A backcountry permit is required for overnight trips. The permits are available at the self-registration box at the trailhead. No camping is permitted within 0.5 mile of the Upper Falls.

Most of the trail is slickrock, steep in places, but not difficult. Cairns mark the way, especially across the slickrock, where no trail is visible. From the ridge at the trailhead, you can see the rock-lined path descending down the slickrock slope to a sandy flat below.

There are several hiker trails along the sandy bench; try to stay on the cairned route to prevent further erosion caused by multiple trails. As you near the falls, the trail splits. The lower left trail goes to the bottom of the falls, the upper to the top. You'll probably want to try both paths.

The return trip to the trailhead gains significant elevation, and the openness of the trail means full exposure to the hot afternoon sun. Adequate time and water are essential for this part of the hike.

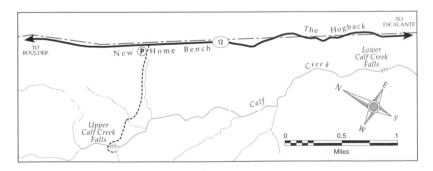

The trail down to Upper Calf Creek Falls

71 | PEEK-A-BOO, SPOOKY, AND BRIMSTONE GULCHES

Distance: 14 miles round trip
Hiking time: 5 to 8 hours
Difficulty: easy to moderate
Season: March to May, September to November
Elevation gain: 330 feet
Maps: USGS Big Hollow Wash, Moody Creek; Trails
Illustrated Canyons of the Escalante
Land Management Agency: BLM Grand Staircase–
Escalante National Monument

Turn off SR 12 onto the Hole-in-the-Rock Road, a signed dirt road east of the town of Escalante. From SR 12 drive 24 miles to the Cat Pasture, where you'll see a sign to Early Weed Bench. Continue about another 2.5 miles on Hole-in-the-Rock Road to a dirt road on the left. Turn and follow this road 1 mile to a parking area and trail register.

A new trailhead is being constructed as this book goes to press. Once complete, the trailhead parking area will be closer to the Hole-in-the-Rock Road, near the word "trail" above section 36 on the Big Hollow Wash USGS map. The trail will also change, heading north from the parking area near the current pack trail shown on the same map. The new trail will drop into Dry Fork Coyote Gulch across from the head of Spooky Gulch, rather than across from Peek-a-boo Gulch as described here for the current trail. Once the new trail is complete, you will drop into the canyon and head upcanyon to Peek-a-boo or downcanyon to Brimstone, after exploring Spooky.

From the current trailhead, follow the worn path over to the rim of a

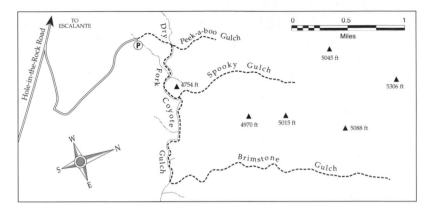

small wash that empties into the Dry Fork Coyote Gulch (the canyon on the left). Find the cairn-marked trail down to the bottom. Look for the water path marked by lighter sandstone—an easy entrance to the canyon.

Upon reaching the canyon floor the entrance to Peek-a-boo Gulch is directly in front of you to the east, across the wash. It is difficult to see at first, as a large sandstone fin juts out into the wash, blocking your view of the gulch. Peek-a-boo enters the main canyon about 20 feet above the wash bottom. Small steps have been chipped out so scrambling up to the canyon is fairly easy. Most people leave their packs at the bottom.

The canyon starts out very narrow and several small potholes collect water. Only one had water when we went through it, but this will vary with the weather. The slot is about 50 feet deep, but stays very narrow as it twists and turns its way through the sandstone. After about 0.25 mile, the walls close in so tight you must chimney up between the walls for about 10 feet. Peek-a-boo Gulch is fairly short—it opens up after about 30 to 45 minutes. Go back through the narrows and climb down the steps.

Spooky Gulch—longer and narrower than Peek-a-boo—enters about 0.5 mile downcanyon, also on the north side. A couple of trails head up into the gulch, one first crossing a sandbank and dropping back in, the second entering the gulch where it drains into Dry Fork Coyote Gulch.

Spooky Gulch narrows very quickly, alternating between tight narrows and short open sections of sandy washbed. Shortly after entering, the walls close in so tightly that you'll need to remove your pack. These narrows are fantastic. In places you'll need to crawl under or over large chockstones, under a small natural bridge, and chimney up where the narrows are too restrictive to pass. If you get to a spot too difficult to pass, you can climb up onto the bench (you may need to backtrack) and rim-walk around the obstacle, then drop back in. You can follow the canyon up for more than 2 miles, or turn around at any time. If you proceed all the way to the top, you'll see a dirt road at Early Weed Bench.

The incredible narrows of Spooky Gulch

Once back to the Dry Fork of Coyote Gulch, head to Brimstone Gulch, which lies about 0.75 mile downcanyon. Between Spooky and Brimstone, the Dry Fork narrows, and you need to downclimb an easy 8-foot chokestone.

Brimstone's narrows are more technical. The walls quickly converge to form a very deep, dark slot with pools of water in the bottom. The narrows continue up for a couple of miles, but beware: at least one person was trapped upcanyon. Deep cold water, log and rock jams, or just plain tight narrows eventually prove too difficult for most within the first 0.5 mile. But the depth and tightness of these narrows make the short, sometimes difficult trip worth the effort. If you plan to ascend through the pools to the point where the canyon becomes impassable, plan your trip in warmer weather and bring a wet suit to avoid hypothermia.

Hiking times and distances vary widely, depending on how far you venture up each of the canyons and how comfortable you are with working your way through and over obstacles. An average hiker could visit all three gulches in 6 to 7 hours. Novice hikers might choose to visit only Spooky and Peek-a-boo Gulches. Spooky's narrows rival any on the Colorado Plateau, and are highly accessible.

72 | COYOTE GULCH

Distance: 28 miles round trip
Hiking time: 2 to 4 days
Difficulty: moderate
Season: March to June, September to October
Elevation gain: 560 feet
Maps: USGS Big Hollow Wash, King Mesa, Stevens Canyon South; Trails Illustrated Canyons of the Escalante
Land Management Agency: National Park Service, Glen Canyon National Recreation Area

From Escalante, drive east on SR 12 to between mileposts 65 and 66. Turn south on the Hole-in-the-Rock Road. Drive about 33 miles south to the Hurricane Wash trailhead. The signposts along the road are in kilometers, so this is just before kilometer post 55. A signed parking area is on the west side of the road. Be sure to obtain a free permit for overnight camping at the Escalante Interagency Visitor Center or at the trailhead.

Coyote Gulch is one of the quintessential and most popular hikes in the Escalante area. Those who enjoy only the most untouched wilderness will likely resent the evidence of past grazing in Coyote Gulch, but for most the beauty of the high canyon walls, the perennial stream, and the two arches and a natural bridge will make this hike a favorite.

Start by following the trail down the shallow, dry Hurricane Wash. About 1.5 miles in, you reach a short section of narrows in the washbed, about 6 to 10 feet wide with 25-foot walls. The section is only about 250 feet long. As the wash nears Coyote Gulch, the wash deepens, and a small stream begins flowing down the wash bottom.

You'll reach Coyote Gulch after 4 miles, where two streams combine to form a stream 4 to 6 feet wide and normally only ankle deep, except in occasional pools. From the confluence it's about 10 miles to the Escalante River.

Continuing downcanyon, you'll spend much of your time alternating

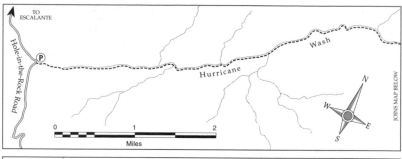

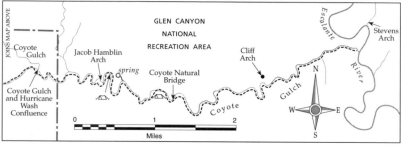

between hiking across sandy bench lands, which cut across the meanders of the stream, and walking directly in the stream. Except in cold weather, stream walking is often preferable.

Three notable scenic wonders await. First is Jacob Hamblin Arch, about 1.5 to 2 miles below the confluence. The arch formed in a tall, long sandstone fin in a meander of the Coyote Creek. Opposite the fin is a huge undercut alcove. There are several seeps on the downstream side of the arch—good sources of water. We recommend filtering all water, even that taken directly from the seeps. Good camp spots abound near the arch.

Two miles below Jacob Hamblin Arch is Coyote Natural Bridge, which spans the creek where the creek finally cut through a sandstone buttress, bypassing an old meander. There are campsites both before and after the bridge. Just after the bridge are pictographs high up on the north wall. Halfway between the bridge and the Escalante River is Cliff Arch.

After the Arch the streambed becomes more interesting. Frequent waterfalls and cascades grace the canyon bottom, offering cool shade, and great scenery. About 1 mile above the Escalante River, the canyon bottom narrows, and a huge boulder blocks the stream course. The trail ascends up on the south side of the stream across steeply sloping slickrock and onto a bench. The bench drops back down near stream level after a short distance. Getting back to the stream requires downclimbing an old log about 6 feet off the bench.

The final section before reaching the river can be a muddy mess,

Scalloped sandstone in Coyote Gulch

especially after rains or floods. Occasionally Lake Powell rises enough to push its waters up this lower section of Coyote Gulch, depositing thick layers of stinky mud. After the waters recede, the mud remains.

Finally, you reach the Escalante River, about 14 miles from the trailhead. Water levels vary widely, but normally the river is fairly easy to cross. Looking north, a short distance upriver, you'll see Stevens Arch.

73 | UPPER GULCH

Distance: 8 to 20+ miles round trip
Hiking time: 1 to 3 days
Difficulty: easy
Season: spring and fall
Elevation gain: 840 feet
Maps: USGS King Bench, Steep Creek Bench; Trails Illustrated Canyons of the Escalante
Land Management Agency: BLM Grand Staircase–Escalante National Monument

The Gulch lies east of Boulder, between the Escalante region and the Waterpocket Fold of Capitol Reef National Park. The best access to the

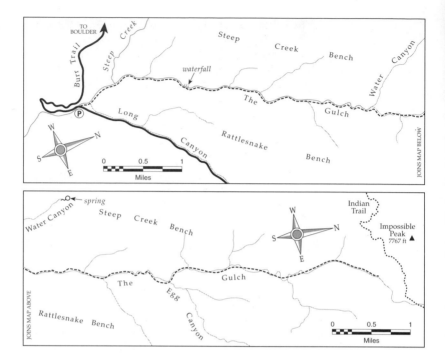

area is from the west. Take SR 12 to the town of Boulder, either from Torrey in the north, or from the west through Escalante. Just south of Boulder the highway makes a sharp 90-degree turn. A road sign at the turn indicates that the paved Burr Trail cuts off to the east right at that turn. Be sure to get a free permit at the trailhead or at the Escalante Interagency Visitor Center.

Take the Burr Trail for about 11 miles to the Gulch trailhead. You'll pass the Deer Creek trailhead and campground, then just before your destination, you'll go down a steep hill and see a parking area and trailhead on the south. This is the trailhead for the Lower Gulch, which joins with the Escalante River. Continue past this trailhead. Once in the flat canyon bottom, you'll find the unmarked Upper Gulch trailhead at a bridge over a small stream that flows through the Gulch. There are several areas to park alongside the road on either side of the bridge. The Deer Creek Campground has good developed overnight camping, or there are several designated campsites near the trailhead; check with the visitor center for locations.

The trail follows the creek for up to 10 miles through a wide and remote sandstone canyon. Although this canyon lacks the spectacular narrows of the other Escalante-area canyons, the relative solitude, sculpted sandstone streambed, and deepening cliff walls make the hike a relaxing foray.

Water falling through a unique undercut sandstone ledge

At first, a definite trail hugs the east bank of the stream through relatively flat terrain. Cottonwoods line the stream course, with large sagebrush on the benches. About 0.75 mile from the trailhead, Steep Creek breaks off to the left (northwest). Trails continue up both canyons. Stay to the right to follow the Gulch.

Another 0.25 mile, and a short slot enters from the left. Exploring this slot takes only a few minutes, as it ends after only 150 feet. Farther upstream it's necessary to bypass a small falls. Climb up and around the falls. A fence crosses the slickrock above the falls, but you can duck under the fence close to the constricted stream course. This is a great place to cool off in the cool water and soak up sunshine as you dry off on the warm rock. For those interested in a day hike, this is a good place to turn around for a 7- to 8-mile round trip.

Above the falls the canyon opens up even more. Bench walking becomes more common. The first large canyon entering from the left is Water Canyon. As its name suggests, it is the source of the water flow in the Gulch. The side canyon merits exploration. Next, two canyons enter from the right. The first is unnamed; the second is Egg Canyon. You can follow Egg Canyon for about 1.5 miles up onto the Circle Cliffs, where there are great views east toward the Henry Mountains.

About a mile past Egg Canyon, an unnamed canyon enters from the left. Be prepared for a major bushwhack if you attempt to head up Indian Trail Canyon. However, for those who make it, Lamanite Arch rewards your efforts. There may be seasonal water in this canyon. The round-trip hike to Lamanite Arch requires 2 full days. Throw in exploration of the side canyons and you can spend 3 or more days in the Upper Gulch.

74 | NEON CANYON

Distance: 12 to 14 miles round trip
Hiking time: 7 to 10 hours
Difficulty: strenuous
Season: March to May, mid-September to October
Elevation gain: 1560 feet
Maps: USGS Egypt; Trails Illustrated Canyons of the Escalante
Land Management Agency: National Park Service, Glen Canyon National Recreation Area

Turn off SR 12 onto the Hole-in-the-Rock Road, a signed dirt road east of Escalante. Drive south about 10 miles to a sign that says "Egypt 10." Turn left on this road and drive approximately 10 miles to the trailhead and parking area at the end of the road. An HCV is required.

This long day hike, or short overnighter, takes you to one of the most spectacular locations in the Escalante region—the Golden Cathedral of Neon Canyon. Above the Cathedral an exceptionally narrow slot once flowed through two deep potholes and over a very high dryfall. Over time the water eroded out underneath the potholes, creating cylindrical shafts through the slickrock. During flash floods the water now routes through the first pothole and drops 60 feet into a large pool below. The adventurous can enjoy a canyoneering adventure through the slot and pothole—a short but technical section for expert canyoneers only.

From the trailhead, follow the trail down off the ridge into the red rock. As you descend the ridge, the trail crosses bare slickrock. In places steps have been carved into the stone. Cairns mark the route down the slope. Once on the bench below the sandstone rim, the trail leads across a sandy bench for about 1.5 miles, then down the north ridge of Fence

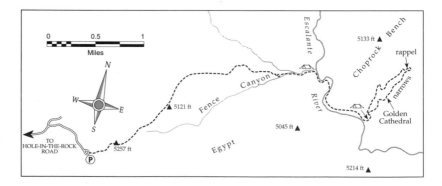

Canyon. You eventually reach the canyon floor, a riparian zone thick with reeds and cottonwood trees. There is a good camp spot as you drop into Fence Canyon. The streambed continues another 0.25 mile to the Escalante River with its highly variable flow. From the trailhead to the river is 3.5 miles.

You cross the Escalante several times as you walk downstream about 1 mile to the mouth of Neon Canyon, the first canyon entering from the left. From the mouth of Neon Canyon to the Golden Cathedral is about 1 mile. At the first big turn in the canyon, look for a faint trail heading up the north side. For those intending to camp, do not do so in the canyon bottom—it is highly susceptible to flash flooding. A few potential camp spots are up on the bench on the slickrock.

If the purpose of your hike is to see the Golden Cathedral from the bottom, simply continue walking up the main canyon. If you're prepared for a technical adventure, head up the trail onto the bench. This trail follows the rim of the canyon for about a mile. Soon the slickrock walls below you slope increasingly steeply downward, then, when only 30 feet apart, plunge into a black slit. Continuing upcanyon on the bench, the slot opens up. You can see the sandy canyon floor and sandstone bench between you and the canyon bottom. Working your way down to the bench will likely require downclimbing. Find a tree or large rock to use as an anchor and rappel about 60 feet to the sandy bottom.

Enter into the technical slot just below the rappel point. The slot begins with a 25-foot class 5 friction climb down into a pool. Once into the pool, it's a 60-foot swim around a couple corners to a sandstone lip, then into another long narrow pool. Pools depths vary, but almost always have sections more than 6 feet deep.

At the end of this pool, a 20-foot dryfall into a deep pool greets you. Chimney about 15 feet out over the dryfall to a log jam, then rappel from the log jam into the deep pool below. This could be a difficult spot if a flash flood flushes the log jam.

This section is the deepest, coldest, and darkest. You swim about 100 feet, then exit out onto dry slickrock. You slide 5 feet down the rock into a wide, deep pool, then onto a sandy beach on the far side. Here the canyon opens up to 60 feet wide with a mostly dry, sandy bottom. The final obstacle, the potholes of the Golden Cathedral, lie immediately downcanyon.

The rappel through the potholes is the highlight of Neon Canyon—not that the slot was forgettable. Attach a web sling around the base of the large boulder just above the slickrock halfpipe draining into the upper pothole. Get on the rappel, then work your way down the narrow sluice toward the pothole. Once into the pothole, the rappel is technically simple, but unlike any other. As you drop through the bottom, it's like entering the netherworld below. It's a free rappel about 60 feet to a large pool. The walls of the Cathedral are moist, with ferns clinging to cracks and dark desert varnish coloring the walls in wide streaks.

The Golden Cathedral of Neon Canyon

To return to the trailhead, simply hike back down Neon Canyon, and retrace your steps up the Escalante River, up Fence Canyon, and back up the steep slickrock rim. Allow sufficient time for the ascent. For day hikers, especially those who do the canyoneering section, this is a long trip with the uphill section at the very end of the day.

75 | ZEBRA AND TUNNEL SLOTS

Distance: 6 to 7 miles round trip
Hiking time: 4 to 6 hours
Difficulty: moderate
Season: March to June, September to October
Elevation gain: 480 feet
Map: USGS Tenmile Flat
Land Management Agency: BLM Grand Staircase–
Escalante National Monument

Turn off SR 12 onto the Hole-in-the-Rock Road, a signed dirt road east of the town of Escalante. From SR 12 drive south about 4.25 miles to the first major wash east of the highway, known as Harris Wash. Continue past the wash. The next drainage you cross is Cottonwood Wash, followed by Halfway Hollow. Park along the road at Halfway Hollow. Do not pull off onto side roads, as these roads are not open to public travel.

Halfway Hollow drains into Harris Wash about 1.5 miles downcanyon from the Hole-in-the-Rock Road, giving convenient access to two good slot canyons draining into Harris Wash from the north. From your parking spot, go down the dirt road, cross Hole-in-the-Rock Road, and drop into Halfway Hollow. Several trails, most made by cattle, run along the dry streambed. Watch for trails heading up onto the benches on the left—these trails shortcut the meanders.

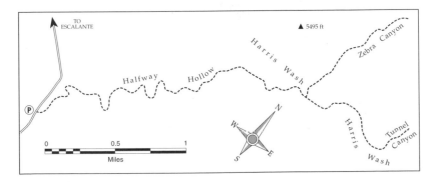

At first you cross a shallow wash surrounded by rolling sagebrush hills. After about 0.5 mile, slickrock appears along the streambanks, and rises higher on the sides as you progress downstream. At about 1.5 miles, the wash meets Harris Wash. Visually note your surroundings so you'll recognize the junction on the return trip.

Where the two washes meet, stand looking north. Across the wash is a wide, shallow, dry drainage emptying into Harris Wash, which turns to head more to the west. Hike up the drainage to the north. This shallow, sandy, dry wash soon turns into the narrow slot of Zebra Canyon. Walk up about 0.33 mile. As you approach the hills, you soon see where the wash enters the slickrock.

The wash bottom is still sandy, but easier walking. The wash narrows to about 15 feet wide at the opening. Follow Zebra upcanyon. Each few hundred feet you proceed upward, the canyon narrows more and more. Soon, the sloping walls are about 50 feet high and the V at the bottom of the canyon is barely wide enough for your feet.

The striations in the sandstone walls give Zebra its name. The stripes zip, zag, and weave their way in fantastic patterns. If you have a day pack, remove it before moving upcanyon; it's easier than trying to fight it against the narrow canyon walls. About 30 minutes into Zebra Canyon, there are three large potholes. More experienced hikers *may* be able to climb around these pools, but if they're deep, or you prefer not to get wet, it's best to turn around here. Above the potholes, the canyon continues for another mile or more. However, those ending the hike at the potholes have seen the most scenic parts of Zebra Canyon.

Return to the confluence of the wash draining Zebra Canyon and Harris Wash. Start hiking down Harris Wash, passing the drainage where you entered (Halfway Hollow), and continue downcanyon for about 0.5 mile. Look for the first real drainage entering from the left (north). At the mouth of the canyon is a small stock pond behind some trees. Hike past the stock pond and into the narrow, but unimpressive, canyon. Very quickly the wash begins to look like a luge run—a sandy, flat-bottomed canyon about 40 feet wide.

As you round a gentle corner to the northeast, the canyon seems to end at a pouroff up ahead. Approach the seeming box-end and you'll discover that the water has formed a unique slot only inches wide at the top, then widening to a 3- or 4-foot-wide "tunnel" below. The tunnel is about 10 feet high, and the bottom is filled with water. To get through the tunnel requires at least wading, and probably swimming. Those experienced with chimneying may be able to avoid the deeper sections by putting their feet against one wall and outstretching their arms against the other. Once into the tunnel, it widens in places, making chimneying difficult, especially for shorter hikers.

Striations in the sandstone give Zebra Canyon its name

This narrow, short slot is cold, wet, and dark. In cool weather this is very cold, so plan this adventure for warm weather. Upcanyon from the 120-foot-long tunnel, the canyon winds its way for some distance with potholes and trees in the canyon bottom.

To return to your vehicle, backtrack to Harris Wash and turn upcanyon. Make sure to turn left (generally west) at Halfway Hollow.

76 | LLEWELLYN GULCH

Distance: 6 miles round trip
Hiking time: 3 to 4 hours
Difficulty: easy
Season: March to June, September to October
Elevation gain: 210 feet
Maps: USGS Nasja Mesa; Trails Illustrated Canyons of the Escalante
Land Management Agency: National Park Service, Glen Canyon National Recreation Area

Llewellyn Gulch is best accessed from Lake Powell, at mile marker 62.5. Rent a boat at Bullfrog Marina, about 1 hour south of Hanksville, on SR 95, then SR 276. Pick up a boater's map with your boat and head west, down the lake. From Bullfrog to the gulch is about 60 miles, 2 to 3 hours by powerboat or longer for houseboats. Follow the canyon until you reach the beaches.

In the spring, before the lake reaches high water levels from spring runoffs, the inlet of Llewellyn Gulch has nice sandy beaches, perfect for securing your boat and setting up camp. Later in the year, the lake water covers the sand, making finding a camp spot more challenging. Spring also has fewer other hikers.

Follow the small stream upcanyon. Although the canyon starts wide near the lake, it quickly narrows. In these lower narrows an active beaver population has created several small pools, which can be waded or

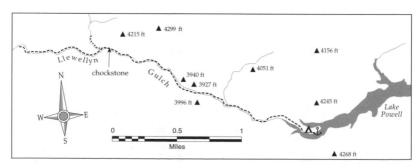

skirted along the banks or in the shallows on the sides of the pools.

Above the beaver ponds, you arrive at a small waterfall that requires bypassing. Climb the banks on the north side and bushwhack onto the bench, then move upcanyon past the falls. Above the falls, you spend much of the time wading in the knee-deep stream or bushwhacking along the banks to avoid deeper water. Thickets of tamarisk, reeds, and grasses complicate progress for about a mile.

The canyon walls continue to close in, eventually choking out the

Reflections of Llewellyn Gulch

vegetation and forming a true slot canyon, with high walls less than 10 feet apart. The stream flow tapers off to just puddles along the rocky bottom before drying out completely.

The slot undulates wider then narrower, almost pulsating with the energy of the bygone flash floods, the scars of which appear in the soft sandstone walls. About 1 mile into the slot, you encounter a chockstone that is about 7 feet tall but easy to scramble over.

A second, more formidable chockstone hangs some 15 feet in the air, wedged between the canyon walls just a short distance later. It is impossible to go around or under the huge boulder. For those unfamiliar with rock climbing, this is a good turnaround point. If you have the climbing skills, chimney up between the walls, now only 3 to 4 feet apart, and through the crack on the left side of the boulder. Send up the most skilled climber in your party first; he or she can lend a hand to get others over the 5.4 crux move at the crack.

For those who want to continue upcanyon but lack climbing skills, backtrack about 100 yards downcanyon and scramble up the steep talus slope on the south side of the canyon. Once on top, follow the canyon rim for about 200 yards west, just past a fork in the narrows, to an entry point—another steep, rocky slope dropping into the canyon.

From here you can follow the ever-narrowing slot for 2 miles or more toward Fifty Mile Mountain—the huge band of cliffs running from the lake all the way north to Escalante. Numerous small side canyons merit exploration, if you have the time.

On the way back, make sure to use the two exit points to get out of and back into the canyon, bypassing the chockstone. Without a rope, getting back down over the chockstone would be very difficult.

77 | FORBIDDING CANYON

Distance: 6 to 8 miles round trip
Hiking time: 3 to 6 hours
Difficulty: easy
Season: late April to late September
Elevation gain: 150 feet
Maps: USGS Navajo Mountain; Trails Illustrated Glen
    Canyon NRA, Capitol Reef NP, Rainbow Bridge NM
Land Management Agency: National Park Service, Glen
    Canyon National Recreation Area; Navajo Nation Parks
    and Recreation

Forbidding Canyon is accessible by car and hiking, but only with great difficulty—accessing the canyon by boat from Lake Powell is far easier. Wahweap

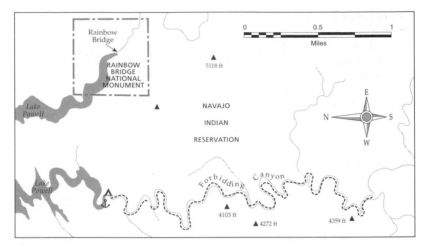

Marina, which sits just north of the Glen Canyon Dam, is the closest marina, but you can reach the canyon from Bullfrog, Hall's Crossing, or Wahweap. Some of the land in this hike is on the Navajo reservation; contact the Navajo Nation Parks and Recreation for information and permits.

See Hike 76, Llewellyn Gulch for information on getting on the lake from Bullfrog. Wahweap is on US 89 east of Kanab, Utah, and just north of the Utah/Arizona border. Pick up your boat from the Aramark concessionaire, and start heading up Lake Powell. Make sure to get a boaters map.

Forbidding Canyon shares its inlet with Rainbow Bridge National Monument at mile marker 50. Plenty of lake signs will guide you to Rainbow Bridge from the main channel. You should definitely visit Rainbow Bridge while you're so close. Once you've turned out of the main channel, you reach a fork: the right goes to Forbidding Canyon; the left goes to Rainbow Bridge. For the hike, take the left branch and follow it to the end of the lake.

Set up camp on the beaches. Because Forbidding is so narrow, you should only camp if there is no chance of storms. Evidence of flash floods is everywhere. The water level of the lake determines how far up the canyon you can go. In the spring, water levels are lower awaiting the spring runoffs, which peak in June. Later in the year, and especially in wetter years, the lake level rises significantly.

Forbidding Canyon is an excellent hike in warmer weather. Simply follow the narrow canyon upstream. Aztec Creek, a perennial stream, offers good clean water (always filter!). Partway up the canyon is a technical obstacle, a 25-foot friction slab from a ledge down to the creek and back up the other side. Most hikers will have no problem, but a rope may help the inexperienced.

There are numerous deep pools, slots carved into the canyon floor, and a 50-foot cascading waterfall, all of which can be enjoyed, then easily bypassed. The water in the pools is always cold, but it's refreshing during

One of many large pools in Forbidding Canyon

hotter weather. You can follow the canyon for many miles and explore the various side canyons, but the most spectacular scenery occurs in the first 3 or 4 miles (again, depending on the water level).

Above the waterfall, which is above the lake's high water mark, Cliff Canyon breaks off to the left (east). Farther upcanyon the walls narrow in again, creating potholes requiring swimming, others more difficult to bypass, and another waterfall. This area is a good point to turn around.

78 | LITTLE DEATH HOLLOW

Distance: 14 miles round trip
Hiking time: 7 hours
Difficulty: moderate
Season: April to September
Elevation gain: 600 feet
Maps: USGS Pioneer Mesa, Red Breaks; Trails Illustrated Canyons of the Escalante
Land Management Agency: BLM Grand Staircase–Escalante National Monument

Use Utah SR 12 to get to Boulder, either going east from Escalante, or south from Torrey, which is near the west entrance to Capitol Reef National Park.

Cooling off in the shade in Little Death Hollow

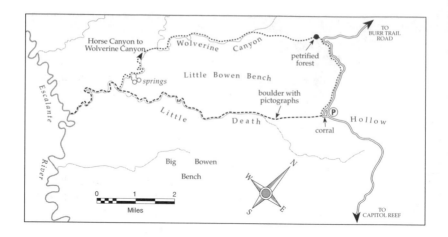

On the south edge of Boulder, take the paved Burr Trail Road to the east. As you exit Long Canyon, you go down a steep grade. Take the second turnoff on the right, marked with a large brown sign giving mileages to the surrounding canyons. Little Death Hollow is 13 miles down this road. A corral is at the trailhead.

The dirt/clay road is in good shape, but road conditions vary after rainstorms. Like many roads in the region, the clay base becomes very slippery and muddy when wet. Use caution in wet weather. Little Death Hollow is also accessible from the east by following the Burr Trail Road out of Capitol Reef National Park, but this involves a long drive on dirt roads.

Beginning at the corral, head west down the well-marked trail. You will be walking the first 2 miles or so in a wide, open canyon. Notice the large boulders on the canyon floor that have dropped from high above.

About 1.5 miles down the trail, a small trail cuts off to the right toward one of the fallen boulders. Follow this trail to a panel of pictographs. The majority of them are on the side facing the trail. The mileage added by the cutoff is negligible and well worth your time.

Soon the walls begin to creep in on top of you, narrowing down to just 6 to 8 feet apart at times. The canyon winds through the Kayenta sandstone, narrowing and then widening. Once in, there are very few ways out, so take necessary precautions to avoid flash floods.

Little Death Hollow eventually meets up with the Escalante River. From here you can either retrace your hike in, or you can follow Horse Canyon out about 2 miles back from the Escalante River where Horse Canyon meets Little Death Hollow. After 2 miles, Horse Canyon splits. Take the right fork, which is Wolverine Canyon. From here it is about 5 miles back to the road and then another 2 miles to the Little Death Hollow trailhead. This route adds several miles to the trip, but allows you to hike through the petrified forest at the top of Wolverine Canyon.

79 | UPPER MULEY TWIST

Distance: 9-mile loop from Strike Valley trailhead; 15-mile loop from Upper Muley Twist trailhead
Hiking time: 4 to 6 hours from Strike Valley trailhead
Difficulty: moderate
Season: February to April, October to November; also warm dry periods December to February
Elevation gain: 520 feet
Maps: USGS Bitter Creek Divide, Wagon Box Mesa; Trails Illustrated Glen Canyon NRA, Capitol Reef NP, Rainbow Bridge NM (not suggested for backcountry navigation because of scale)
Land Management Agency: Capitol Reef National Park

From Green River go west on I-70 to the junction with SR 24 at exit 147. Take SR 24 south through Hanksville. From Richfield, take SR 24 east through Torrey. Go through Capitol Reef National Park. Just east of the park's east boundary sign, turn south on Notom Road. The road changes from blacktop to dirt after about a mile. The dirt road should be passable for most cars.

The drive south along the Waterpocket Fold gives a great view of the earth's folded crust. After about 60 miles, you reach a junction with the Burr Trail Road. Turn right (west) and follow the road through a set of steep switchbacks that take you right up and through the fold.

The Upper Muley Twist Canyon road is approximately 1 mile west of the switchbacks. Follow this road 0.5 mile north to a parking area. From here, 4WDs and most HCVs can drive another 3 miles up the riverbed to the Strike Valley Overlook trailhead. If you start from the first trailhead, remember to tack 6 miles onto the total mileage.

From the Strike Valley Overlook trailhead, follow the wash upcanyon. After about 1.75 miles, you reach Saddle Arch. You can see the arch up and

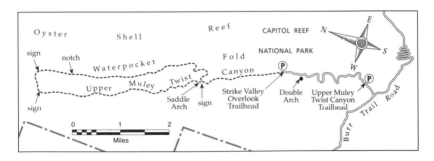

to the left on the west side of the canyon. If you're observant, you'll see another arch on the west wall before you reach this point. From Saddle Arch, a sign marks the trail up to the rim. You can go up here, but we recommend you continue up the canyon; the trail loops back to this junction.

The riverbed continues to meander up through the canyon for another 2.25 miles or so. There are a couple more arches on the west wall as you continue up the canyon. The canyon walls begin to narrow, and the canyon makes a wide turn to the left (west). The trail turns up out of the canyon bed, and up onto a bench to bypass a set of narrows and chokestone. Watch for cairns marking a path up a ramp and onto a ledge. This is a good place to drop your pack and go exploring.

Upcanyon, soon after the walls narrow, there is a chokestone. (If you make it here without spotting the cairns, backtrack about 100 to 150 yards and look for the cairns just upcanyon from the turn.) With a little scrambling you can get over the chokestone. Continuing upcanyon, you will soon reach a pouroff. To bypass it, use the small steps carved into the sandstone on the right. This is a good place to stop if you're uncomfortable with climbing. A short distance above this pouroff, the narrows even-

Sandstone domes in Upper Muley Twist

tually become impassable, and you have to return to your pack.

Follow the cairns up the east side of the canyon. You will soon drop back into the canyon upstream of the narrows. From here go about another 0.5 mile to a sign marking the trail to the rim. The trail then turns east and goes up several hundred feet.

As you go up, it's hard to tell where the top will be, but suddenly the entire length of the Waterpocket Fold will pop into view. Once your mouth closes, take in the spectacular views of the nearby Henry Mountains to the east and Tarantula Mesa below them. To the south you can see all the way to Lake Powell (although you can't see the lake), and to the southwest, Navajo Mountain looms darkly on the horizon. Few views on the entire Colorado Plateau beat this one.

From your perch on the ridge top, you'll see another sign marking the trail. From here, watch closely for cairns, because the slickrock you're crossing has no worn path to follow, and you can easily wander off the trail. If you go more than 100 feet or so without spotting the next cairn, backtrack to the last one you saw and scan forward. The trail takes you up along the rim of the fold for several miles. There are many times when you can see back to the west. Notice how over the years water has formed beautiful domed formations in the Wingate sandstone on the west side of the canyon. You may also spot a few arches you didn't notice on your way in on the canyon bottom.

About 0.75 mile from the sign, you pass a notch in the ridge top. Be careful here—you need to scramble up the slickrock slope on the far side of the notch. Watch for cairns so you don't get off the trail. In another mile the ridge top flattens out, and you work your way up the side of the ridge to get on top. In winter, this ascent can be tricky because snow covers the northeast-facing side of the ridge.

Once on the flat mesa top, routefinding becomes even more important. The ridge top is wide and there is more vegetation, so it's easy to get off-trail. After a while you begin to wonder how you're going to descend the sheer sandstone cliffs back into the canyon. You can anticipate where the trail will be by watching for Saddle Arch on the west canyon wall. If you remember, you passed the trail junction earlier in the day just after Saddle Arch. Eventually, you will reach the trail's descent and then get back to the riverbed at the exit sign by the arch. From here you are 1.5 miles from the Strike Valley Overlook trailhead and a little more than 4.5 miles from the Upper Muley Twist Canyon trailhead.

SOUTHEAST

80 | PRICE RIVER

Distance: 13 miles round trip
Hiking time: 5.5 to 7 hours
Difficulty: moderate
Season: February to April, October to November
Elevation loss: 220 feet
Maps: USGS Cliff, Jenny Canyon
Land Management Agency: BLM Price Field Office

On US 6, go south out of Price to Woodside, a gas station just north of a bridge over the Price River; 0.2 mile north of the bridge, take a dirt road to the north. The road crosses a wash within the first 0.25 mile; after a rain this could be slick. Drive on the dirt road for 5 miles. There are good flats with a few cottonwood trees that make good camping spots. Cars may want to stop here. Between miles 5 and 6 there are a couple of rough spots that require HCVs. Continuing past the sixth mile, the road leaves the river and starts up onto a ledge. At the top of the ledge is a large parking area with no shade. All but small-wheel-base 4WD vehicles should stop here. Rocks block much of the road ahead.

The Price River has a surprisingly large stream flow considering the dry, desolate-looking surroundings. Your path parallels the river into a stark, desolate, remote, and wild region. Walk down the road about 4 miles to Trail Canyon. The road takes you off the ledge onto the canyon floor, staying between the cliffs and the river on the north side.

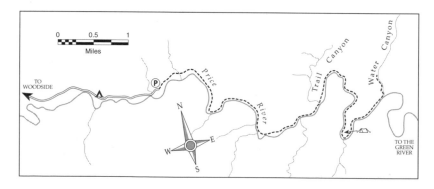

The headwall of Water Canyon

Just after Trail Canyon, the road crosses the river and heads up the south side. A foot trail continues along the north bank; stay on the foot trail. A sign indicates you are entering a wilderness study area. As you round the bend to the south, the trail gets squished between the rocky cliff and the river. At one point, just as you pass under a large overhanging rock, the trail splits. The lower trail stays next to the river for a bushwhack through thick tamarisks. The upper trail climbs up through some small boulders onto a ledge about 20 feet above the river. Take the upper route. The sometimes faint trail continues on; keep high as you round the bend to stay above the thickets next to the river.

Farther downstream, before reaching Water Canyon, several wide benches with cottonwood trees would make excellent camp spots for an overnight trip. After 6 miles, you reach Water Canyon entering from the left. Turn up the canyon and hike in the streambed for about 0.5 mile to a large headwall with a high pouroff. At the base of the heavy alkali cliffs is a very small seep, the source of Water Canyon's name. The water is barely enough to wet the ground, so don't count on refilling your water containers here.

Opportunities for side trips include Trail Canyon, which has a double track trail that ascends to the top of the Book Cliffs in a Wilderness Study Area. A second alternative is to take 3 or more days to hike down to the Green River and back out, or continue down the Green into the town of Green River. The latter would be a long hike into very remote backcountry.

81 | LITTLE HOLE CANYON

Distance: 5 miles round trip
Hiking time: 2 to 4 hours
Difficulty: easy
Season: February to April, September to November
Elevation loss: 310 feet
Map: USGS Agate
Land Management Agency: BLM Moab Field Office

Take I-70 east about 40 miles from Green River to exit 202. Follow SR 128 for 2.8 miles. While the highway turns to the south, continue straight ahead to the ghost town of Cisco. After 2.6 miles, you'll see the BLM sign indicating the turnoff to Cisco Landing and Fish Ford. Follow the road another 2.9 miles to a Y intersection and turn to the left toward the Cisco boat launch.

After 1.9 miles, you arrive at the Cisco boat launch. On the left, just before the turn into the parking area, is a dirt road marked with a small BLM sign indicating the Kokepelli Trail. Follow this road north to Agate—an old house foundation and fenced corral—and continue to a Y intersection 5.5 miles from the beginning of the dirt road. Take a right onto

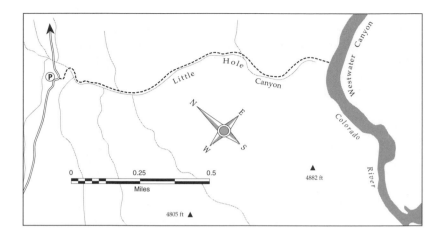

the road paralleling the telephone poles on the Kokepelli Trail.

This section goes through a wash with water, requiring an HCV. There is also a gate to open in a rocky stretch right after the wash. Be sure to close the gate. At 1.5 miles take the road turning to the right, leaving the Kokepelli Trail. After 0.2 mile an old house foundation sits on the left with a road turning off toward it. Stay to the right and continue another 2.2 miles to a fork. Take the right fork for another 3.5 miles to another fork. You should be able to see the top of Little Hole Canyon to the east. Go left (east) for 0.4 mile. Ignore the several roads and 4WD tracks here; just park and hike from here. Plan on 45 minutes to 1 hour to get from the freeway exit to the trailhead. Follow these directions carefully. It's easy to get lost on the maze of roads, especially at night. In the day you can see the top of Little Hole Canyon, which serves as a guide to the trailhead.

Follow the wash to the canyon rim. From the rim look to the west and you can see the trail down below. Follow the rim right (west) to where the trail follows a break in the rim down. This part should be easy and the trail obvious. Once down to the level of the large alcove, you can either follow a trail that stays up on the bench or drop down into the wash bottom—they meet about 0.25 mile down the canyon. A canyon enters from the right at the point where the two trails meet.

Now you just follow the hiker trail down the wash bottom, and occasionally up on the bench, toward the Colorado River. Another canyon enters from the left about halfway to the river. Just before you reach the river, you'll see dark granite protruding from the canyon bottom. The Colorado River has eroded away the top sandstone layer to expose the lower level granite. This is one of the few areas where the granite substrate is exposed. The next point is along the Colorado at Granite Falls in the Grand Canyon, hundreds of miles to the southwest.

Reaching the river, look downstream at the huge canyon walls on the

Overlooking the Colorado River at Little Hole Canyon

west side. You can hear the sound of a small rapid echoing off the walls. You can also see a large grassy bench on the south side of the river and high cliff walls beyond. The area south of the river is little traveled by humans. It is only reachable from the east on roads beginning in Colorado, or by river runners. This is one of the most remote areas in the Colorado River Basin and part of the Westwater Wilderness Study Area.

You gain some elevation on the return trip, but the short distance makes this a pleasant and relaxing hike in beautiful and unique surroundings.

82 | ROBBERS ROOST CANYON

Distance: 15 to 30 miles
Hiking time: 3 to 7 days
Difficulty: strenuous
Season: March to early June, September to October
Elevation gain: 970 feet
Maps: USGS Angel Point, Angel Cove, Point of Rocks East
Land Management Agency: BLM Henry Mountains Field
Station

From I-70, take SR 24 south toward Hanksville. Just after milepost 137, turn off SR 24 onto the dirt road to the Hans Flat Ranger Station, part of Canyonlands National Park's Maze District. At 24 miles you arrive at a signed fork. Go right towards Hans Flat. Continue 33 miles from SR 24 to another fork. Hans Flat lies farther down the road to the left; the road to the right goes to Robbers Roost Spring. Take the middle road to a ranch. Stay to the right and go past the ranch. As you near the rim of the South Fork of Robbers Roost Canyon, you pass an airstrip. Keep heading west. Eventually the road ends at a parking area on the edge of a mesa. This is the Angel Point trailhead. An HCV is recommended, especially for the last mile or so of the road.

The trail drops right off the edge of the mesa, losing elevation rapidly on its way down to the Dirty Devil River. Since much of the trail crosses slickrock, the only markers are rock cairns. In places where the trail

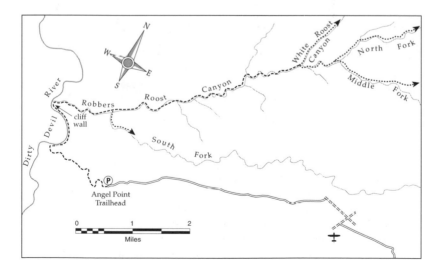

becomes hard to follow, you need to backtrack to find cairns. Good route-finding skills are important for this hike. After descending 500 feet from the rim in about 2 miles, you reach a shelf 100 feet above the river. If you go straight west, you can't descend the cliff band down. Instead, work your way north to the small canyon that protrudes into the bench. The trail goes down into this canyon to reach the river.

Once on the riverbank, follow any one of several footpaths to the north. The going gets tough in spots, as thickets of tall bushes with 1-inch thorns line the bank. You should be able to work your way upriver without getting wet. After 1.75 miles upriver, you arrive at the mouth of Robbers Roost Canyon, the first major drainage on the east side of the river. Just before reaching the canyon is a huge sheer cliff wall on the west side, with acoustics that rival a great music hall.

Going up Robbers Roost Canyon is simple and somewhat uneventful for several miles. Intermittent water runs in the canyon floor. In many spots the water's sulfur content lessens its desirability as a source of drinking water; watch for spots with greater flow. Also, some of the small side canyons and clefts in the high walls contain seeps with cleaner water. These are usually evidenced by increased vegetation, especially cottonwood trees, and occasionally by footpaths that seem to lead nowhere.

The South Fork takes off to the right about 1.5 miles upcanyon. You can follow the main canyon for another 5 miles to the confluence of White Roost Canyon, a narrower drainage to the left. The North and Middle Forks break off 1 mile above White Roost. All the canyons narrow significantly in the upper reaches, and all end as box canyons with high impassable pouroffs. The North Fork and its side canyons offer the best narrows—if you have

View of the Dirty Devil River from Angel Point trailhead

the time to reach its upper end. Each of the forks offers multiple possibilities for exploration. To explore them all would require as much as a week in the canyon.

Perhaps the greatest attraction of this canyon is its remoteness and attendant solitude. Wildlife is most prevalent and signs of humanity infrequent.

83 | HORSESHOE CANYON

Distance: 5.5 to 6 miles round trip
Hiking time: 3 to 6 hours
Difficulty: easy to moderate
Season: September to May
Elevation gain: 580 feet
Maps: USGS Sugarloaf Butte; Trails Illustrated Canyonlands National Park/Glen Canyon National Recreation Area
Land Management Agency: Canyonlands National Park, Hans Flat Ranger Station

Horseshoe Canyon is located in southeast Utah, in the western section of Canyonlands National Park, also called the Maze District, a more remote and much less visited region. The Green River divides the park into eastern and western sections; the western side is more difficult to reach. Rather than accessing the park from the Moab area, as you would the Island in the Sky or Needles sections, you access the Maze District off SR 24 west of Green River on I-70.

From Green River, head west about 15 miles to the SR 24/Hanksville exit (#147). Going south on SR 24, turn left 0.5 mile past the signed Goblin Valley State Park Road. This is a graded dirt road with a sign indicating the mileage to the Hans Flat Ranger Station. From the turnoff to the first junction is 24 miles. At this fork, you'll see a sign indicating the road to the right goes to Hans Flat. The left fork goes to Horseshoe Canyon. It is 5.5

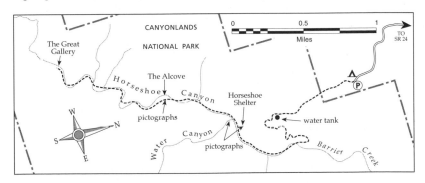

The Holy Ghost Panel at the Great Gallery

miles from the fork to the turnoff to the trailhead. There you'll see a road signed for Horseshoe Canyon, which turns off to the right. The trailhead is 1.5 miles from the turn.

The trailhead has an outhouse, information kiosk, and a large parking area. You can camp at the trailhead parking area, or back on the main road, before you turn onto the Horseshoe Canyon Road (i.e., outside the National Park boundary). It is best to bring binoculars for better viewing of some of the pictographs.

The trail is well marked with cairns all the way through the canyon. It follows an old jeep trail, first descending about 830 feet to the canyon floor. The road was built in the 1920s and continues up the other side of the canyon. The road is now closed on the north side, but remains open on the south. However, in the 1990s a slide blocked the south road, and it is no longer possible to descend into the canyon by jeep.

Once in the canyon bottom, follow the cairns upcanyon (right). The canyon walls are sheer cliffs a couple of hundred feet tall. The canyon is not narrow, but its depth gives it a feeling of isolation.

Moving upcanyon, keep your eyes open for a panel of pictographs high up on the cliff face on the south side of the canyon. If you follow the cairns, you're more likely to see the panel. If you stay in the creekbed, you may miss it. The first panel is about 0.5 mile up the canyon. Almost directly across the canyon from the first panel is the Horseshoe Shelter, a set of pictographs just up off the canyon floor. This site was shared by the older Desert Archaic culture and the more recent Anasazi/Fremont cultures.

Water Canyon enters from the south shortly after the second panel. Continuing upstream about 0.5 mile, you come to a large alcove on your right (north side), with several smaller pictographs from the Archaic period, between 2000 and 9000 years ago.

The Great Gallery lies 0.5 mile beyond the Alcove. As you walk upstream around a bend, you'll see the Holy Ghost pictograph looking down on you from the north wall. As you approach the site, you'll see an increasing number of figures. In all more than fifty images cover a span of 300 feet. The best viewing time is when the panels are in the shade in the afternoon.

The National Park Service (NPS) bills Horseshoe Canyon as possibly having the best pictographs in North America. NPS rangers provide guided tours on Saturday and Sunday mornings from April through October. The guides offer a wealth of knowledge that adds significantly to the experience. As at other panels in the canyon, the Great Gallery has chain barriers to keep visitors back away from the images. Respect the preservation efforts by not crossing over the barriers.

The best time to hike Horseshoe Canyon is from late fall to spring. You can hike in winter as long as you are prepared for the cold, watch out for storms, and make sure the road is dry. Like many southern Utah roads, it can quickly become impassable when wet.

84 | MAIDENWATER CANYON

Distance: 7-mile loop
Hiking time: 4 hours
Difficulty: moderate
Season: October to March
Elevation gain: 570 feet
Map: USGS Black Table
Land Management Agency: BLM Henry Mountains
Field Station

From Hanksville, head south on SR 95, then turn onto SR 276 heading toward Bullfrog. Park along the road after milepost 9 and near the cattle guard in the road.

State Route 276 runs right over the top of Maidenwater Canyon. From the east side of the road, the trail drops steeply into the bottom of the canyon. There is no real distinct trail, but the canyon can be identified by a

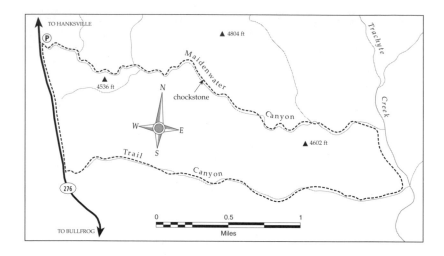

large hole, or tunnel, in the sandstone at the bottom of the canyon that allows water to run under the road. From here the trail starts downcanyon in an open wash.

The wash remains fairly shallow. As it continues down, the trail runs along the wall on the right side. About halfway between the trailhead and Trachyte Creek, water seeps begin to appear, allowing a more abundant plant life. The canyon narrows down just after the water's appearance and is blocked by a chockstone. Depending on the water level, it is an 8- to 12-foot drop to the water. Although the jam can be downclimbed with some effort, a 15- to 20-foot rope is suggested for lowering packs. The water level varies significantly, from chest deep to as much as 8 to 10 feet deep, depending on the time of year, recent storms, and the water year. In low water, the pool is an easy wade; in deep water, it's a cold swim.

From the rock jam, the trail frequently crosses the stream, requiring wading shoes. The canyon floor is also full of brush that often requires minor bushwhacking. For afternoon hikers, the high wall to the south provides good shade.

At just under 3.5 miles, Maidenwater Canyon joins with Trachyte Creek, where the trail heads south along the creek. After 0.5 mile, the trail turns to the west and heads up Trail Canyon. Water flows in this canyon, but not as steadily as in Maidenwater. However, there seemed to be more wildlife in the lower sections of Trail Canyon.

As the trail works its way back up toward SR 276, the canyon bottom becomes very rocky. Walking on the cobblestone can be arduous, but at times trails cut the meanders in the wash, offering a softer path. Sturdy footwear is essential. From the confluence of Trail Canyon and Trachyte Creek to SR 276 is 2.5 miles. Once you get back on the road, walk north along the highway about 1 mile back to your car.

Wading through the pool in Maidenwater Canyon

85 | LOST SPRING CANYON

Distance: 12-mile loop
Hiking time: 6 to 7 hours
Difficulty: easy
Season: February to May, September to November
Elevation loss: 900 feet
Maps: USGS Mollie Hogans; Trails Illustrated Arches
National Park
Land Management Agency: Arches National Park

The entrance to Arches National Park lies a few miles north of Moab along US 191. From the north, take exit 180 south off I-70 toward Moab to the Arches National Park entrance. There you'll need to pay the park's entrance fee. The Lost Spring Canyon trailhead begins at the Broken Arch/Sand Dune Arch trailhead, about 15 miles from the park entrance. The trailhead is signed and has a paved pullout/parking area on the east side of the main park road.

Begin following the Broken Arch Trail. After 450 feet, a footpath veers to the right off the main trail. This footpath overlays a buried pipeline, which you follow for the next 5 miles. From this junction, you can look back toward the paved road and see an orange-and-white-striped pole marking the pipeline. These poles serve as trail markers for much of the hike.

Follow the path eastward. At about 0.5 mile, you reach the rounded edge of a small mesa and start dropping down a gentle slope. From here you'll enjoy good views into the Salt Wash, Clover, and Lost Spring Canyon drainages. From here the footpath turns into a noticeable double track as it slowly descends toward Clover Creek.

Large flint and chert rock beds protrude from the sand throughout this area. Native American inhabitants made arrowheads, knives, and spear

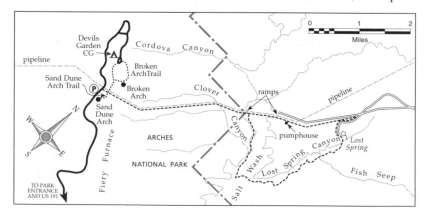

Taking a break in Lost Spring Canyon

points from this glasslike rock. Note also the layers of colored sand as you descend. First you pass through a deep red sand layer, with sparse vegetation and less rock. The next layer consists of yellow-white sand with larger rock outcroppings. After about a mile, you near the head of Clover Canyon, a box canyon with steep walls. When you reach the Clover Creek wash, turn off the trail to follow the wash to the right to a 75-foot pouroff, overlooking Clover Canyon. Be careful as you approach the edge, the canyon walls are sheer.

Continue to follow the pipeline and occasional barbershop-style marker poles. Soon you approach Salt Wash, a wide drainage eroded about 100 feet below the surrounding terrain. Drop off the man-made ramp, apparently blasted out of the canyon walls during pipeline construction, and onto the canyon's flat floor. In the spring, you'll need to cross Salt Wash's moderate flow. A log across the stream assists you. In other seasons, the stream is smaller and you can easily jump across. Several trails branch north and south here, most made by grazing cattle. Approaching the east side of the canyon, you'll notice signs demarcating the north boundary of the Lost Spring Canyon Wilderness Study Area (WSA). The pipeline you're following is the north boundary of the WSA. Your loop into Lost Spring Canyon rejoins the pipeline in the flats of Salt Wash.

Ascend the steep pipeline ramp up the east canyon rim. At the top, follow the well-developed road east past the pumphouse. From this vantage, be sure to take in the views of the Colorado River cliffs and La Sal Mountains to the south.

Continue east on the road. After 0.75 mile, the road splits, with the pipeline road veering to the left (northeast). Follow a road to a white-tufted rock outcropping jutting about 15 feet up on the right. At the rock outcrop the road splits. Take the right, southern branch toward the canyon rim on your right. The road crosses slickrock, then begins to descend into Lost Spring Canyon. The road turns back to the southwest, then hairpins back to the east to an old, but still-used corral. Just beyond the corral to the north, in a small north-south crack, you'll find Lost Spring. Cattle heavily use this small spring, so filter or treat any water from the trough before drinking.

There is no clear trail from Lost Spring to the canyon bottom. Just pick out a path down the small shelves toward the cottonwood trees and the wash bottom. Just below the spring are a couple of very small waterfalls. In winter, these falls form beautiful icefalls.

From here, multiple paths lead down to Lost Spring Canyon. In places, particularly at the head of the canyon, there seems to be a predominate trail, but throughout the canyon there are many cattle trails, which all seem traveled with equal frequency. Choose your path either along the wash bottom, or along the cow paths on the flat benches. When bench walking be sure to stay on established paths and avoid the black cryptobiotic crust, which dominates benches despite the heavy grazing.

The next 3 to 4 miles down Lost Spring Canyon and up Salt Wash to rejoin the pipeline trail are the most scenic of the hike. The red sandstone walls deepen and form interesting caves and domes. Take your time here and enjoy the canyon. As you exit the canyon mouth where it joins Salt Wash, turn right (north) upcanyon. Follow the canyon until you see the ramps to your left and right. Make a left and head up the ramp and retrace your steps back to your car.

86 | DEVILS GARDEN LOOP

Distance: 5.5- to 8-mile loop
Hiking time: 3 to 6 hours
Difficulty: easy to moderate
Season: February to June, September to November,
     December and January during warm dry weather
Elevation gain: 740 feet
Maps: USGS Mollie Hogans; Trails Illustrated Arches
     National Park
Land Management Agency: Arches National Park

Arches National Park sits on US 191 just north of Moab, the slickrock capital of Utah. Take exit 180 heading south off I-70 toward Moab for about 25 miles. About 5 miles north of town, you reach the Arches National Park entrance, where you'll pay the park entrance fee.

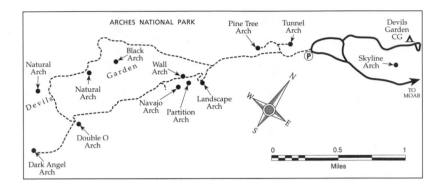

The trailhead lies at the far north end of the park's main road just under 20 miles from the park entrance. Heavily signed, the trailhead has a large parking area. The Devils Garden Campground is about 1 mile from the hiking trailhead.

You'll have a lot of company on this trail, especially in the spring and fall. In summer it's unbearably hot—actually dangerous if you're unprepared. Winter's cold drives away most casual hikers, offering a more solitary experience. Take care on the primitive portion of the hike when snow or ice is on the trail. A couple of sections have slight exposure and a slip in icy conditions would be dangerous.

The trail passes at least nine named natural arches along its course and gives perhaps the best overall hike in the park. The arches themselves are spectacular; the primitive trail section offers an intimate view of the land formations that comprise the area.

The first section, from the trailhead to Landscape Arch, hardly deserves the trail moniker. It's the equivalent of an interstate highway for hikers—wide, graveled in places, and all the "exits" are signed.

From the trailhead it's about 0.25 mile to the Pine Tree Arch side trail, a 0.5-mile trail to the right with two arches, then another 0.75 mile to Landscape Arch and the junction where the loop trail rejoins the main trail back to the trailhead. Take the left branch. The trail deteriorates a little here, mostly because it crosses slickrock. The going is still easy and rock cairns mark the way. With literally thousands of hikers of all skill levels taking this hike every year, it's almost impossible to lose the trail. In 0.75 mile, you arrive at another side trail, this one to Navajo and Partition Arches, a 0.75-mile round trip.

From the Navajo Trail junction, continue on the main trail for 0.75 mile to Double O Arch, with one arch directly above another. From Double O Arch you can take a primitive side trail to Dark Angel Arch, one of the least visited arches in the park. The round trip to Dark Angel adds 1 mile. After Double O a sign warns, "Primitive Trail—Difficult Hiking." The hiking is not all that difficult, although one section on the loop requires descending

Walking atop the fins in Devils Garden

a very short slickrock slab. If you had a hard time coming down the last group of sandstone boulders before Double O Arch, you may want to turn around, but you'll miss some excellent scenery.

The primitive trail from Double O Arch back to the loop junction at Landscape Arch is just over 2 miles. It takes you across the top of some high fins with views of the broken country to the east, then drops down into wide areas between finlike sandstone ridges. After winding through this jumble of jutting sandstone, the trail emerges in sage flats east of the Devils Garden area, then rejoins the trail "highway." You retrace your steps for 1 mile back to the trailhead.

If you take all of the side trails and the full loop, the hike length is just under 8 miles; the loop alone is closer to 5.5 miles.

87 | FISHER TOWERS

Distance: 4 miles round trip
Hiking time: 2 to 3 hours
Difficulty: easy
Season: spring and fall, winter dry periods
Elevation gain: 665 feet
Maps: USGS Fisher Towers; Trails Illustrated Moab East
    Mountain Biking and Recreation
Land Management Agency: BLM Moab Field Office

Turn east onto SR 128 on the south side of the Colorado River bridge, located on the north end of Moab. Follow the highway about 18 miles east through Castle Valley to the turnoff. A BLM State Recreation Area sign marks the dirt access road to the Fisher Towers parking area and trailhead. It's about 2 miles of graded dirt road to the parking area. Passenger cars

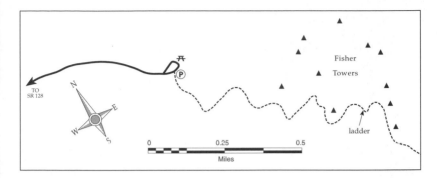

should keep their speed down—several sections of washboard prove pretty bumpy. The trailhead has ample parking and good outhouse facilities, but no running water. A campground sits just to the east of the parking lot.

The trailhead starts at the top of a small ridge on the west edge of the parking area. The trail is well marked; just follow the rock paths and cairns. Logs or rocks block the few side paths that veer off.

The trail follows the ridge to the west, then drops into a relatively wide drainage. There are several paths down the ridge, some more difficult than the main trail. If you start down the ridge and feel the trail is getting difficult, you've probably taken the wrong path.

Once in the wash bottom, the trail turns back to the southeast. From here the trail winds up and down a series of ridges between dry washes, which drain the Fisher Towers area. As you proceed, each successive drainage gets deeper and deeper. The trail rims larger drainages to their heads before crossing. In one place you need to descend a secure metal ladder about 8 feet to cross the head of one of the narrower washes.

After about 30 minutes you approach the base of the first tower. These towers are fins, or monoliths, that extend hundreds of vertical feet upward with sheer cliff faces. The tower walls are unique—they look like the edges of huge sandcastles smoothed by scraping fingers down the walls. The towers are remnants of a mesa that eroded over eons. Above the towers to the east, the mesa top rises hundreds of feet higher.

The trail follows benches between the base of the towers and the edges of the washes below. After 2 miles, you reach the end of the trail at an overlook with several large boulders on which to sit, eat lunch, or sun yourself.

The area is subject to frequent winds, so on cooler days make sure to take a jacket. There are good views to the north and west over Castle Valley and to the southwest down a series of drainages falling away through brown and yellow layers of earth.

We don't' recommend this hike in summer's heat. The best times to hike are spring and fall. You can hike in the winter (December through February) during warm, dry periods, but if snow is on the ground, there is danger of slipping off the trail near the heads of some drainages.

The spires of Fisher Towers

88 | HIDDEN VALLEY

Distance: 5.5 to 6 miles round trip
Hiking time: 3 to 4 hours
Difficulty: moderate
Season: September to May
Elevation gain: 840 feet
Map: USGS Moab
Land Management Agency: BLM Moab Field Office

Hidden Valley's trailhead is one of the most easily accessible around. Its proximity to Moab makes it easy to get up early in the morning, hike to Hidden Valley, and be back in town for lunch.

Take US 191 south out of Moab to Angel Rock Road. Turn west on Angel Rock for 2 blocks to Rimrock Road. This street dead-ends at the signed trailhead.

Most of the hard work will be done in the first 0.75 mile, straight up the cliffs that frame the west side of Moab. Do not despair—Hidden Valley, which can't be seen from the bottom of the cliffs, does not require climbing all the way to the top of the Moab Rim. Rather, the trail starts with a series of steep switchbacks climbing about 700 feet up the talus slope at the base of the cliffs.

At the top of the switchbacks, the trail crosses a saddle into a small valley about halfway up the cliffs. The valley, which is about 0.25 mile wide and extends for almost 2 miles, is completely hidden from view from the valley below. The trail stays in the middle of the valley, but you can walk to

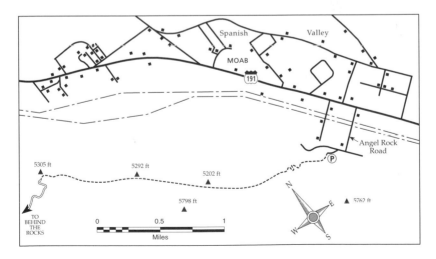

Barrel cactus in Hidden Valley

the east edge for excellent views of the Moab Valley. Although the area is hidden, you'll likely encounter other hikers, trail runners, and mountain bikers, especially in the long open valley.

At the far end of the valley, the trail ends at a 4WD road that extends into an area of sandstone fins called Behind the Rocks. You can follow the 4WD road all the way to the Colorado River, but we recommend returning back to the Hidden Valley trailhead.

89 | SHAY MOUNTAIN TRAIL

Distance: 6.5 to 7 miles round trip
Hiking time: 3 to 4.5 hours
Difficulty: moderate
Season: June to October
Elevation gain: 2835 feet
Maps: USGS Shay Mountain; Trails Illustrated Manti-La Sal National Forest
Land Management Agency: Manti-La Sal National Forest, Monticello Ranger District

From US 191 in Monticello, turn west onto North Creek Road. As you head away from town, you can see the Blue Mountains. Follow the road for 11.5

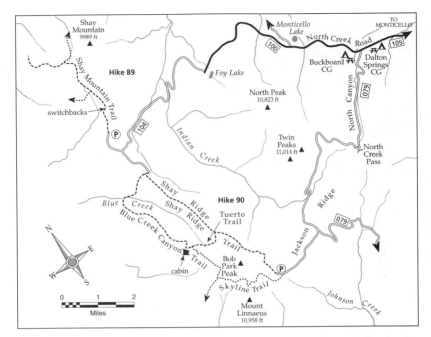

miles to where the pavement ends just before you reach Foy Lake. At the lake the road forks; go right. The road descends into upper Indian Creek and continues past two other forks—stay to the right on both—for a total distance of about 5 miles. About 0.25 mile after the second fork the road ends. There is a pullout at the trailhead for parking.

This hike is for experienced hikers familiar with routefinding and map reading. Shay Mountain is heavily grazed, so expect cows in summer. Despite the bovine intrusion, this area is one of the least traveled in this book. Be sure to take the USGS maps and a compass (if not a GPS) for this hike—the Trails Illustrated map is good for general directions, but not for routefinding once you're on Shay Mountain. Even the USGS maps do not include all of the roads and trails you'll encounter, but it will help you identify key terrain features.

The first couple of miles of the trail were once a jeep road, so it is wide but quite rocky. The trail quickly takes you up via a series of steep switchbacks. After ascending a few hundred feet, you can look back to the southeast and see the Blue Mountains and Shay Ridge.

The trail soon begins to level out as it goes through the aspen trees. If you look closely, you can see the groves of trees extending into the meadows manifested by the saplings along the groves' edges. Expect to see evidence of grazing.

After about 1.5 miles over relatively level terrain, the trail forks. The main trail turns right, heading toward Shay Mountain Peak (9989 feet). Take this

A panoramic view of Canyonlands from Shay Mountain

right fork and continue a little more than a mile to a meadow, where you'll find another fork. This time go left. This trail leads you toward the west edge of the mountain and your goal, one of the best views of the entire canyonlands area anywhere.

The trail joins with other trails crossing the flat mesa top. Follow the main trail south and west. At the end of the trail, you can see the southwest shoulder of Shay Mountain. Walk off-trail across the mesa top to the point where you can't continue south or west any farther without downclimbing the cliffs. Depending on the route you take, the distance will be 0.75 to 1 mile.

Below you lie steep cliffs forested with aspens and pines on top, then pinyon-juniper, giving way to the underlying red sandstone cliff strata from which the entire canyonlands area has eroded.

90 | SHAY RIDGE TRAIL

Distance: 12.25-mile loop
Hiking time: 10 to 12 hours
Difficulty: strenuous
Season: July to October
Elevation gain: 4590 feet
Maps: USGS Shay Mountain; Trails Illustrated Manti-La Sal National Forest
Land Management Agency: Manti-La Sal National Forest, Monticello Ranger District

See map on page 231.

From US 191 in Monticello, turn west onto North Creek Road. Go 5 miles to a graded dirt road forking left just past the Dalton Springs Campground. Take this road for 9 miles. At 4 miles, you go over North Creek Pass, at

10,370 feet. Continue another 5 miles to a small pass at 9685 feet. There's a fork to the right. If you start down a steep hill, you've gone too far. Turn right at the pass and go 2 miles, ascending to 10,300 feet. At the top, is a parking area on a ridge overlooking Blanding, Recapture Lake, and Comb Ridge—an imposing cliff line extending north to south almost to the horizon west of Blanding. A sign at the parking area confirms you've reached the right place.

The Shay Ridge Trail is a beautiful mountain hike that gives incredible vistas of Canyonlands to the northwest and Cedar Mesa to the southwest. Parts of the trail are open to ATVs, so these sections are fairly wide and smooth. Other sections, particularly at the far end of the loop hike, are infrequently traveled and consequently less distinct.

There are two trails parting at the trailhead. The Skyline Trail skirts the base of the Bob Park Peak heading west. The Shay Ridge Trail goes northwest, climbing about 600 feet to nearly 11,000 feet in the first mile on an old jeep road. You top out, then drop down through the trees. The area is a haven for wildlife, including deer, elk, falcon, owl, and wild turkeys. Along with wildlife, also note a unique pink skyrocket, rosehips, and a large variety of wild mushrooms.

Over the next 1.5 miles the trail drops 1100 feet along the Shay ridgeline to a fork in the trail coming in from the left. Stay right here, but remember this junction, as this is where you'll rejoin the main trail on the loop. The main trail continues its steep drop, as it parallels Blue Creek Canyon to the left of the trail, from 9800 feet at the fork to 8400 feet, passing from high alpine aspen and pine to a pinyon-juniper forest. About 2.75 miles from the fork, you reach the north end of the trail at a junction with a dirt road, the same road that you travel to get to the Shay Mountain trailhead, Hike 89.

Bob Park Peak from the Shay Ridge Trail

Follow the road left (west). Soon it turns into a trail and after 0.75 mile it crosses Blue Creek. There's a small pond where the trail crosses the creek, and you may have to bushwhack above or below the pond to avoid getting wet. Ascend some sandy hills then reach a fork at 0.25 mile from the stream crossing. Turn left and begin to ascend Blue Creek Canyon.

Get ready for a long climb back to the trailhead, from 7650 feet to almost 11,000 feet. The first 1.25 miles climb 900 feet to a small lake in a meadow. The next mile has a gain of 500 feet to a small cabin. The cabin is private property, so stay away. Both maps show the junction of three trails near this cabin. However, these trails are very hard to find.

You can take the trail straight ahead (south)—if you can find it—up to the Skyline Trail, then east to the trailhead. The easiest trail to find is the Tuerto Trail, which follows a lodgepole pine fence east down into the canyon. It is 1.25 miles and 800 feet up the steep side of Blue Creek Canyon back to the junction with the main trail, and another 2.5 miles back to the parking area.

91 | RED LAKE CANYON

Distance: 14 miles round trip; 22 miles round trip to Colorado River
Difficulty: moderate, strenuous to the river
Season: mid-September to early June
Elevation gain: 1150 feet
Maps: USGS Spanish Bottoms, The Loop; Trails Illustrated Canyonlands National Park, Needles and Island in the Sky
Land Management Agency: Canyonlands National Park, Needles District

From Moab, head south on US 191 toward Monticello. After about 40 miles, take the turnoff to the right (west) onto SR 211 toward the Needles District of Canyonlands National Park. (Do not mistakenly take the road to the Needles Overlook.) You work your way down a ridge with switchbacks and then out into the canyon bottoms. Along the way you may want to stop at Newspaper Rock, a large boulder with many pictographs.

From the turnoff it's about 40 miles to the Canyonlands Visitor Center. Once there, stop and get your hiking permit, then take the main road past the Squaw Flat Campground. Turn right onto a well-graded dirt road marked "Elephant Hill." After 2 miles the road opens up into a parking and picnic area with tables and outhouses.

Red Lake Canyon is a remote and dry part of Canyonlands National Park. Because of this very few people visit this area. Be prepared to pack

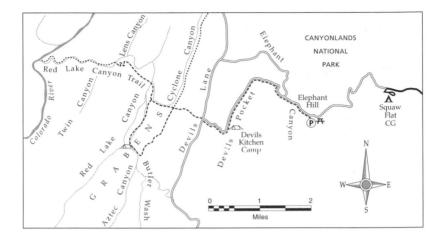

all the water you will need for this trip because there is nowhere to filter once you are in. Along with being dry, the canyon can be very hot in summer. Plan to do this hike between late fall and early spring. In winter warm spells the snows melt off the trail, but still lingers in shaded places. The snow makes a welcome alternate water source in an emergency.

The hike begins at the parking area. Follow the road up and over Elephant Hill. After 1.5 miles you reach a fork in the road. Take the left fork and follow the road for another 2 miles through Devils Pocket to the Devils Kitchen camp. Ordinarily this camp is reserved for 4WDs only, but hikers may camp here in the winter months.

From March to October, the Elephant Hill Road from the picnic area to the camp, is open to 4WDs, but because of the difficult terrain we suggest hiking or biking this section. During the winter, the road is closed to all mechanized vehicles, including bikes.

Just before reaching the camp, there is yet another fork in the road. Take a right here toward Devils Lane Road. After a mile, you reach another road that runs perpendicular to the road you're on. Stay to your right and you'll see a sign marking a footpath that heads west toward a sandstone ridge. The path takes you to the top of the ridge, then down and into Cyclone Canyon. This section of the trail is about 1 mile.

Cross the Cyclone Canyon Trail, which was once a jeep trail, and enter into a side canyon heading west. The trail drops several hundred feet over the next mile and ends up in Red Lake Canyon.

You will now be in what's called the Grabens. Camping here is at large, but you must have a backcountry permit issued by the National Park Service and you must camp at least 1 mile away from the established trail. We suggest hiking upcanyon toward Butler Wash.

If you have the time, follow the trail down into Lower Red Lake Canyon. The trail takes you up along the southern rim of the canyon. From

At the top of Lower Red Lake Canyon

here you can look hundreds of feet down to the bottom. After about a mile the trail makes a dramatic drop to the bottom of the gorge and continues down to the Colorado River.

If you choose, you can follow Butler Wash out of Red Lake Canyon rather than hiking out the way you came in. You can walk up Butler Wash, but after about 2 miles you reach an impassable pouroff. We suggest you exit the canyon about 0.5 mile up the wash from Red Lake Canyon. You'll see a canyon entering high up on the left. Scramble up the rocks and follow what will noticeably be a dried water path. This will take you to the south end of the Cyclone Trail. From here it is only a mile back to the trail you came in on.

92 | CHESLER PARK

Distance: 11.5-mile loop; add 0.75 mile for the Joint Trail
Hiking time: 6 to 8 hours
Difficulty: easy
Season: February to early June; September to November
Elevation gain: 1260 feet
Maps: USGS The Loop, Druid Arch; Trails Illustrated Canyonlands National Park
Land Management Agency: Canyonlands National Park, Needles District

Follow the instructions for Hike 91, Red Lake Canyon to the Elephant Hill trailhead in the Needles District of Canyonlands National Park. Our description assumes you do not have a 4WD and do not want to brave the difficult 4WD road over Elephant Hill. The hike shortens significantly from the 4WD roads, but do your heart and soul some good—hike the whole trail!

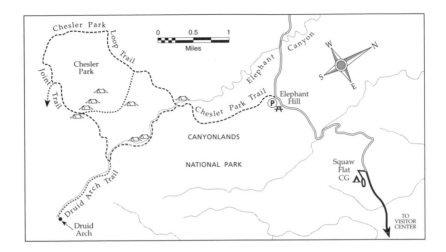

Most people hike this area in April, May, or September—all great times to visit Canyonlands, but it's usually crowded. Consider an off-season trip in October/November or February/March. Canyonlands does get snow during these times, but the 4WD roads are closed and few hikers brave the park, even though conditions are excellent during warm and dry periods.

The signed Chesler Park Trail leaves the far end of the parking area heading south. At 1.5 miles the trail meets another coming in from Squaw Flat. Turn west and proceed 0.5 mile to another junction in the bottom of Elephant Canyon. The Druid Arch Trail breaks off to the south; continue west for another half mile and yet another trail junction. Go south (left) for 0.25 mile. You pass through a narrow crack between tall spires that form the northern edge of Chesler Park, a circular, flat "park," or meadow, nestled amid towering, striped sandstone pinnacles. Please stay on the trails here; hikers do significant damage to the area when they explore off-trail.

You can do the loop around Chesler Park in either direction—we recommend going counterclockwise. Follow the trail west 1.25 miles to the Devils Pocket Trail (an old 4WD track), then south 1 mile along the road. At the road junction, go back east toward the Joint Trail, which you arrive at in 1.5 miles.

Don't miss the Joint Trail! It's a short 0.75-mile loop spur that rivals Chesler Park as the highlight of this hike. The trail crosses slickrock for about a 0.5 mile then drops into a cavelike crack in the rock formation. For the next 0.25 mile the trail wanders through increasingly narrow cracks, or joints, between huge sandstone blocks. Side cracks offer plenty of opportunity for exploration. Some of the cracks dead-end; others can lead up on top of the blocky sandstone. A set of human-carved steps leads out of the joints to rejoin the Chesler Park Trail. A short spur trail at this junction rises up onto a ledge for a better view of the park.

Continuing your circle around Chesler Park, keep hiking east. In 0.75 mile, you arrive at a junction with the Elephant Canyon Connector Trail, which breaks out of the circle and heads east to join the Druid Arch Trail. You can continue to circle Chesler Park, another 1.5 miles to the point where you began your circle, then retrace your steps back to the trailhead—a distance of about 4 miles—or connect with the Druid Arch Trail and follow it back to the trailhead. The latter route repeats less of the ground you've already covered, but is about 0.25 mile longer and a little more rugged. Very strong hikers might also take in Druid Arch, which adds another 4 miles.

We recommend the side trail. Go 1 mile east to join the Druid Arch Trail in the bottom of Elephant Canyon. The trail rises slightly to exit Chesler Park, then drops 350 feet over slickrock as it works its way down into Elephant Canyon. This section can be difficult in winter; snow or ice on the trail helps the slickrock live up to its name. Once in the wash, turn north (left) 0.5 mile to a junction, then continue north another mile where you rejoin the Chesler Park Trail. Turn right (east) for 0.5 mile, then turn north for the final 1.5 miles back to the trailhead.

There are several backcountry campsites in Chesler Park and in Elephant Canyon, so also consider an overnight trip. Chesler Park sites 2, 3, 4, and 5 are near the Elephant Canyon Connector Trail, a little more than half way into the trip. Reservations for the campsite need to be made at the visitor center. During peak seasons, spring and fall, the sites are often booked well in advance. Also, scarce water sources mean you should always pack enough water for the entire trip.

The Needles of Canyonlands

93 | UPPER SALT CREEK

Distance: 28 miles round trip
Hiking time: 3 to 4 days
Difficulty: moderate
Season: March to June, September to November
Elevation gain: 1890 feet
Maps: USGS Cathedral Butte, South Sixshooter Peak; Trails
Illustrated Canyonlands National Park, Needles and
Island in the Sky
Land Management Agency: Canyonlands National Park,
Needles District

Follow the instructions for Hike 91 to Red Lake Canyon to get to the
Canyonlands National Park Visitor Center, where you'll need to get your
backcountry permit. Call or visit the park's website to make reservations
(see Appendix).

Once you have your permit, backtrack to the east on SR 211 (i.e., the
road you came in on). Pass the park boundary and a dirt road turning off
to the south with a sign indicating it goes to Lavender and Davis Canyons.
Continuing east, the road makes a wide turn and heads more to the south.
About 14 miles from the visitor center, is a well-graded, signed dirt road
on the right heading toward Elk Mountain and Beef Basin. This road is just
before (north) the Dugout Ranch, also on the right.

In the first 0.25 mile the road crosses Cottonwood Creek, an easy crossing
for most vehicles, except during high water or immediately after rainstorms.

Follow the road 17 miles. Just past Cathedral Butte—the dominant feature in the area—you'll see a turnout and parking area on the right signed
Bright Angel Trail and Salt Creek.

The view from the trailhead is spectacular, another of the canyonland

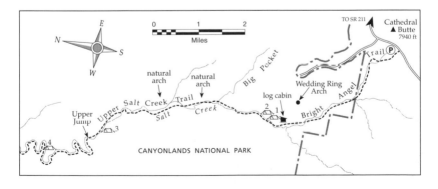

An unusual pictograph in Salt Creek Canyon

area's notable viewpoints. Below you, the wide-bottomed, deeply incised Salt Creek Canyon and its tributaries, spread out like cracks in dried mud. Sheer thousand-foot cliffs drop from the mesa tops exposing thick layers of sandstone. The erratic erosion has formed many scenic and visually appealing features in the sandstone, including several natural arches. The area's abundant water, flat canyon bottom, and concealed alcoves made Salt Creek an ideal home to the Anasazi, whose ruins and rock art dot the Salt Creek region.

The trail immediately drops over 1000 feet to the bottom of Salt Creek Canyon. This section is rocky, but the trail is easy to follow. The hard part is the ascent back up on your way out. The bottom is wide, sandy, and quite open. There is no water in the wash at this point, but soon there will be. The trail crosses the wash and follows the west side along the flat bench.

After the water starts flowing in the wash, brush along the creek gets thick in places. Sagebrush grows to 8 feet high, or more, and the trail in places weaves its way through dense stands.

The first leg of the trip, from the trailhead to campsites 1 and 2, is about 4 miles. About halfway there, you pass Wedding Ring Arch. Just before the side trail to the campsites, you pass an old log cabin. Campsite 2 is the best site in Salt Creek, out of sight behind a sandstone outcrop and surrounded by juniper and pinyon trees. By this point there is flow in the stream for a water source.

Moving on downcanyon, about 1.5 miles from the campsites, Big Pocket opens up to the southeast. This area is a large relatively flat "pocket" formed by stream erosion. Big Pocket is heavily populated with ruins. It is also off the trail and requires a little scrambling to get up a ledge into the pocket area. Exploring Big Pocket will add a day to your trip.

From campsites 1 and 2 it is 5 miles to the Upper Jump, an area with small trees, thick undergrowth, and small cascades, where the water pours over small ledges in the stream channel. In places, you'll work your way through tall, dense thickets, where mosquitoes can be a problem. Numerous ruins are on both sides of the canyon, some right on the canyon floor, others higher up. Binoculars will help you spot those set back from the trail up in the canyon walls. Campsite 3 sits in an open sandy flat about 0.25 mile upstream from the Upper Jump.

The canyon walls begin to narrow after the Jump and the stream meanders. Its about 3 miles to campsite 4, a clearing amid a few cottonwood trees on a bench about 75 feet off the trail. If you don't watch for the faint side trail and sign up on the right bank, it is easy to hike right past them.

Another 2 miles from campsite 4 and you reach the old dirt road coming up from Lower Salt Creek Canyon. You can hike the old road another 8.5 miles to the Peek-a-boo Camp Trail, or continue another 3.5 miles to the end of the old road, near the Cave Spring trailhead. For most, however, the better option is to return to your vehicle at the trailhead at the base of Cathedral Butte.

94 | ROAD CANYON

Distance: 8- to 9-mile loop
Hiking time: 5 to 7 hours
Difficulty: moderate
Season: March to June, September to October
Elevation gain: 990 feet
Maps: USGS Snow Flat Spring Cave, Cigarette Spring Cave; Trails Illustrated Grand Gulch Plateau
Land Management Agency: BLM Monticello Field Office

Road Canyon is located on Cedar Mesa, west of the town of Blanding. Take SR 95 west from Blanding. At the junction of SR 95 and SR 261, follow SR 261 south 4 miles until you reach the Kane Gulch Ranger Station. Stop to get your permit for all Cedar Mesa canyons. Expect to pay a usage fee.

The Seven Kivas Ruin in Road Canyon

From the ranger station, continue south on SR 261 to the signed County Road #239 or Cigarette Spring Road, which turns off the east at milepost 19. The sign states that Cigarette Spring is 9 miles from SR 261.

Take note of your mileage. Go 0.9 mile to a gate and large parking area. There is a trail register, but no place to pay your fee. At 1.3 miles, a road and camp area is to the north. Continue on the main road, 1 more mile where a road turns off to the south. Immediately after the turnoff to the south is another turnoff to the north, which goes a short distance to the trailhead.

From the parking area and trailhead, follow the hiker trail northeast toward the rim of the canyon. Drop into the dry washbed and follow it down. Shortly after dropping in, attentive hikers will spot several Anasazi ruins on the north side of the canyon. As you follow the canyon down, you have to bypass a dryfall on a bench on the south side.

Continuing downcanyon, you'll encounter intermittent water. About 4 miles in you arrive at one of the most significant ruins in Cedar Mesa—the Seven Kivas Ruin. The ruin is impressive, but more so if you are familiar with the meaning of kivas to the Anasazi. Reading up on the Anasazi and their rituals before hiking Road Canyon will greatly heighten your experience. Kivas were the center of Anasazi ceremonial life. A single kiva could serve several families. Seven kivas in a single location indicates that this spot was especially sacred, perhaps serving as a spiritual center not only for those living in the immediate vicinity, but also for a larger, more regional area. The kivas are well preserved, with the log roof timbers still in place and the slip (paint) still on the inside walls.

For most the hike ends at the Seven Kivas Ruin. Returning the way you came, you may spot a route out of the canyon on the south side. Exiting to the mesa top doesn't save any distance, but makes for faster hiking once you connect with the Cigarette Springs Road, which you can follow west back to your car. In hot weather, hiking the mesa top is very hot and dry.

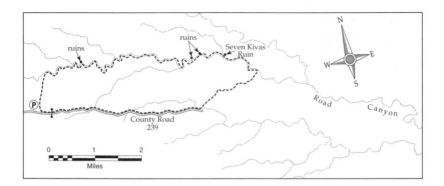

95 | GRAND GULCH

Distance: 23 miles one way
Hiking time: 3 days
Difficulty: moderate
Season: March to June, September to early November
Elevation gain: 1505 feet
Maps: USGS Cedar Mesa North, Pollys Pasture, Kane Gulch;
    Trails Illustrated Grand Gulch Plateau
Land Management Agency: BLM Monticello Field Office

Kane Gulch Ranger Station is about 4 miles down SR 261, south of the SR 95 junction, on the east side of the road. You get to SR 95 heading west from Blanding or south out of Hanksville. Hiking permits should be acquired at the ranger station before entering the canyon. Advance permits are recommended during prime spring weekends. Leave a shuttle car at Kane Gulch. After about 7.5 miles south on SR 261, turn west on San Juan County Road 251. The trailhead at Bullet Canyon is approximately 1 mile in on this dirt road.

The trail begins heading west and quickly drops into Bullet Canyon. It then follows the dry canyon bottom, working its way over ledges and slickrock boulders. Watch closely for rock cairns marking the trail down. At times it is necessary to bypass 10- to 20-foot drops. This section of the hike is by far the most difficult because of both the elevation loss and the rough terrain.

The trail soon passes the Perfect Kiva Ruin, and then Jailhouse Ruin at about 4.75 miles. Both Anasazi ruins are in great condition and can be found on the right hand side of the trail. Notice the painting above Jailhouse Ruin for which it was named.

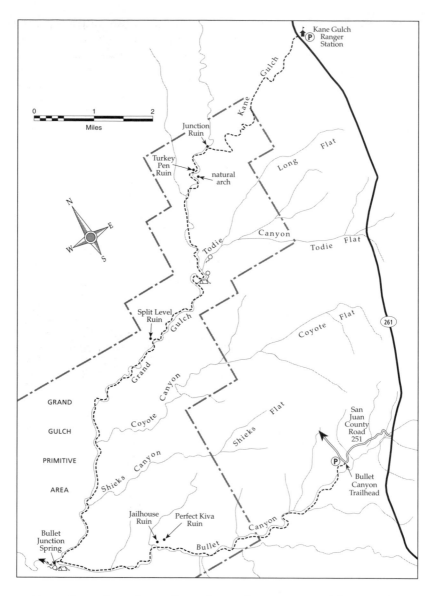

From the ruins, the trail continues downcanyon. After 2 miles it reaches the junction with Grand Gulch. Bullet Junction Spring provides needed water, making this a prime location for the first night's camp.

On the second day, the trail heads up Grand Gulch for 8 miles to the junction with Todie Canyon. Along the way, careful observers will see signs of ancient life. The most prominent ruin along this stretch—Split Level Ruin—

can be found 5.5 miles from the Bullet Canyon and Grand Gulch junction. It lies on the left hand (north) side of the canyon. This ruin is well worth the stop.

Fine camp spots can be found at the junction with Todie Canyon, with water up Todie about 0.25 mile.

Turkey Pen Ruin is 2 miles upcanyon from the junction of Todie Canyon on the left side (north) wall. The ruin is just around the bend from the natural arch on the right side wall. Junction Ruin is just 1 more mile upcanyon. Both ruins are high traffic areas; however, they still command a certain sense of reverence.

One of many Anasazi ruins in Grand Gulch

From Junction Ruin, follow Kane Gulch out of Grand Gulch. The trail leads you up out of the canyon toward the Kane Gulch Ranger Station for 4 miles to complete the hike.

96 FISH AND OWL CREEKS

Distance: 16- to 17-mile loop
Hiking time: 2 to 3 days
Difficulty: moderate
Season: March to June, September to November
Elevation gain: 1620 feet
Maps: USGS Snow Flat Spring Cave, Bluff NW; Trails Illustrated Grand Gulch Plateau
Land Management Agency: BLM Monticello Field Office

Take SR 95 west from Blanding. At the junction of SR 95 and SR 261, follow SR 261 south 4 miles until you reach the Kane Gulch Ranger Station, where you get your permit and pay your usage fee. Continue south on SR 261 another mile. Then take a left on San Juan County Road 253. The dirt road continues another 5.5 miles to the trailhead.

The BLM recommends hiking down Owl Creek and out Fish Creek. This avoids some difficult routefinding encountered when hiking the reverse direction. However, we prefer descending the droppoff into Fish Creek Canyon. The following description assumes that you begin on Fish Creek and exit via Owl Creek.

Begin the hike by following the single-track trail north overland toward Fish Creek Canyon. After 2 miles you reach the canyon rim. Here there is a 15-foot downclimb where most will find a 20-foot cord useful for lowering

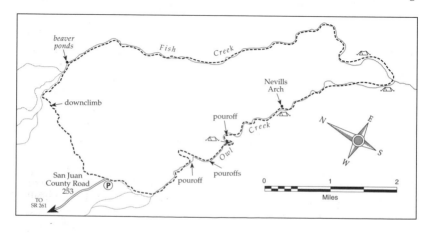

Nevills Arch in Owl Canyon

packs. After the downclimb, the cairned trail switches back and forth, dropping to the bottom of the canyon.

Springs in the canyon provide water for several beaver dams in the upper reaches of Fish Creek. Also, the observant hiker will find many pristine ruins high on the canyon walls. Binoculars enhance the viewing experience.

Continuing downcanyon, the trail crosses over the water several times. However, crossings aren't deep enough to warrant separate wading shoes.

Six miles downcanyon, the trail turns due south. Trees and brush line the canyon floor, and there are several spots for the night's camp. Or, several camping spots are at the confluence with Owl Creek, about 8 miles from the point where you arrived at the floor of Fish Creek Canyon. However, water sources diminish in the last mile before the confluence. There is also little water for a mile or two up into Owl Creek Canyon.

The second day is spent hiking up Owl Creek back to the trailhead. About 2.5 miles upcanyon from the confluence is Nevills Arch, perched high on the north wall. Conveniently, in addition to the arch, this area also has water, making it a great spot for campers wanting to spend more time in the canyon.

Another 2 miles upcanyon is a pouroff that requires a long bypass up the canyon to the right. Good campsites are abundant here, as is water. For a short overnight trip, you can drop from the trailhead to this waterfall area, then hike out the next day. The trail scrambles up the canyon on sandstone and then returns to the main canyon above the pouroff. Good routefinding skills are needed to find the exit route out of Owl Creek Canyon. From here it is another 2 miles back to the trailhead.

97 | CHEESEBOX CANYON

Distance: 7 miles round trip
Hiking time: 5 to 7 hours
Difficulty: moderate
Season: March to early May, September to October
Elevation gain: 610 feet
Maps: USGS The Cheesebox, Dark Canyon and Natural Bridges National Monument
Land Management Agency: BLM Monticello Field Office

Take SR 95 south from Hanksville, or west from Blanding. At milepost 75 on SR 95 is a dirt road that pulls off to the east. Follow the dirt road to its terminus at the rim of White Canyon. The road is passable by passenger car and has several pullouts suitable for car camping. A rock cairn and tree branch–lined path to the right of the road mark the trailhead.

Following the cairns, the trail winds down the west wall of White Canyon. Don't expect to go straight down. There are several spots on the trail where minor scrambling is involved. We didn't use rope, but an accessory cord may be useful to lower packs. The trail reaches the bottom of the canyon about 200 feet north of the Cheesebox confluence.

A large forking tree marks the beginning of Cheesebox Canyon. Shortly after entering the canyon, you'll find the wash bottom route ends at a large pouroff with a pool of water. To avoid this, backtrack to the tree at the confluence and make your way up the right side. After ascending an un-

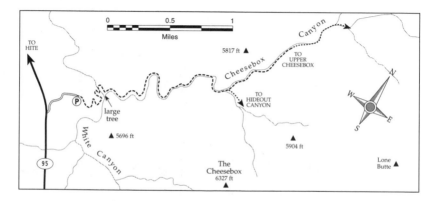

A narrow slot in Cheesebox Canyon

avoidable 15-foot scramble, follow the canyon to the right. Below, you can see the twisted, convoluted slot below. The steep wall will soon come to the point where you can safely walk down to the canyon floor.

From here, you can walk upcanyon with fairly few obstacles. In spots, large boulders make for some mild scrambling that helps give variety to the canyon floor, but there is nothing technical. One section has a very tight slot a couple hundred feet long in the floor of the canyon, but you can walk right past this on the slickrock streambed on either side. To descend this short section would require swimming deep holes and rappelling over dryfalls.

About 2.5 miles in, a canyon forks to the right. Bypass the dryfall by scrambling on the right side. It is possible to follow this fork up out of the canyon, giving a great view of The Cheesebox and Lone Butte to the southeast. It is then possible to cross over into Hideout Canyon, returning to White Canyon. To take this route would be about 7 miles back to the spot where you entered the canyon. Hideout Canyon may have technical narrows sections, so be prepared if you elect to make this loop.

It is also possible to continue several more miles up Cheesebox Canyon (left at the fork), which offers more of the beautiful canyon and some interesting narrows.

98 | NATURAL BRIDGES NATIONAL MONUMENT

Distance: 8.5-mile loop
Hiking time: 5 to 7 hours
Difficulty: moderate
Season: March to May, September to November
Elevation gain: 1040 feet
Maps: USGS Moss Back Butte; Trails Illustrated Dark Canyon and Natural Bridges National Monument
Land Management Agency: Natural Bridges National Monument

Take SR 95 south of Hanksville. At the junction with SR 276, stay on SR 95 toward Hite, where you cross Lake Powell at its upper end. The bridge over the Colorado (Lake Powell) is between mileposts 47 and 48. Continue past the lower connector to SR 276, coming from Halls Crossing. The next junction is the turnoff to Natural Bridges on SR 275. From Hanksville to this turnoff is just over 91 miles. You can also get to the monument by heading west from Blanding for about 40 miles on SR 95.

Several dirt roads turn off the highway between the SR 276 junction and the Natural Bridges turnoff where you can camp. There is no camping or overnight parking at the trailhead. From the turnoff it's 4.4 miles to the

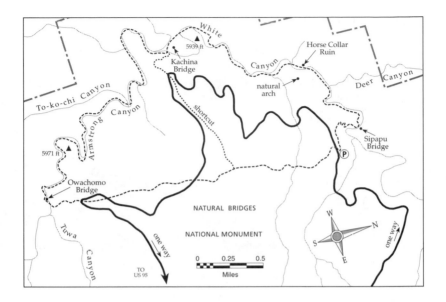

visitor center, where you'll need to pay the park entrance fee. The trailhead is at the parking area for the Sipapu Bridge, about 0.5 mile beyond the Sipapu Overlook.

There are several hiking options here. We present the longest hike in the park, a loop hike that passes three large natural bridges.

From the Sipapu trailhead, the trail drops quickly as it skirts along ledges along a cliff. There is little exposure, but the trail does go down quickly enough that you have to descend several sections with handrails and ladders. These present few problems for most hikers.

Once at the bottom, the trail heads downstream, following the convolutions of the meandering stream. The white sandstone canyon walls tower hundreds of feet high. The trail is obvious and has no significant obstacles. Although you have to cross the small stream a few times, you will not need to get wet. From Sipapu to Kachina is 3.25 miles.

Kachina Bridge sneaks up on you on the right side of the canyon. It is smaller than the high, arching Sipapu Bridge, but both are spectacular. The trail passes under the bridge. On the far side you can see that two canyons—White and Armstrong Canyons—meet here. The stream continues down White Canyon on the right making its way to Lake Powell, but you turn up Armstrong Canyon to the left. A sign and trail register under the bridge, on the downstream side, point the way. A short distance upcanyon, you'll see a sign indicating that the trail heads up onto a bench. There is still a trail in the canyon bottom, but don't follow it—it dead-ends at a pouroff a few hundred yards ahead.

Instead, follow the ranger-made steps up onto a bench. Soon you reach

Owachomo Bridge

a sign indicating a junction. The left trail rises to the Kachina Bridge trailhead. You can cut your hike short by heading up to the overlook and then another 2 miles overland to your car.

To continue to Owachomo Bridge, turn right, staying on the bench upcanyon. Soon you see the pouroff on the right. This section of the trail is less maintained, but still evident and well marked. It is obvious that fewer people hike this section. The scenery changes—the canyon is less deep than the high white cliffs of White Canyon that you see in the section between Sipapu and Kachina.

The trail begins to loop back to the southeast. After 2.5 to 3 miles, as you near the next natural bridge, you'll see a sign on the left side indicating the trail starts up onto a bench above the streambed. Take this trail, as the canyon narrows ahead and there is a large pool that you'd have to swim to cross. The section on the bench goes for 0.25 to 0.5 mile. As you round a bend the Owachomo Bridge spans right above you on the left wall, paralleling the canyon rather than crossing it. The trail proceeds under the bridge and a short distance up to the overlook. The total distance from Kachina to Owachomo is about 3.25 miles.

The trail back to the Sipapu parking lot starts on the far side of the road from the Owachomo parking area. It is about 2.25 miles back to your car. You cross three small canyons on your way back. Although small, the ups and downs can be tiring if you aren't used to walking this distance. There is substantial sun exposure in this section, so be sure you've taken enough water to last the entire trip.

After about 1.5 miles you reach the signed junction with the trail from the Kachina Bridge trailhead. Slightly less than a mile ahead, you can see White Canyon and your car directly below you. As you drive the loop road to leave the park, consider stopping at the Horse Collar Ruin overlook, a short hike to a view of an ancestral Puebloan ruin high up on the cliff side of White Canyon, just past the Sipapu trailhead.

99 | HOG SPRING

Distance: 3 to 4 miles round trip
Hiking time: 1.5 to 2.5 hours
Difficulty: easy
Season: February to early May, September to November
Elevation gain: 215 feet
Map: USGS Hite North, Black Table
Land Management Agency: BLM Henry Mountains Field Station

Go south from Hanksville on SR 95 for 33 miles. Between mileposts 33 and 34, you'll see the Hog Springs parking area and picnic site on the west side of the road. The site has restrooms and a picnic area, but no running water.

For those looking for an accessible, easy hike Hog Spring is a great choice. It's one of the easiest hikes in this book and is suitable for anyone, as long as you don't mind walking across some marshy ground and through knee-high grasses.

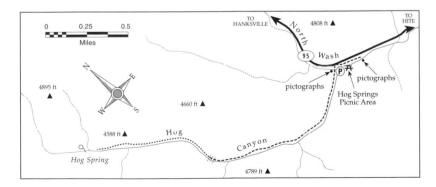

Pool in Hog Canyon

The trail starts right next to the picnic area pavilion. It follows the small year-round stream upcanyon. Near the picnic area the canyon is tall and narrow. It widens as you proceed upcanyon. The trail is obvious at the beginning as it meanders from side to side of the stream. After about 0.75 mile, you reach a small pool. The trail passes it on the right side. Continuing farther, the trail becomes less marked. Grasses and reeds line the streambed, and in some places the trail consists simply of bent reeds or grasses. You may get your shoes wet here, as the entire canyon bottom becomes marshy, especially in the spring.

You pass a few small side canyons, but at each one follow the main canyon and stream, always to the right at each junction. One larger fork seems to have water coming down its streambed, but it is just a spring at the base of the sandstone at the junction. Keep to the right here. Although you'll see a trail ascending up onto a bench into this side canyon, it goes only about 300 feet, where you can look into a series of box canyons. The main trail continues through the reeds and grass. Shortly after this junction, you reach a large pool at the base of a waterfall. For most people the trail ends here. It is possible to skirt the falls and continue upcanyon to its end at Hog Spring, but you've seen the best parts of the canyon by the time you reach the pool.

When you get back to the trailhead, be sure to check out the pictographs on a panel just north of the picnic area. There is a fence around the area at the base of the panel. There are more pictographs in a large alcove about a quarter mile south of Hog Springs picnic area. There is a trail into the alcove, but only a couple of images are on the walls there.

100 | DARK CANYON

Distance: minimum 12 miles
Hiking time: 2 to 5 days
Difficulty: strenuous
Season: February to early April, late September to early
  November
Elevation gain: 3240 feet
Maps: USGS Indian Head Pass, Bowdie Canyon West, Trails
  Illustrated Dark Canyon and Natural Bridges National
  Monument
Land Management Agency: BLM Monticello Field Office

Traveling south out of Hanksville on SR 95, turn east onto a dirt road just south of milepost 49, shortly after the Colorado River bridge. At 4.0 miles a road enters from the right; stay left. Roads join from the right at 4.2 and 4.3 miles. In both cases stay left. At 6.5 miles a road exits to the left; keep right.

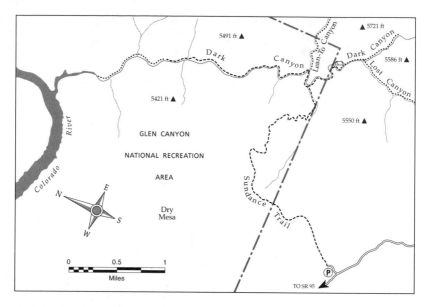

A signed fork at 7.2 miles shows a faint trail arrow pointing right. At 7.6 miles a road joins from the right; continue straight. At 8.4 miles there is a signed junction; go left. The final junction, at 10.7 miles, has a sign, which indicates the trailhead is 0.2 mile to the left. The Trails Illustrated map has a good inset that shows most of the roads and mileages.

Start at the trail register, following the worn trail and cairns. As you cross the slickrock, watch for the cairns, otherwise follow the trail as it works its way across the flats, then turns west and drops down slickrock into a small basin. There is one 25-foot section with steep slickrock, but it is easy walking. The trail crosses an old 4WD road; do not follow the road.

Soon, off to the right, you can see a deep canyon. The trail follows this canyon for about 0.75 of a mile. There is one short downclimb, which should be easy for almost everyone, but novice hikers may have difficulty. As you approach the rim, you can see deep into Dark Canyon, a spectacular sight into the wide, deep canyon 1400 feet below.

When you arrive at the rim, watch carefully for cairns. There are multiple trails down the steep face. Choose the one you are most comfortable with. The going is slow and tedious, but not as bad as the trip back up will be! You descend 1100+ feet down a 50-percent boulder-strewn slope into the bottom of a dry drainage that joins Dark Canyon about 0.25 mile farther downcanyon.

Once you arrive at Dark Canyon, with its perennial stream, look for a camping spot. There are several good spots in the next mile upstream

Deep canyon walls in lower Dark Canyon

toward Lost Canyon. Once you've settled in at camp, you can start your explorations of Dark Canyon.

The most popular day trip is down Dark Canyon toward Lake Powell. Leaving camp, you quickly pass the side canyon you entered from (assuming you camp upstream). Dark Canyon narrows down with alternating bands of sandstone and limestone. For 1.5 miles, you walk in the narrow canyon bottom, crossing in and out of the stream.

There is a waterfall that you have to bypass—the best path is to the left. Shortly after, the walls narrow more. Watch carefully for cairns leading you up on the ledges on the right side. You have to traverse a small ledge, about 1-foot wide with about 20 feet of exposure, to proceed downstream. Although it sounds difficult, most will find the traverse easy. If you are uncomfortable, this is a good place to turn back. The trail stays up on the ledge, climbing to over 100 feet above the canyon floor. There are frequent spots with exposure to the canyon floor, but the going is easy.

The trail follows the ledges for 0.75 mile, passing many pools and narrow sections in the canyon floor below. Soon the trail approaches a canyon entering from the right. The trail abruptly drops to the canyon floor at this confluence. The canyon is narrow and very deep here, the walls extend more than 1500 feet high and are less than 0.33 mile apart at the rims. You follow the slickrock streambed downcanyon, soon approaching a beautiful, small waterfall and large pool. You can bypass the pool on the left.

If are hiking this section on the same day you dropped down into Dark Canyon, this is a good turnaround point for a moderately long day. If you want to continue down to the lake, keep hiking down the canyon floor. There is one more cairned route where you need to rise up on the right-side ledges before you arrive at the lake. Depending on the lake's water level, the bottom of the canyon can be very mucky in sections.

For multiday backpacking trips, try exploring Lean-To Canyon, which enters Dark Canyon just below and opposite the point where you entered the canyon. You can also travel upcanyon about a mile to Lost Canyon. Farther up Dark Canyon are more narrows and pools. It's about 6 miles up Dark Canyon to the confluence with Youngs Canyon.

On your return trip, backtrack out of Dark Canyon the way you entered. Be sure not to get caught ascending up the rocky talus slope in hot weather. The climb is hard enough without the intense heat of the sun and heat rising from the rocks. In warmer weather start your ascent as early as possible in the morning to take advantage of cooler temperatures. Plan on 2.5 to 4 hours from the confluence to the trailhead.

APPENDIX: CONTACT INFORMATION

NATIONAL PARK SERVICE
www.nps.gov/

Arches National Park
P.O. Box 907
Moab, UT 84532
(435) 719-2000
www.nps.gov/arch/index.htm

Bryce Canyon National Park
P.O. Box 170001
Bryce Canyon, UT 84717
(435) 834-5322
www.nps.gov/brca/index.htm

Canyonlands National Park
Reservation Office
2282 Southwest Resource Boulevard
Moab, UT 84532
(435) 719-2313 (General Information)
(435) 259-4351 (Backcountry Reservation Office)
(435) 259-2652 (Hans Flat Ranger Station)
(435) 259-4711 (Needles District)
www.nps.gov/cany/index.htm

Capitol Reef National Park
HC 70 Box 15
Torrey, UT 84775
(435) 425-3791
www.nps.gov/care/index.htm

Cedar Breaks National Monument
2390 West Highway 56, Suite 11
Cedar City, UT 84720
(435) 586 9451
www.nps.gov/cebr/index.htm

Dinosaur National Monument
P.O. Box 210
Dinosaur, CO 81610
(435) 789-2115
www.nps.gov/dino/index.htm

Glen Canyon National Recreation Area
P.O. Box 1507
Page, AZ 86040
(520) 608-6404
www.nps.gov/glca/index.htm

Natural Bridges National Monument
HC 60 Box 1
Lake Powell, UT 84533
(435) 692-1234
www.nps.gov/nabr/index.htm

Zion National Park
Springdale, UT 84767
(435) 772-3256
www.nps.gov/zion/index.htm

U.S. FOREST SERVICE

Ashley National Forest
www.fs.fed.us/r4/ashley/

Flaming Gorge Ranger District
P.O. Box 279
Manila, UT 84046
(435) 784-3445

Roosevelt Ranger District
244 West Highway 40 Box 333-6
Roosevelt, UT 84066
(435) 722-5018

Dixie National Forest
www.fs.fed.us/outernet/dixie_nf/

Cedar City Ranger District
P.O. Box 627
Cedar City, UT 84721-0627
(435) 865-3200

Pine Valley Ranger District
196 East Tabernacle Street, Room 40
St. George, UT 84771
(435) 652-3100

Teasdale Ranger District
138 East Main
P.O. Box 90
Teasdale, UT 84773
(435) 425-3702

Manti-La Sal National Forest
www.fs.fed.us/r4/mantilasal/

Monticello Ranger District
496 East Central
P.O. Box 820
Monticello, UT 84535
(435) 587-2041

Uinta National Forest
www.fs.fed.us/r4/uinta/

Heber Ranger District
2460 South Highway 40
P.O. Box 190
Heber City, UT 84032
(435) 654-0470

Pleasant Grove Ranger District
390 North 100 East
Pleasant Grove, UT 84062
(801) 785-3563

Spanish Fork Ranger District
44 West 400 North
Spanish Fork, UT 84660
(801) 798-3571

Wasatch-Cache National Forest
www.fs.fed.us/wcnf/

Evanston Ranger District
1565 South Highway 150, Suite A
P.O. Box 1880
Evanston, WY 82931-1880
(307) 789-3194 (winter)
(435) 642-6662 (summer)

Kamas Ranger District
50 East Center Street
P.O. Box 68
Kamas, UT 84036
(435) 783-4338
www.fs.fed.us/wcnf/kamas/index.html

Logan Ranger District
1500 East Highway 89
Logan, UT 84321
(435) 755-3620

Mountain View Ranger District
321 Highway 414
P.O. Box 129
Mountain View, WY 82939
(307) 782-6555

Salt Lake Ranger District
Discover Public Lands Information Center
(Inside REI store)
3285 E 3300 South
Salt Lake City, UT 84109
(801) 466-6411
www.fs.fed.us/wcnf/slrd/

BUREAU OF LAND MANAGEMENT
www.ut.blm.gov/

Cedar City Field Office
176 East D.L. Sargent Drive
Cedar City, UT 84720
(435) 586-2401
www.ut.blm.gov/cedar_city/index.html

Fillmore Field Office
35 East 500 North
Fillmore, UT 84631
(435) 743-3100
www.ut.blm.gov/fillmore/index.html

Grand Staircase–Escalante National Monument
180 West 300 North
Kanab, UT 84741
(435) 644-4300
www.ut.blm.gov/monument/
www.ut.blm.gov/gsenm/index.html

Henry Mountains Field Station
P.O. Box 99
Hanksville, UT 84734
(435) 542-3461
www.ut.blm.gov/richfield/index.html

Kanab Field Office
318 North 100 East
Kanab, UT 84741
(435) 644-4600
www.ut.blm.gov/kanab_fo/
www.ut.blm.gov/kanab/index.html

Moab Field Office
82 East Dogwood
Moab, UT 84532
(435) 259-2100
www.blm.gov/utah/moab/index.html
www.ut.blm.gov/moab/index.html

Monticello Field Office
P.O. Box 7
Monticello, UT 84535
(435) 587-1532 (Reservation Office)
www.blm.gov/utah/monticello/index.html
www.ut.blm.gov/monticello/index.html

Price Field Office
125 South 600 West
Price, UT 84501
(435) 636-3600
www.blm.gov/utah/price/information.htm
www.ut.blm.gov/price/index.html

Red Cliffs Desert Reserve
197 East Tabernacle
St. George, UT 84770
(435) 634-5759

St. George Field Office
345 East Riverside Drive
St. George, UT 84790
(435) 688-3246
www.ut.blm.gov/st_george/index.html

UTAH STATE PARKS
http://parks.state.ut.us/parks/www1/

Goblin Valley State Park
P.O. Box 637
Green River, UT 84525-0637
(435) 564-3633
http://parks.state.ut.us/parks/www1/gobl.htm

Snow Canyon State Park
1002 Snow Canyon Drive
Ivins, UT 84738
(435) 628-2255
http://parks.state.ut.us/parks/www1/snow.htm

Wasatch Mountain State Park
P.O. Box 10
Midway, Utah 84049-0010
(435) 654-1791
http://parks.state.ut.us/parks/www1/wasa.htm

OTHER AGENCIES AND PHONE NUMBERS

Escalante Interagency Visitor Center
P.O. Box 246
Escalante, UT 84726
(435) 826-5499

Navajo Nation
Parks and Recreation Department
Box 9000
Window Rock, AZ 86515
(520) 871-6647

Utah Avalanche Forecast Center
(801) 364-1581

Zion Canyon Transportation
(877) 635-5993

INDEX

ABOUT THE AUTHORS

Steve Mann is a widely published outdoor and technology writer and photographer. He has written nearly 200 published articles on outdoor gear, computer technology, and travel destinations. As a native of Utah, he has spent many years exploring Utah's backcountry doing environmental impact statements, archeological surveys, and botanical investigations. He serves as the president and managing editor of GearReview.com *(www.gearreview.com)* the leading website for expert reviews of outdoor gear. Mann received a BA in Behavioral Sciences, with emphasis in Anthropology and Archaeology, from Southern Utah University and holds a Master's Degree in Experimental Psychology from the University of North Dakota.

Rhett Olson is a native of Utah and graduated from Brigham Young University with a B.A. in Communications Marketing. A long-time outdoor enthusiast, Olson has spent years exploring the canyon country of southern Utah. He is a principal and contributing editor at GearReview.com and has also been responsible for much of the company's website management and development. Olson's writing focuses on hiking, footwear, and canyoneering. He has spent the last three years of his professional life in the Internet development industry and currently works in marketing at GeoDiscovery.

Steve Mann   *Rhett Olson*

THE MOUNTAINEERS, founded in 1906, is a nonprofit outdoor activity and conservation club, whose mission is "to explore, study, preserve, and enjoy the natural beauty of the outdoors...." Based in Seattle, Washington, the club is now the third-largest such organization in the United States, with 15,000 members and five branches throughout Washington State.

The Mountaineers sponsors both classes and year-round outdoor activities in the Pacific Northwest, which include hiking, mountain climbing, ski-touring, snowshoeing, bicycling, camping, kayaking and canoeing, nature study, sailing, and adventure travel. The club's conservation division supports environmental causes through educational activities, sponsoring legislation, and presenting informational programs. All club activities are led by skilled, experienced volunteers, who are dedicated to promoting safe and responsible enjoyment and preservation of the outdoors.

If you would like to participate in these organized outdoor activities or the club's programs, consider a membership in The Mountaineers. For information and an application, write or call The Mountaineers, Club Headquarters, 300 Third Avenue West, Seattle, WA 98119; 206-284-6310.

The Mountaineers Books, an active, nonprofit publishing program of the club, produces guidebooks, instructional texts, historical works, natural history guides, and works on environmental conservation. All books produced by The Mountaineers Books fulfill the club's mission.

Send or call for our catalog of more than 450 outdoor titles:

The Mountaineers Books
1001 SW Klickitat Way, Suite 201
Seattle, WA 98134
800-553-4453
mbooks@mountaineers.org
www.mountaineersbooks.org

The Mountaineers Books is proud to be a corporate sponsor of Leave No Trace, whose mission is to promote and inspire responsible outdoor recreation through education, research, and partnerships. The Leave No Trace program is focused specifically on human-powered (non-motorized) recreation.
Leave No Trace strives to educate visitors about the nature of their recreational impacts, as well as offer techniques to prevent and minimize such impacts. Leave No Trace is best understood as an educational and ethical program, not as a set of rules and regulations. For more information, visit *www.LNT.org* or call 800-332-4100.

Other titles you may enjoy from The Mountaineers Books:

100 HIKES IN™ SERIES: Fully detailed, best-selling hiking guides with complete descriptions, maps, and photos. Chock-full of trail data, including access, mileage, elevation, hiking time, and the best season to go; safety tips, and wilderness etiquette.
75 HIKES IN™ NEW MEXICO, Craig Martin
100 CLASSIC HIKES IN™ COLORADO, Scott S. Warren
100 CLASSIC HIKES IN™ ARIZONA, Scott S. Warren
100 HIKES IN™ CALIFORNIA'S CENTRAL SIERRA & COAST RANGE, Vicky Spring

HIKING THE SOUTHWEST'S CANYON COUNTRY, Second Edition, Sandra Hinchman
Features the most enjoyable trails and dramatic scenery of the Four Corners region. Included are maps for nearly 100 hikes and information on distance, time required and level of difficulty.

MAC'S FIELD GUIDES SERIES, MacGowen & Sauskojus
Two-sided plastic laminated cards with color drawings, common and scientific names, and information on size and habitat.
SOUTHWEST CACTI, SHRUBS, AND TREES
SOUTHWEST PARK/GARDEN BIRDS

SELECTED CLIMBS IN THE DESERT SOUTHWEST: Colorado & Utah, Cameron M. Burns
From today's favorites like Touchstone Wall to forgotten classics like Gentleman's Agreement in Zion, these 132 routes, compiled by an expert rock climber, represent the best of the desert Southwest.

BEST HIKES WITH CHILDREN® Series: Fully detailed "where-to" and "how-to" guides to day hikes and over-nighters for families. Includes tips on hiking with kids, safety, and fostering a wilderness ethic.
BEST HIKES WITH CHILDREN® IN UTAH, Second Edition, Maureen Kielty
BEST HIKES WITH CHILDREN® IN COLORADO, Second Edition, Maureen Keilty
BEST HIKES WITH CHILDREN® IN ARIZONA, Lawrence Letham
BEST HIKES WITH CHILDREN® IN NEW MEXICO, Bob Julyan

UTAH STATE PARKS: A Complete Recreation Guide, Jan Bannan
Where to go hiking, boating , swimming, camping, bicycling, fishing, and information on park seasons, hours, fees, facilities and reservation procedures.

ANIMAL TRACKS OF THE SOUTHWEST, Chris Stall
The handy pocket-sized guide helps you identify the desert, mountain and trail animals of the southwest region with life-size drawings of the animal's characteristic footprints.

BACKPACKER'S EVERYDAY WISDOM: 1001 Expert Tips for Hikers, Karen Berger
Expert tips and tricks for hikers and backpackers selected from one of the most popular *Backpacker* magazine columns.